THOMAS CROMWELL

Tudor Minister

THOMAS CROMWELL

Tudor Minister

B. W. BECKINGSALE

ROWMAN AND LITTLEFIELD
TOTOWA, NEW JERSEY

First published 1978 by
THE MACMILLAN PRESS LTD
London and Basingstoke

First published in the United States 1978
by Rowman and Littlefield, Totowa, N.J.

Printed in Hong Kong

Library of Congress Cataloging in Publication Data

Beckingsale, B   W
    Thomas Cromwell, Tudor minister.

    Bibliography: p.
    Includes index.
    1.   Cromwell, Thomas, Earl of Essex, 1485?-1540.
2.   Great Britain — History — Henry VIII, 1509-1547.
3.   Statesmen — Great Britain — Biography.   I.   Title.
DA334.C9B42   1978   942.05'2'0924 [B]   77-29057
ISBN 0-8476-6053-2

To Anne

CONTENTS

PREFACE

This book will, I hope, provide a palatable *hors-d'oeuvre* to the great feast of specialised works on Thomas Cromwell and the reign of Henry VIII for which it aims to stimulate the appetite of its readers. In selecting the ingredients I have tried to give some hint of the variety and flavours of the main dishes which await the gourmet with a taste for early Tudor history. In its preparation I have depended much on the work of such scholars as G.R. Elton, A.G. Dickens, S.E. Lehmberg and R.B. Merriman. My debts to them and to others I can only briefly acknowledge in the notes and list of books for further reading, where a mere mention must suffice to indicate all that I owe. I wish also to thank my wife for all the encouragement which she has given me during the writing of this book.

Newcastle upon Tyne
May 1977   B.W. Beckingsale

CROMWELL'S PORTRAIT

Hans Holbein is one of those artists who almost persuades us that there is something in Thomas Carlyle's assertion that a good portrait 'is superior in real instruction to half a dozen written biographies'. From the best copy of Holbein's lost portrait of Thomas Cromwell we get the sense that we could recognise Cromwell on sight as he was in his late forties in 1534.[1] But the portrait is more than a likeness. Holbein presents the details which make the observer cast Cromwell not only as a character but also as an actor in a particular role. The artist makes a psychological and a social estimate of his sitter.

Holbein knew where to place Cromwell in the hierarchy of Henry VIII's court in portraying the King's 'trusty and well beloved councillor'. Cromwell with a firm dignified expression displayed the public face of an official who had cultivated an authoritative presence. This was the presence at whose approach the London street gangs ceased brawling and slipped away through the side alleys.[2] In the heavy countenance there is the unflinching resolution of a man who has learned to obey and command. Holbein catches the guarded reserve and self-awareness of a politician playing his public role under the watchful eye of the royal predator. Despite the stolid mask of officialdom Cromwell's vitality and force is not obscured.

Cromwell is seated, half turned to his right, gazing out with narrow pouched eyes. Around his sitter Holbein has thrown an air of abstraction which keeps the observer at a distance and suggests the remoteness of high office. The averted gaze preserves the detachment of a man who is pondering the mysteries of state and conveys the concentration of a far-sighted intellect. The brown eyes neither challenge nor confide. They see beyond persons to the ideas and emotions which drive them.

The penetrative distant gaze of the wise counsellor hints at the visionary in Cromwell. Amidst the sordid struggles of court politics he did retain a vision of a great monarchy, a prosperous commonwealth and a religion, purged of superstition. His capacity to visualise the means and consequences of action tempered his preference for drastic solutions. His activist temper and his impatience to 'make or mar' were controlled by his desire to survive and his ability to judge the odds. A

1

sense of calling sanctified his faith in himself. His intelligence demanded intellectual support for his boldest claims. Above all he sought the vindication of legality. The discipline of religious, intellectual and legal justification controlled and gave form and purpose to his dynamism and vision.

Cromwell possessed the ruthlessness of the reformer. He combined his realism with an optimistic enthusiasm. He recommended legislation to the king as 'the most noble, profitable and most beneficial thing that ever was done to the commonwealth of this your realm'.[3] Thinking in superlatives, he could describe Henry as 'the mirror and light of all other kings and princes in Christendom'.[4] He believed in his own rhetoric and so tempted others to believe in it. Rebuffs made him more cautious but did not shatter his confidence. To the end he was proud of his service to the King. Like many reformers, convinced that future good would justify present ills, he wished to turn a blind eye to the suffering and destruction which he had wrought and to be remembered for all his constructive efforts, his 'edification'.[5]

Intimacy was not an ingredient of the court portrait. Holbein's portrait lacks the animation of Cromwell's private face. The expressive mobility of his features, when he engaged in lively conversation, the twinkle in his sidelong glance, as he watched for response to some witticism, are not shown. His tears of frustration, when he seemed about to lose all that he had worked for, the flash of anger as he wished his enemies to the devil, the look of sympathy for an old servant could not appear. Neither his charm for Chapuys, the imperial ambassador, and for Coverdale, the biblical scholar, nor his embarrassing humour at the expense of Gardiner or Cranmer were Holbein's subject.[6]

The intellectual and physical power of Cromwell with his large head and heavy frame are caught in alert suspense. Holbein suggests their latent force by the cramped surroundings of the massive figure which heighten the sense of compressed energy. He puts this black bull of a man in a narrow pen. He depicts the powerful physique which sustained Cromwell in long hours of work at his desk and gave him the energy to ride off to urge on workmen to repair flood damage[7] or to marshal an outdoor reception in the depth of winter for Anne of Cleves.[8] Cromwell worked obsessively and rarely took a holiday. His stamina was mental as well as physical. He did not suffer from self-doubt. His misgivings arose from practical considerations, not from any uncertainty of purpose.

His need to assert himself and achieve his aims often made Cromwell aggressive and arrogant. He relished face to face encounters. He was prepared to put himself 'in the press' to discover what men thought of him and, when he deemed it necessary, he was ready to let others know what he thought of them with surprising frankness. In his heyday he commanded favours, took liberties and bullied with all the assurance of the great, when they were tempted to abuse the deference and obedience upon which society rested. But he knew when and to whom to show the arrogance of power.

Holbein reflects the social discretion of Cromwell in 1534. The coat of arms, granted two years previously, is not paraded in the portrait. He neither assumed the dynastic airs of a gentleman nor the overweening ostentation of a parvenu. But there is no trace of false humility in the assured mien of the royal servant who could distinguish between the trappings and substance of power. The fact that he sat for his portrait indicated his satisfaction with his progress and prospects. His is the plump face of the middle-aged politician who thrives upon responsibility and hard work. It radiates the self-assurance of a self-made man who was proud to have climbed so far and was confident of climbing higher.   *Assurance*

Cromwell's sedentary pose, his clean-shaven face, and black cap and gown are the marks of the *togati*, the clerics and lawyers of officialdom. Elizabeth I's secretary, Sir William Cecil, had himself portrayed with his sword at his side, standing by a table in a known pose of aristocratic authority. In 1534 Thomas Cromwell made no such pretensions. It was as well that he adopted the pose suitable to his station for he would not have made a well poised standing figure with his high shoulders, bulky body and clumsy gait. He lacked the elegance of a courtier. He had not won the King's favour by appearances. *Not won favour by Appearance*

Without flaunting the spoils of office, the rewards of Cromwell's service to the King are apparent. The gold ring, the fur collar, the finely made gown and cap were indications of an affluence befitting a councillor. The scene of the portrait was not set in the Flemish mercantile splendour of his home but in the utilitarian surroundings of a working functionary. The panelled bench and heavy table are serviceable rather than decorative. The hints of opulence in the figured damask wall hangings and Turkey carpet on the side table are subdued. The impression is of a plain solid man in plain solid surroundings. It is a picture of Cromwell at work, poised in momentary reflection in the midst of transacting the King's business.

On the table before the practitioner of statecraft lie the symbols of his administrative and legal skill: the quill, the inkpots, the papers and parchments and a book. His element is the literate world. He wields his power with the pen, drafting legislation, writing directives and memoranda. The bejewelled book suggests his love of learning and his patronage of scholars and printers. It was a token of the power of the printing press which he used so well to educate himself and influence others. The papers and documents, the living tissue of bureaucracy, reveal another source of Cromwell's authority for one of them is addressed, 'To our trusty and right well beloved councillor, Thomas

Power in Pen

Cromwell, Master of our Jewelhouse'. Holbein made the King spell out the identity of the sitter. It was an apt device, for Cromwell's existence and authority depended on acknowledgement by the King.

Holbein's composition draws attention to the broad capable left hand of Cromwell. It holds the symbol of bureaucratic power, a missive, perhaps, the personal directive of a councillor. But of equal significance to contemporaries was the ring on the index finger. The King gave Cromwell such a ring as a New Year's gift in 1532. Courtiers would see it as the sign of royal approval and protection, like the royal ring which later preserved Cranmer from his enemies. Among the people it was rumoured that Cromwell possessed the magic ring of King Solomon which endowed him with power.[9] Even if the ring was one of Cromwell's own occasional purchases or Holbein's invention, it was symbolic of the mystery of great authority.

In his choice of Holbein to present him to his contemporaries and to posterity Cromwell showed an appreciation of visual propaganda which was rare for him. Although the original Holbein portrait disappeared at the time of Cromwell's fall, the surviving copies preserve the artist's composition in its essentials. They reveal Holbein's ability to depict the relationship between the individual and society, between the particular and the typical, between the man and his function, between the instant and the age. His portrait of Cromwell is not without what Carlyle called 'real instruction'. It has proved influential evidence in shaping historical estimates of Cromwell.

Holbein portrayed Cromwell in 1534. How different a portrait might have been painted a mere six years later in April 1540. In the scarlet gown, trimmed with miniver, of the Lord Privy Seal, or the blue mantle of the Order of the Garter, Thomas Cromwell, Earl of Essex, would have left an image upon the eye of posterity very different from that of the portrait of 1534. It would have reflected the rapid change in Cromwell's political and social status, the transformation from sober official to magnificent officer of state and the metamorphosis of Master Cromwell into the holder of one of the most respected and ancient titles of nobility.

By 1540 Cromwell had achieved social as well as political greatness. His wealth was equal to an earldom. His landed property was extensive, including the King's gift of the Manor of Wimbledon, extending over seven parishes, and his share of the proceeds of the dissolution of the abbeys of Lewes, St Osyth, Launde, Michelham, Modenham and Alcester.[10] While his plurality of offices provided a comparatively small income, it opened the way to a rich haul from unofficial fees, gifts, perquisites and patronage. Cromwell had been used to making money through money-lending, commerce and law and he continued to take his opportunities when he entered royal service. By 1535 his income was nearly £4000 a year, an income, which even at the end of the sixteenth century after threefold or more inflation, was considered sufficient for an earl. Yet even in 1539, when his income had further increased, it did not match Wolsey's income which was some four or five times as great in his heyday.[11] The overheads of greatness were heavy and there was some surprise at the smallness of the assets which Cromwell left. He had been generous in supporting his son, his staff and followers, in meeting the debts of friends and in giving alms.

In his greatest extravagance, building, Cromwell had followed the example of Wolsey and the King. Although a widower from 1527 onwards, he continued to expand his domestic establishments. He acquired houses in Hackney, Stepney and Islington and at Ewhurst in Hampshire and spent much upon altering them to his taste. Yet it was in the fashionable Austin Friars, where he had bought a house as a budding lawyer and servant of Wolsey, that he built his most ambitious residence to establish his prestige and presence in London.[12] It was a house to match those of the episcopal administrators, like Stephen Gardiner.

Close to the centre of power, Cromwell was at home in London. He lived there most of the time in his house at Austin Friars or in the Rolls House, which he continued to use even after his resignation as Master of the Rolls. He had no time or incentive to build a rural seat at which to play the provincial magnate. What he might have built as Earl of Essex, had he lived, cannot be known. The destruction of his great house in London has deprived his memory of its architectural monument, while the manner of his death denied him the commemoration of a worthy tomb.

His household offered the expected hospitality to the rich and some two hundred poor received alms daily at his gates.[13] Although he kept a good table and appreciated delicacies and knew, as the treatment of a Pope showed, that the way to a man's heart is through his stomach, he did not indulge in the vanity of playing host at purely social banquets. He discussed business over dinner and invited Gardiner to a meal, when he wished to improve relations with a too successful enemy.[14] Until his last days he lacked the status and the fortune to copy Wolsey in entertaining the King and his court in princely magnificence.

Cromwell preferred small parties, where as host he could choose the topic and set the tone of conversation. His chosen acquaintances were active men, merchants, officials, reformers and creative intellectuals. His close friends were few and of long standing and to them he could show a spontaneity and range of emotion which was denied expression in his public life. Yet even for his political opponents he could show human concern, as he did for Thomas More, and preserve a cordiality, as he did with the Duke of Norfolk.[15] His deepest loyalties centred upon Wolsey and the King.

As he became absorbed in politics Cromwell showed less emotional dependence on women and made no effort to marry again after his wife's death. He stood aloof from the gallantries of the court where affairs of the heart were dangerous to the head. The Duke of Norfolk tempted him with offers of a mistress, but there was no sign that Cromwell shared the Duke's aristocratic tolerance of the sins of the flesh.[16] It was significant of his attitudes that he chose to attack Anne Boleyn for her unfaithfulness and the monks for their immoralities. His bible reading in his middle age had given him a sense of morality which suited his activist temperament. The standards of moral conduct, good learning and religion in Cromwell's household were such as to prompt protestant-minded gentlemen to entrust their sons to his upbringing.[17]

Towards the visual arts Cromwell showed a puritan suspicion, nourished by the contemporary emphasis upon the didactic nature of art. He launched the official campaign against the superstitious abuses of art which destroyed so much of the artistic heritage of the Church. But, if he was sensitive to the moral and religious message of art, he did not lack an appreciation of the arts. His walls were hung with paintings on religious subjects and among his possessions was a statue of the child Christ.[18] He was less fond of pictures on subjects of pagan mythology than Wolsey. He patronised Holbein whose portraiture avoided both popish superstition and pagan licence. In music he showed an English taste for vocal rather than instrumental music, as was shown by the inclusion of a dozen singing boys in his household and his choice of plain song to beguile a Pope.[19] He made a friend of Wyatt, the lyric writer and poet. His furnishings revealed his taste for rich gilded pieces and things of intricate workmanship. He could appreciate the architectural qualities of Wolsey's Oxford college. He admired jewellery and his office as Master of the King's Jewel House gave him the opportunity to cultivate his judgement. As pastimes he indulged in the arts of card playing and dicing, in archery and in hunting and hawking in his purple riding coat.[20]

In intellectual circles Cromwell had to win acceptance among the highly educated by the force of his intelligence, his prodigious memory and self-taught knowledge. Unlike many of his contemporaries he was not prepared for the active life by a formal education at a university. His membership of Gray's Inn acknowledged rather than contributed to his legal learning. His wits had been sharpened by travel, business and the practice of the law by the time he began to compete in Wolsey's learned entourage. He did not approach politics with academic assumptions and end up like Sir Thomas Elyot as a mere maker of books.[21] He was not an intellectual in politics, although he did become an intellectual politician.

To the command of Italian and French and a smattering of German acquired on the continent, he added a knowledge of Latin and a little Greek. He mastered the educated English style of the court to convey information with clarity and express emotion with dignity. He deployed a wide vocabulary, replete with latinisms, and the fashionable trick of repetition for the sake of emphasis.[22] His careful construction and revision of his work revealed a lawyer's appreciation of words, a humanist's sense of rhetoric and a reformer's powers of persuasion. He could compose forceful letters and persuasive speeches. He was a skilled editor of legal texts. By his own efforts he had learned to wield the pen. Yet he did not emulate Dudley, More or Gardiner in the writing of treatises. Although he had made himself literate and articulate, his chosen method was to embody his ideas in legal rather than in literary form. It was a method suited to one who was by nature a man of action rather than of letters.

Cromwell's personal interests included politics, history, divinity and law. They were the favourite subjects of the humanists. Among his books were Petrarch's *Triumphs*, Castiglione's *Courtier*, Machiavelli's *Prince* and *History of Florence*, presented to him in 1537, and Erasmus' edition of the New Testament.[23] If, as Pole claimed, Cromwell admired the realism of Italian writers on statecraft, it was to Marsilio of Padua, the fourteenth-century imperialist, and not Machiavelli that he turned for his political theory. He looked to the Bible for his divinity and, judging by his patronage, to Erasmian and Lutheran works.[24] He gained his information on the Anglo-Saxon Church from Bede and monastic muniments. He possessed an astronomical globe but he abhorred astrology.[25] The gift of a map of Hungary from Edward Hall, the chronicler, calls attention to Cromwell's geographical interests, which might be expected in a man who had been a great traveller in his youth.

Cromwell's interests drew him to intellectuals and his patronage drew intellectuals to him. He maintained Wolsey's cultivation of humanist scholars and perpetuated the New Learning which was too well established in England to be checked by the death of Thomas More or the conservatism of the universities. His power to act made him the hope of both Erasmian and protestant reformers. He promoted the New Learning in its concern with the moral, social and economic stability of the commonwealth but he emphasised the division of Erasmian opinion on the merits of novel religious practices and beliefs. Whereas Thomas More had used the New Learning to cleanse and defend the Church of Rome and Christendom, Cromwell used it to reform and justify the Church of England and the imperial realm.

In private life Cromwell's keen intellect and discipline of mind enabled him to enjoy study and ideas for their own sake. His table-talk included the discussion of biblical interpretation.[26] He gained a reputation for learning which was remembered in Elizabethan Cambridge.[27] In relaxation he was prepared to play the academic with scholars who aspired to the active life. Although as a self-taught man of affairs he could not resist scoring off the learned, he did not hold scholars in contempt. If in his public role he did not defer to intellectuals and submitted their proposals to the criteria of political practicability, he did not neglect the theory behind what he did put into practice. Like the King, he recognised the importance of winning the battle of ideas in politics and he followed his royal master in picking academic brains for useful material to justify or inspire policy. Having a better grasp of conceptual thought than Henry, he was able to provide a more profound intellectual basis for policy and to make better use of intellectuals.

Cromwell's reputation for originality is based on his readiness to apply the central notions of Erasmian reform and of imperialist theory to political action and on his receptivity to ideas current among the advocates of what was known by contemporaries as the New Learning. With a masterly selectivity he put together his programme for action and the justification for it. Of the quality of the mind, which he applied to that task, there is the recognition by such men as Reginald Pole, Thomas Cranmer, Thomas Starkey and among others the King, himself, who was used to being served by brilliant men. Sir Thomas Elyot claimed that it was 'excellent virtue and learning' that enabled 'a man of base estate of the communalty, to be thought worthy to be so much advanced'.[28]

Lacking noble birth, Cromwell, nevertheless, had the aspirations of a dynast. He arranged the marriage of his son Gregory, to Elizabeth, sister of Jane Seymour, the Queen, and widow of Sir Anthony Oughtred.[29] In the event the marriage probably helped to save Gregory's inheritance which had been forfeited at his father's fall. Cromwell did not up to the time of his death attempt to win an aristocratic bride for himself. The story of his plan to marry Mary Tudor was intended to involve him in treason but it also recognised his need of high connections to offset his humble origins which were a persistent disadvantage to him.[30]

Cromwell had to suppress his military abilities and be content to be a politician rather than a soldier. As his speech for the Commons in 1523 showed, he had a grasp of strategy.[31] He concerned himself with organising the military preparedness of the realm, knowing that he lacked the social status to exercise command of a royal army in the field. Remaining at Court, while his rival, Norfolk, was sent to face the hazards of insurrection, suited Cromwell. Both his nephew, Sir Richard Cromwell, and his son, Gregory, were able to uphold the family name at the joustings.[32] It was in their company that Cromwell himself appeared on parade before the King at the head of a great force mustered in London. It was an appropriate command for, if he had a home territory, it was London, the most important city in the realm.[33]

His brief tenure of his earldom, before his downfall, did not allow Cromwell time to establish himself as Earl of Essex and impress himself upon history as a great lord. His reputation owes nothing to his titles and he has been known to historians as Thomas Cromwell. It is, perhaps, appropriate that the existing portrait of him was taken while he was a commoner. It is not in the brief splendour before his going down that we can sense visually what manner of man he was, but in the clear morning light of his ascent, when Holbein pictured him with a realism that conceals the subtlety of his study.

1 WAYS TO ADVANCEMENT

Thomas Cromwell had but a short time in which to leave his mark upon the history of England. For him the wheel of fortune turned fast. He gained great influence with Henry VIII by 1532 but that same King sanctioned his execution in 1540. Compared with other notable servants of the Tudor dynasty, such as Cardinal Wolsey or Lord Burghley, his effective political career was brief. Born about 1485 he gained power at a comparatively advanced age when he was in his late forties. Without the advantage of gentle birth, clerical office, or title he entered royal service as the protégé of a fallen minister. He had neither the academic distinction of Wolsey nor the literary reputation of Thomas More. Thomas Cromwell had to achieve greatness.

Thomas was not born great. His grandfather and father had lived in humble circumstances on the outskirts of London, a magnet for men from the provinces with fortunes to make or mend. Thomas' father, Walter, belonged, liked William Shakespeare's father later, to that class of men who raised themselves above the poverty of the smallholder by pursuing a variety of occupations. In his time Walter was a brewer, a smith and a fuller in Putney. He held a few virgates by copyhold in the manor of Wimbledon. His modest success in taking his opportunities gave him some standing. He was Constable of Putney in 1495 and he had served as a juryman. He married his daughters successfully: the elder, Katherine to a lawyer, Morgan Williams, from a rising Welsh immigrant family in the neighbourhood, and the younger, Elizabeth, to a farmer with the reassuring name of Wellyfed.

But the strains and temptations of the life of a jack of all trades, haunted by hopes of affluence, appear to have overcome Walter Cromwell's scruples. He descended to petty dishonesty. For his contraventions of the Assize of Ale he was brought to the manor court forty-eight times between 1475 and 1501. He abused his common rights as a tenant of the manor. In 1514 he practised a serious fraud by altering the documents relating to his copyhold tenure, and was evicted from his manorial tenancy. He often drank heavily and in 1477 he had been convicted and fined for assault.[1] Not surprisingly he was unable to control his young son Thomas.

If his father's weakness influenced Thomas, it may have disposed him to venerate authority and father figures. Thomas was remarkably loyal to Wolsey at the time of his fall and defended the Cardinal's memory in after years.[2] Later Henry VIII fulfilled the parental role. In one of his last letters to the King he wrote, 'For your majesty hath been the most bountiful prince to me that ever was King to his subject, yea and more like a dear father, your majesty not offended, than a master.'[3] His words may have been those of a skilful advocate but they seem to be charged with an emotion, going beyond the common acknowledgement of royal paternalism, which Cromwell even feared might offend the King. Such speculation is, perhaps, justified, if it calls attention to the evidence of Cromwell's devotion and loyalty in the service of his masters and of the pressures of his formative years.

Whatever the effects of his father's conduct on his future, Thomas made an early break with his family and went abroad. He may have been fleeing from an intolerable father or from the results of his own misconduct. It was said that he was briefly imprisoned. In after life Cromwell divulged little of his early days. He once told Cranmer that he had been a ruffian in his youth.[4] Whether his admission was made with a nostalgic self-approval or with some regret, it was fair comment, for only a tough boy could have survived and profited by the risky enterprise on which he embarked.

Like some hero in a sixteenth-century picaresque story, Thomas ventured abroad and attached himself to a foreign army. It says much for Cromwell's subsequent fame and for his early adventurous career that the Italian novelist, Bandello, should have referred to the story of Cromwell's youth in which he was said to have joined the French army, probably as a page to some man-at-arms, and to have found his way to Italy and to have been present at the battle of Garigliano in December, 1503. There is no reason to doubt the story.

By some combination of initiative and luck Thomas later found work with the merchant banking family of the Frescobaldi. Their international connections, no doubt, made them ready to accept a young foreigner. But Cromwell must have shown evident promise to secure employment with such shrewd merchants. Whatever education Thomas had had in his boyhood, it had clearly made him both literate and numerate. He showed a facility in acquiring fluency in languages and skill in accountancy. His new career was a striking demonstration of his opportunism and intelligence.

His experience of military life with a conquering army and of commerce in such cities as Venice, Florence and Pisa was likely to impress upon Thomas the elemental and materialistic traits of human nature. It was significant that he preferred the calculating temper of a merchant house to the violent emotions of the camp. If he sowed wild oats, the expense of spirit appears to have left him with a distaste for licence. Thomas spent his impressionable years in the hard but sophisticated ways of Italian mercantile life.

The young Cromwell, earning his living in competitive business, was far from enjoying the advantages of a favoured scholar, such as Thomas Winter or Reginald Pole, studying abroad. But he did enjoy some of what were recognised as the educative influences of travel. Italy gave him a different perspective from that which he had known in Putney. He knew at first hand the impact of the Renaissance upon the society which had generated it. He acquired a familiarity with those Italianate attitudes which were being consciously cultivated in the North by intellectuals and courtiers. In later years his early experiences gave him an understanding of and sympathy with the humanist thinking which he encountered in English intellectual circles. It was in England in middle age that his ability to speak Italian, his acquaintance with Italian authors and his awareness of Italian ways and ideas were to appear as the attributes of a cultivated and educated man.

Although Cromwell was to cherish his knowledge of Italy, he did not become the Italianate Englishman, so abhorred later by English moralists. He did not find Italy so attractive as to wish to settle. As soon as he had learned enough of the international cloth trade, he moved confidently to the Netherlands. With his good financial and business head, he made a place for himself among the English merchants there. He visited the great mercantile centres such as Antwerp, Bruges and the fair at Middelburgh. Yet his years on the continent he counted as his apprenticeship. His ambition was to return to England.

About 1512 Cromwell decided to settle in England. For one equipped with a knowledge of European commerce and business methods England with its booming cloth trade was a land of opportunity. After some years of moving around on the continent, Cromwell, already in his late twenties, determined to marry. His bride was a well-to-do widow of a yeoman of the guard, Elizabeth Wykys, the daughter of a shearman, who had served as a gentleman usher to Henry VII. His marriage opened the way to a place in his father-in-law's business in the cloth trade. Cromwell had followed a well known way to business success through matrimony.

After his marriage Cromwell prospered. He added to his interests in the cloth trade, by dabbling in estate management and money lending. He lived in the mercantile world of London which had commercial, financial and intellectual contacts throughout Europe and with all the layers of society which it served.

In 1517-18 he made a return visit to Italy on behalf of the Guild of Our Lady of St Botolph's Church, Boston, to obtain certain indulgences from the Pope. Cromwell contrived to evade the tedious and costly bureaucratic proceedings of the curia by catching the attention of the Pope, while he was making his accustomed journey from his hunting lodge, by a performance of an English 'three man's song'. The unusual serenade gained Cromwell and his party an immediate audience with the curious Pope. Cromwell then completed the second part of his plan by producing English jellies 'such as kings and princes only in the realm of England use to feed upon' in order to please a Pope, renowned for his fastidious palate. The Pope was delighted and then and there granted the requests of the guild.[5] The skilled choice of means revealed Cromwell's insight into human nature but more significantly his estimate of the Papacy as a human institution. In Italy he had learned to regard the Pope as one more Prince and the Curia as one more administration to be managed with the wiles of earthly wisdom.

In his dealings with all sorts and conditions of men Cromwell gathered money and ideas. He avoided the outright heretical circles in London which had been exposed in the celebrated scandal of the death of Richard Hunne, the Mercer, in the Lollard's Tower, but he was attracted by the fashionable Erasmian circles. He read and learned by heart the Latin version of the New Testament by Erasmus soon after its publication in 1516 and by 1519 he had struck up an acquaintance with Thomas Elyot, the future author of *the Governour*, and friend of Thomas More.[6] The prospects of intellectual activism were broadening before him. His interests and acquaintances indicate that Cromwell was mixing with lawyers. Since his return to England he had studied the law and increasingly pleaded in the courts and by 1520 he had something of a legal reputation.

Cromwell's opportunity for legal studies came from the availability of printed law books, the proximity of the Courts at Westminster, and the concentration of lawyers in London. If social ambition or sheer intellectual energy led him on, it was the dependence of his business on legal transactions which initiated him into the law. Litigation was a means of getting a settlement, of establishing an advantage and of securing a deal. He learned the law at a mature age as a method of dealing with men and situations in business rather than as an academic pursuit. It was the first systematic discipline to which he had applied his intellect and it had a profound impact upon his ways of thinking and acting. If his travels had broadened his outlook and his mercantile expertise had sharpened his wits, it was the law which enabled him to concentrate all his experience behind an effective legalistic approach to problems. It qualified him for new employment. The years between 1512 and 1520, when Cromwell developed a legal mind, were the most formative and significant for his future.

In 1520 the great Cardinal Wolsey employed Cromwell on legal business concerning an appeal to the Papal Curia against a finding in the Prerogative Court of Canterbury. It was a sign that Cromwell's reputation as a lawyer could attract the most exalted patron. Even if he did owe his opportunity to his cousin, a vicar of Battersea, known to the Cardinal, his employment was an important recommendation in a world where advancement depended on patronage. Over the coming years Cromwell's legal activities increased while his interests in the cloth trade dwindled. He was attorney for William Popley in a matter before the King's Council. He handled the English affairs of a Hansa merchant. He was to be patronised by the nobility. Lady Dorset and Viscount Rochford's sister consulted him on business and legal matters. The cases multiplied.[7] His letters were clear and polite or forceful, as occasion required. His expanding practice was a tribute to the confidence which he inspired in his clients. He had confidence in himself for, when the chance came to enter parliament in 1523, he was among the ambitious lawyers who eagerly took it.

For his début in the High Court of Parliament he prepared a set-piece.[8] He constructed a speech which would arouse controversy and call attention to its author. His argument was designed to dissuade the King from his plan to lead in person a large army in the conquest of France and so to remove the need for the massive subsidy which Wolsey was demanding from the Commons. Opposition to taxation was usually welcome to the Commons and in 1523 there was little enthusiasm for the King's attempt to revive the glorious days of Henry V. Cromwell was following in the footsteps of another lawyer, Thomas More, who in his youth had opposed the demands of Henry VII for taxes. It was a good way for a new member to establish himself in the Commons.

But Cromwell's speech was not mere obstruction. He may have wished to ingratiate himself with his fellow members in the Commons but he had no wish to offend the King or Wolsey. His use of flattery towards the King was a masterly exercise in sycophancy but what was more impressive was the array of arguments demonstrating his grasp of domestic and foreign politics, of the strategy and tactics and economic aspects of warfare. While allowing the necessity of meting out retribution to the provocative Francis I and accepting the King's commitment to war as an ally of the Emperor, he argued that a series of small expeditions were both militarily and financially preferable to a massive invasion of France under royal leadership. He pressed the need for the King to remain in England for the well-being of the realm and in order to avoid the disastrous consequences of injury or capture.

He questioned the feasibility of sustaining a large army on the continent without reducing the realm to impotent exhaustion. He demonstrated the military weaknesses of marching a large army to Paris and he dismissed encouraging parallels with past English victories in France by pointing out that they had been won under very different conditions. Finally he boldly suggested that the King's objective should be the conquest of Scotland and its union with England.

As his clerk wrote it down, Cromwell's speech was a *tour de force*. But whether Cromwell ever managed to deliver such a long and ambitious maiden speech is not known. He had obviously taken his début in parliament very seriously and had found the seventeen weeks of the three sessions exhausting. A few days after the Commons were dismissed in August he could not resist writing about parliament to his gushing business friend, John Creke, in Bilbao.[9] Obviously he wanted to avoid the appearance of boasting by representing the whole business as tedious. He reeled off an impressive list of the topics of debate but concluded that nothing had been achieved and that the King had got his subsidy, because as usual parliament had proved ineffective. As a new member, Cromwell, no doubt, had had some of his illusions shattered and was disappointed that members of the commons seemed to have so little influence. With pride and disillusion mixed, he took the wordly wise course of depreciating his new experience to a friend from whom he could expect both admiration and sympathy.

It is, of course, possible to take Cromwell's little note to Creke *au pied de la lettre* as a cynical dismissal of the role of parliament in government. But it can hardly be insisted that such an interpretation established Cromwell's life-long and considered opinion on such an important constitutional matter. Such an opinion was consistent neither with his learning and expectations as a lawyer nor with the use he made of his future opportunities in parliament. In their context his comments look like the irony of a momentarily disenchanted new member rather than the final verdict of an experienced member on the utility of parliament.

If Cromwell in parliament had failed to change the world, parliament had helped to change him. It had demonstrated that his business in cloth and practice in the law had given him a grasp of greater affairs. He revealed a political sense. In the eighteen months following the end of parliament in August, 1523, there was an important change in Cromwell's status. He was referred to as a gentleman when he appeared among merchants, haberdashers and mercers. The right worshipful Mr Cromwell had crossed the social divide between the governed and the governors. His election to Gray's Inn during 1524 gave him professional respectability as a lawyer. He served as a subsidy commissioner in Middlesex. But most important of all he had recommended himself for employment in the entourage of Wolsey. By the winter of 1524 Cromwell was being addressed as 'Councillor to my Lord Legate'.[10]

In the household of the Cardinal, Cromwell was in one of the most important centres of power in the Kingdom. It was Wolsey's personal extension of the royal government and the hub of his legatine authority over the Church. Here Cromwell could observe how the procedures of control in both church and state were operated. He became familiar with the manners and ways of those in authority. He shared discussions which ranged over the problems of the commonwealth and the philosophy of politics. Erasmus, himself, had praised the learning of the Cardinal's household. There were opportunities to become the cultivated man of affairs. Cromwell had a place in what was recognised as a school for politicians, administrators and diplomats. The stimulating atmosphere, known to the young Thomas More in the household of Cardinal Morton, was now being breathed in the household of Cardinal Wolsey by Cromwell, near the end of his thirties. He proved that it was not too late for him to learn.

Although suited for diplomacy by his familiarity with the continent and its languages, Cromwell lacked both lay or clerical status and the knowledge of civil law which were required by a diplomat. He did not lack the interest in foreign policy as his speech for parliament in 1523 showed. Wolsey, however, did not employ him in diplomacy. Fortunately for his future advancement Cromwell's life abroad had equipped him with the experience which others had to acquire as diplomats. His employment in the Cardinal's personal and domestic business was, therefore, not the obstacle to high office which it might have proved, if he had not been abroad. In the event what he learned of legal and ecclesiastical matters at home turned out to be a valuable complement to his knowledge of European affairs.

Wolsey chose Cromwell to execute his cherished plan to establish a college at Oxford and a school at Ipswich. It was a measure of Cromwell's efficiency that this project was the one of the Cardinal's many proposals for reform that made the most significant progress. The importance of the scheme for Cromwell was that it demonstrated his administrative and legal skill and identified him as an active and capable, if ruthless, reformer. It gave him a reputation at Court as one of Wolsey's most forceful agents.

The redeployment of monastic revenues to endow educational establishments was not without precedent, but Wolsey's scheme to put such revenues to 'better use' was on an unprecedented scale. It was to involve the suppression of twenty-nine religious houses. Cromwell began his survey of the first five houses in January, 1525, and for the next four years he was principally occupied in the business of dissolving the monasteries and building the college and school. He supervised the sales of lands and moveables. The measure of his task was in part revealed, when he handed over to the dean of the Oxford college thirty-four bags of documents, relating to suppressed houses in August, 1526. By the middle of 1528 the school at Ipswich and the college at Oxford were being built and Cromwell reported, 'The buildings of your noble college most prosperously and magnificently doth arise in such wise that to every man's judgement the like thereof was never seen nor imagined, having consideration to the largeness, beauty, sumptuous, curious and substantial building of the same'.[11] He added that the services in the chapel were 'so devout, solemn and full of harmony that in mine opinion it hath few peers'. His enthusiasm for the great project of reform was evident.

The operation roused opposition. Wolsey had won royal and papal approval and the support of Erasmian reformers who believed that the education of the clergy was the surest way to purify religion and combat heresy. But the suppression of religious houses had disturbed many interests and the Cardinal's enemies took the opportunity to attack the methods which he had employed. There were complaints about the conduct of Cromwell and his agents. As receiver-general, Cromwell had managed the finances of the operation and, like any administrator or lawyer, he had counted unofficial gifts, fees and perquisites as payment for his services and acceptable sources of income. Obviously there was room for differences of opinion concerning what dealings were fair and what transactions were corrupt. The court faction hostile to Wolsey made the most of their ammunition. Stories of threats to Cromwell's life and rumours of his disgrace and imprisonment were circulated. Incredible things were being said at court in 1527 about the malpractices of the Cardinal's men.

The attack upon Cromwell was part of the assault upon his master. In 1527 Henry was beginning to take a personal interest in his matrimonial predicament and to show that he was prepared to take matters out of Wolsey's hands and act on his own initiative. Such a situation encouraged opponents of the Cardinal. Norfolk, Suffolk and the Boleyns attempted to exploit the divergence on policies between the King and the Cardinal. Meanwhile 'the right worshipful Mr Cromwell, my lord Cardinal's servant and of his council' was an obvious whipping boy. For Cromwell it was an ironic turn of fate that, so soon after he had managed to establish himself in Wolsey's favour, his good lord's position was being undermined.

Despite the threat that hung over his future, Cromwell continued to prosper and he continued to display my Lord Cardinal's arms in gilt on canvas in the hall of his house at Austin Friars.[12] His correspondents became ever more deferential and tokens of their gratitude, a hundred marks, six dozen quails, a gelding, were a tribute to his influence. His interest was sought in legal cases, in matters of patronage and one petitioner wanted him to give his protection by putting the neighbourhood 'in fear'. His wealth grew and an anxious friend recommended fixing a great chain on the door of his house as a precaution against theft. With a greater trust in providence one suitor informed Cromwell that God provides for those who help the poor 'as I do understand by my brother-in-law your mastership is provided'.[13]

Cromwell was becoming known in legal, ecclesiastical and court circles. Reginald Pole, the future Cardinal, Stephen Gardiner who was to be Secretary to the King, Miles Coverdale who later produced an English translation of the Bible, Lord Berners, the translator of Froissart's Chronicle were typical of the variously influential men with whom he was acquainted. The household of Wolsey attracted the great and those aspiring to be great. Cromwell himself was attracting able followers and servants, like Stephen Vaughan the merchant and financier who kept him informed on foreign affairs and domestic news, and Ralph Sadler who acted as his secretary. During the 1520's Cromwell had established himself among a group of men of affairs in the governing circle. With the intellectuals and the administrators he had proved that he could hold his own in argument and in effective action.

But as the circle of his outside acquaintances increased, his family dwindled. In 1527 his wife died. Her sister too was dead. He then lost his 'little daughters', Anne and Grace. Only his son Gregory, born in 1513 was to remain to Cromwell as his constant hope and disappointment. He sent Gregory to Pembroke Hall, Cambridge, along with his cousin, Christopher Wellyfed, and Sadler's son Nicholas. He was hopeful of great progress from 'my scholars'. But they did nothing more notable than set fire to their rooms. Cromwell's frustration was vented upon their luckless tutor, John Chekynge, who had to defend his competence and his need for funds when the irate Cromwell was reluctant to acknowledge either.[14] He was unfair to Chekynge, but, like most parents, he found it hard to admit that the defects were in his child rather than in the teacher. His awkwardness over paying for the futile attempt to make a silk purse out of a sow's ear indicated his strong parental feeling. His concern for his family was shown in a will, drawn up in 1529, which carefully guarded the interests of his relatives in his estate.[15]

The will which revealed the substantial worldly gains of his successful past was prudently drawn up at a time when Cromwell's future was beginning to look less assured. At the end of July, 1529, the legatine court which had been called to pronounce upon the validity of the marriage of Henry VIII and Catherine of Aragon was adjourned. Wolsey was blamed for failing to secure the annulment which the King required. Henry withdrew his favour from the Cardinal and Wolsey's enemies became more confident that they could bring him down. Cromwell had to wait on events. But in his service to Wolsey he had acquired the ambition and endurance to survive in public life.

2 IN THE KING'S SERVICE

Wolsey had predicted that the adjournment in late July, 1529, of the legatine court, dealing with the annulment of the King's marriage, and the avocation of the case to Rome would 'utterly destroy him for ever'. For the next sixteen months Cromwell witnessed the slow fulfilment of that prediction. Stephen Gardiner, Wolsey's secretary, was summoned to be secretary to the King. There could be no such immediate escape to royal service for Cromwell. Gardiner had dealt with Wolsey's public affairs, while Cromwell had been concerned with the Cardinal's personal business. Having to stay on the sinking ship, Cromwell may have shared his secretary's animosity towards Gardiner, who seemed to have deserted Wolsey.[1]

When through his fellow Cardinal, Campeggio, Wolsey obtained an audience with the King, Cromwell received an over optimistic account of it. It was fleeting comfort. He was required by the King's lawyers to furnish information for the preparation of a charge of *praemunire* against his master. In October Wolsey was indicted. Fear that the alternative might be attainder in parliament drove Wolsey to admit the offence of *praemunire* and to throw himself upon the King's mercy without which he would incur the penalty of life imprisonment and forfeiture of all his possessions. Stripped of the office of Chancellor, Wolsey was in a desperate plight.

By November the gravity of his patron's position was torturing Cromwell. Cavendish, Wolsey's usher, found Cromwell by the window of the Great Chamber of Wolsey's residence at Esher.[2] With his primer in his hands, he was praying, while the tears ran down his cheeks. In seeking the consolations of religion, Cromwell was not play-acting for Cavendish's benefit. He had been moved by the services in Wolsey's college chapel and in his recent will he had left money for prayers for his soul. But, if Cromwell was earnestly seeking the aid of God, he was also resolving to help himself.

When Cavendish enquired whether Cromwell was sorrowing for his own or his master's plight, Cromwell bluntly replied that he was lamenting his own 'unhappy adventure'. He was worried that the ill name that he had earned in the service of the Cardinal would prove his own undoing. He complained that Wolsey had not provided for him by the grant of any income or office. Finally he announced his intention 'to ride after dinner to London and so to court where I will either make or mar ere I come again. I will put myself in the press to see what any man is able to lay to my charge of untruth or misdemeanour'.

While at dinner before he left for London, Cromwell reminded Wolsey of the loyal service of his lay servants and of the rewards due to them. When Wolsey replied that he had nothing left with which to recompense them, Cromwell suggested that the clerics in Wolsey's service, who had been given rich livings, should provide. After dinner he reminded everyone that he had not been granted a penny towards the increase of his income and he then gave generously to a fund for the lay servants and called upon the clerics to do the same. Cromwell's envy of 'idle chaplains' had matured into a sense of injustice and a grudge against the clergy.

When Cromwell did return to London, he decided to test the King's attitude towards him by seeking a seat in parliament, which was timed to meet on 3rd November. He was obliged to approach the King through the Duke of Norfolk, Wolsey's rival and a great borough patron. Learning from Sadler, his secretary, who conducted the negotiations for a seat, that the King was well content that Cromwell should be a burgess, he acted upon the King's assurance.[3] Without waiting upon Norfolk, he tried to obtain a seat at Orford through his friend Sir Thomas Rush but both seats had been promised. He turned to Sir William Paulet, Wolsey's steward in the see of Winchester, who with one day to go before the opening of parliament secured Cromwell's nomination for Taunton, where Wolsey had exercised patronage. Independent of Norfolk's favour, Cromwell took his seat in the Commons through royal favour and the residual influence of Wolsey.

With the success of his last minute bid to enter the Commons, Cromwell was in a position to speak where he would be heard by everyone of influence. He could save his own fortunes, while serving both the King and Wolsey. He was determined to rescue whatever might be saved from the wreckage of his own and his patron's prospects. When Cromwell took his seat in the Commons, Wolsey had lost the King's favour but had won the King's mercy by loyally surrendering himself as the King's subject. He was still Archbishop of York. Some of his forfeited wealth had been restored to him. Henry, it seemed, was not prepared to be hustled into executing Wolsey as he had been into executing Empson and Dudley.

The fact that Wolsey's fate had not been sealed incited his enemies to further efforts to destroy him. Their attempt to secure Wolsey's attainder in parliament was thwarted by the King. In early December they put a petition before the Commons in which Wolsey's misdeeds were rehearsed. If the absence of any mention by Hall of a debate on the petition in the Commons indicates that there were no further proceedings, then Cavendish's story of Cromwell's loyal defence of his master in the debate is suspect.[4] While Cavendish's memory may have erred over the occasion of the debate, it did not fail him over the impression of loyalty to Wolsey which Cromwell gave to the Commons. Throughout the session Cromwell was in close touch with Wolsey and did some parliamentary business for his master. If Gardiner too tried to help Wolsey, it was Cromwell who gained the reputation of being a loyal servant.

Having survived the attack in parliament, Wolsey could not be regarded as having entirely lost Henry's favour. Although it was risky to continue to defend Wolsey, Cromwell was not defending a defiant cleric against the King, but trying to excite the King's mercy for a man who had submitted as an obedient subject and had admitted the error of his ways. He had every incentive to clear his own name, tarnished in the Cardinal's service. Yet to have remained in Wolsey's employ could only have been possible, while it could be believed that the King would not wholly abandon Wolsey to his enemies. Even so it was a gamble requiring courage and political calculation. No doubt Cromwell knew as well as Chapuys, the imperial ambassador, that Henry would not allow parliament to settle Wolsey's fate or anyone to determine who should be his counsellor.[5] Yet in standing by his good lord Cromwell was not choosing the easiest way to survive. Thomas More and Stephen Gardiner had shown the easier way to royal favour.

Cromwell continued to serve Wolsey. In February 1530 he gained a royal pardon for his master which he declared had cost him personally a thousand pounds to arrange.[6] He also obtained money for Wolsey to finance his move to York in March. Until Wolsey moved North, Cromwell constantly visited him. As the most able servant prepared to remain in Wolsey's service, he became the manager of Wolsey's affairs and his agent at Court. He had daily access to Norfolk and made every opportunity to have audience with the King. In dealing with Norfolk, he was not defecting to Wolsey's bitterest enemy. Like his master, he was simply recognising the political necessity of approaching the most influential figure at Court. It was not for his own purposes that he sought to curry favour with the Boleyns. Wolsey himself had addressed Anne Boleyn, requesting her intervention on his behalf with the King.[7] Only by developing a tolerable working relationship with those in a position to sway the King could Cromwell hope to serve Wolsey or himself.

At some time before the end of April, 1530, Cromwell was sworn into the royal service. It was a sign that Cromwell realised that Wolsey would not regain the King's confidence. His personal concern for Wolsey remained but his political loyalty had changed. From now on he never encouraged Wolsey to believe that he could regain power. It was now a matter of his master's survival. He urged Wolsey not to provoke his enemies and to comply with the King's wishes. He encouraged Wolsey to follow his declared intent of cultivating the pious life. When he advised Wolsey to be content with his lot and seek spiritual solace, it was not mockery.[8] He was trying to make sure that Wolsey would stay out of politics. The irony of such advice lay not in the intentions of the giver but in the character of the recipient.

Cromwell had at last accepted the permanence of Wolsey's disgrace. Wolsey still cherished optimistic illusions between bouts of despair. Cromwell had the task of conveying the harsh facts to his old master who was never able fully to accept them. He spared Wolsey the indignity of a servant's pity but not the unpleasant truths. Cromwell's exasperation with his master's behaviour is apparent in his letters. In October, 1530, his resentment at Wolsey's signs of mistrust flared out.[9] The hard tone of Cromwell's letters was partly due to the fact that he could not comment freely for fear of destroying his position as Wolsey's broker at Court, and partly due to his efforts to shock Wolsey into a recognition of his real position. The pathos in the great man's decline must not be allowed to obscure the fact that his constant changes of mood, ambitious self-assertion alternating with abject self-pity, were enough to try the patience of the most loyal of servants. In all he did during this dangerous period, when Wolsey was in disgrace, Cromwell cannot be accused of having injured his master's true interests. When he became convinced that Wolsey's power could not be restored, he tried to ensure his survival and he continued to manage affairs to Wolsey's advantage.

Cromwell's chief business for Wolsey at Court was the management of his remaining assets and of the stewardship of the monastic lands, allocated to Wolsey's educational foundations, in which the King had confirmed him. Wolsey still had revenues from which he could grant annuities and, as a great pluralist, he still had extensive ecclesiastical rights which he could exercise. Although the King might make grants at Wolsey's expense, no recipient could feel secure in the royal gift without confirmation from Wolsey. Cromwell exercised a considerable patronage on behalf of his master.

From such patronage Cromwell had to make what he could, look after the interests of Wolsey, comply with the King's demands and seek to appease his master's enemies. By the skilful award of annuities and the exploitation of Wolsey's clerical rights, Cromwell appears to have created a favourable impression among even the most hostile suitors for Wolsey's favour and to have avoided the displeasure of his master and the King. Besides the pickings from these transactions, Cromwell gained reputation at Court for courtesy and efficiency. He had done well for himself and for his master, as Wolsey on occasion was prepared gratefully to recognise. From a potentially dangerous situation he had drawn some advantage for all concerned. His success obscures the difficulty of his link with a disgraced minister. He had contrived to preserve the appearance of manners at the vulture's feast and had given such honours as there were to Wolsey, the involuntary host.

Cromwell had been fortunate that his particular business had kept him at Court. Whatever he knew of Wolsey's intrigues with the King of France and the Emperor, whatever he knew of Wolsey's contacts with the Papal Curia, he was not directly involved. Wolsey's actions in summoning the Northern Convocation and preparing for a grandiose enthronement as Archbishop of York were his own. These moves which provoked suspicion of Wolsey's disloyalty to the King did not concern Cromwell. When Wolsey died in late November, 1530. while under escort on his way to the Tower, it was, perhaps fortunate for Cromwell. His loyalty to Wolsey had been tested so often. It was not to be given a final test in the notoriety which would have accompanied a trial of his old master for treason. Cromwell had done nothing to destroy Wolsey: he could not save him.

It was significant of Henry's recognition of Cromwell's loyalty to Wolsey that it was not until after his master's death that the King considered giving Cromwell the sort of employment which Cromwell could expect in accordance with the conventions of goodlordship. It was usual for the King to recruit his professional servants from those who had been trained in the service of great men. Wolsey's men had not been sacrificed with their master. Henry had found patronage for everyone from Wolsey's secretary, Stephen Gardiner, to his usher, Cavendish, and from his yeomen to his fool.[10] It remained to be seen whether the man who had been the 'lord Cardinal's servant and of his council' would be given similar status in the service of the King.

Cromwell could expect opposition to his advancement from those who held that he shared in his master's guilt. Sir John Wallop, perhaps at Norfolk's instigation, denigrated Cromwell before the King. But no great names are mentioned as being in open opposition to him. Those who are recorded as having recommended him to the King were Sir Christopher Hales, a legal officer of the Crown, and Sir John Russell, a trusted soldier and diplomat.[11] Cromwell, already in the service of the King, had access to the King. But his association with Wolsey had isolated him and he had no great patron. He had been unable or unwilling to attach himself to any other great patron. He was at the King's disposal and, if the King chose to advance him, he would be wholly the King's man.

In retrospect Cromwell's success in winning the King's favour and advancement appeared to be rapid and complete. The Imperial ambassador, Chapuys, who was knowledgeable about the court factions, recorded that Cromwell obtained an audience with the King to clear himself of accusations being made against him by Sir John Wallop.[12] Furthermore he added that Cromwell had so won the King over with promises to make him rich that Henry had thereupon taken him as his secret adviser until he was ready four months later to make him an official councillor. In the political eyes of Chapuys it had been a personal triumph for Cromwell over court intrigue, won by playing on the King's need for wealth. It was the explanation of a practical politician concerned with the material requirements of government.

Reginald Pole described things differently.[13] He detested Cromwell and saw him as an emissary of the devil who had cunningly tempted the King with visions of wealth and power and with a proposal to create a royal supremacy over the Church in England. Pole's Faustian vision cast the responsibility for the disasters of the Roman Church in England upon Cromwell and pictured him as the archtype of evil counsellor. Cromwell appeared as the scapegoat for the King who might yet be saved. Pole created the elaborate machiavellian arguments with which he imagined that Cromwell had been able to seduce the King. He represented Cromwell's success as the conquest of the King's mind by brilliant but evil persuasion. It was an intellectual's view of politics.

John Foxe tells how the King, when he heard that Cromwell could give him good legal advice on how to undermine papal authority, arranged to meet him in the palace garden in Westminster.[14] There Cromwell argued that the bishops' oath to the Pope divided their loyalty and prejudiced their obedience to the King and the law. He also assured the King that he was entitled to take the wealth of the Church. Foxe felt that Cromwell's well justified arguments had won over the King and had advanced the reformation of the Church in England. Foxe had found a place for Cromwell in the providential plan which led to the establishment of true religion in England. It was the protestant historian's vision of politics.

These accounts reflect something of the sense of mystery which surrounded the apparently sudden elevation of Cromwell. They read like a mixture of rumour and hindsight, condensing the effects of Cromwell's contacts with and services for the King into the impact of a single dramatic meeting. They suggest that Cromwell advocated from the beginning the policies for which he was later generally held to be responsible. They give the impression that Cromwell went to Henry with a plan for the dissolution of the monasteries and for the creation of the royal supremacy. Moreover, they imply that these schemes were original and brought about an immediate change in the King's policies.

All three accounts mention the enrichment of the King. But the exploitation of ecclesiastical resources was not new or the sole financial expedient open to the Crown. Suffolk and Norfolk had openly claimed in 1529 that they would dispossess the Church on Wolsey's fall.[15] Cromwell, after his experience of the violent reaction to Wolsey's dissolution, would have been cautious, as he was five years later, about embarking upon an appropriation of monastic property. Cromwell, no doubt, showed concern about the traditional aim of endowing the Crown and displayed enough financial expertise to obtain his first offices in the financial administration. Yet it is not likely that Cromwell produced any ideas of which the King had not already heard. The King knew how to tax, fine and appropriate clerical wealth before Cromwell gave him advice and he continued to tap those sources when Cromwell became a councillor.

The policy of asserting royal authority at the expense of the clergy and the Pope was likewise not Cromwell's novel idea. The arguments, attributed to Cromwell by Pole, would have been found shocking but their aims in the different guise of Henry's imperialism had already been mooted. Even Pole found it difficult to explain why the King and those about him were prepared to accept amoral advice, which he alleged Cromwell had given, and he put it down to the power of the devil working through his advocate, Cromwell. Foxe created a more plausible argument for Cromwell from hindsight. Henry himself, however, already had views about the powers of his imperial crown over the clergy. He had authorised Wiltshire and Suffolk to speak to the papal nuncio and Norfolk to speak to the imperial ambassador in terms which left little doubt that Henry claimed control in ecclesiastical affairs.[16]

Cromwell did not win royal favour by propounding a novel master-plan or offering original solutions to Henry's problems. Henry was more likely to have been concerned to find out whether Cromwell loyally assented to the royal policies than to have, as a King of twenty years experience, sought instruction from a newcomer. In accepting Cromwell into his council he was strengthening support for views which he already entertained. Cromwell was not offered a great office of state or the chance to step into Wolsey's shoes in order to carry out any plans which he might have put to the King. He did, however, have an opportunity to advise and serve the King.

By early January, 1531, Cromwell had been officially sworn into the Council and for some time before that the King may have been informally sounding Cromwell and assuring himself of his new adviser's loyalty, as is suggested by Chapuys' report that Henry treated Cromwell as a secret adviser.[17] Yet Chapuys' words hint that Henry concealed his favour to Cromwell because of the faction situation at Court. Perhaps, the King wished to be sure of Cromwell, before he would be prepared to disturb the Norfolk faction by appointing an outsider to the Council. When he did officially enter the Council, Cromwell's presence increased the number of professional men of affairs. It represented a small but significant shift in the balance of power between the King and the aristocratic faction which had moved into the vacuum left by Wolsey's fall. If the King was looking for new men through whom to act, Cromwell's appointment had come at a moment of opportunity.

The fall of Wolsey had revealed how deep was the King's personal concern with the policies that involved his marriage, his dynasty, and his authority. Since July, 1529, Cromwell had witnessed the King's efforts to secure the annulment of his marriage to Catherine of Aragon and to escape the frustrating consequences of papal jurisdiction over the case. He must have discussed the King's 'great matter' with his acquaintances among the King's own legal advisers. Sir Christopher Hales knew and approved of his views. As one of a group of politically minded lawyers it might have struck him that the only moves which the King had been able to make, which had been in any way effective and decisive, were those which he had taken through the courts of common law and the High Court of Parliament. The efforts of the King's theologians, his civilian lawyers, his nobles and his diplomats had all come to nothing. The case in Rome was not proceeding with any hope of success. The response of the Universities of Christendom to the King's appeal for support for his case was proving costly and inconclusive. Even the outsize parchment loaded with the seals of the nobility and the bishops in which the King had addressed the Pope in threatening terms had been dismissed by the Papacy.

Through his lawyers, however, the King had driven Wolsey to submit to the charge of *praemunire*. Only, perhaps, because Wolsey had refused to defend himself with ecclesiastical weapons and had surrendered did the common law triumph with such ease. It was the threat of attainder in parliament which persuaded him to choose to put himself at the King's mercy. The combination of the use of the due process of common law and the threat of the legislative powers of parliament had disposed of a papal legate and Lord Chancellor. It was an impressive display of the legal armoury at the disposal of the King. Cromwell had seen his mighty patron stripped of wealth and power.

In the 1529 session of parliament Cromwell had witnessed Henry's response to the call for royal leadership in the reform of the Church. Wolsey's fall seemed to all kinds of reformers to have removed the chief obstacle to the realisation of their hopes and they welcomed the royal lead. In the opening speech, delivered by Thomas More, the King expressed his desire for reform.[18] Without demur from any domestic quarter and regardless of papal sanction Henry assumed the fallen legate's responsibility for rectifying the failings of the Church. For their part the Commons expected the King as a matter of course to remedy their grievances against the clergy. If Fisher deplored the anticlerical, not to say heretical, aims of the Commons, no one challenged their ancient right of petition or the legality of the ensuing legislation to establish a scale of fees for probate and administration, and mortuary dues, to limit pluralism, non-residence, and trading and commercial farming by the clergy and finally to reserve the right of dispensation in all these matters to the King. Through parliament the King had not only encroached upon the autonomy of the clergy but had also extended his royal authority at their expense.

That Cromwell noted for future reference the complaints of the Commons against various legislative, judicial and financial practices of the clergy was a sign that he recognised the initiative of the Commons as well as the power of the King. The session of 1529 convinced him that parliament was accepted both by the King and the political nation as the means by which the grudge against the clergy could find satisfaction. It also made clear that the preoccupation of the political nation was with the state of the Church rather than with the condition of the royal administration. If the complaints against the clergy had been itemised by Cromwell's fellow lawyers, they were not their invention, but an expression of a feeling which was being loudly voiced that the Church had become the prime source of the ills of the commonwealth and an obstacle to the efficacy of the royal government. The right of the Commons to petition the King in parliament was not only justified by tradition but was also fortified by the universal disposition of reformers to call upon the King to act. At the end of the session in December 1529, it was anticipated that the King would use the proposed spring session in 1530 to settle his matrimonial case. There appeared to be a continuing role for parliament and an expectation of further reform. The potential of parliament to support the King in removing ecclesiastical abuse and papal obstruction was recognised at Court by the end of 1529.

Cromwell was among those ready to exploit that potential. He had entered the Commons in 1529 in order to stay upon the political stage. His fortunate election to the Commons gave him the opportunity to keep himself at the centre of affairs and avoid the ostracism which Wolsey suffered. The prorogation in December, 1529, gave him hope of using the Commons as a platform in future. Although the calling of parliament was postponed all through 1530, Cromwell remained ready to resume an active part in the Commons and to keep the possibilities of legislative action under consideration. When he became a councillor in 1530, he could look forward to enjoying a greater authority in the Commons. He had no important office other than that of royal councillor and member for Taunton and it was in the handling and preparation of parliamentary business that he was able to demonstrate his expertise and to gain an influence over the making of policy. He needed parliament in order to create for himself a distinctive place among the King's advisers.

Yet Cromwell's concern with parliament went beyond political opportunism. As a lawyer he was convinced of the need for the sanction of the law both as a means of enforcement and of legitimation. He had a sense of parliament's role in government and a respect for its authority. He understood the political value and constitutional point of a tradition which required the assent of the King, Lords and Commons to statutes. Harmony and balance among different estates of the realm was the pervasive political notion which encouraged him and the political nation to look to the King in parliament.

When Cromwell became a councillor, it was predictable that his training, his personal experience and his position would incline him towards the use of parliament to accomplish the King's business. In the light of the session of 1529 he could anticipate the fruitful cooperation of the King, Lords and Commons in overcoming the difficulties posed to the King and his subjects by the rights and abuses of the Church. The development of Cromwell's influence depended on the opportunity to legislate and the persuasion of the King that statute provided the lawful and most effective means to realise his concept of his Kingship and to settle his matrimonial and dynastic affairs.

At the beginning of 1531 Cromwell began to serve the King with the same ruthless devotion with which he had served Wolsey. He aimed to identify his own interest with that of the King. It was a taxing exercise in persuasion and self-denial. On his task he focused his emotions and intellect. It absorbed him in his loneliness. His wife had been dead since 1527. His son and his nephew engaged his affection but they could not share his life. He reserved his emotional commitment for his chosen symbol of paternal authority, the King. From his bible he drew a sense of vocation and authority. He had sublimated his personal ambition into a vision of the realm and the commonwealth fashioned and justified by law. He existed now as a political being.

3 THE MAKING OF THE SUPREMACY

What he Started to do.

When Cromwell entered the ruling circle about the King early in 1531, the two matters which occupied Henry's deepest personal and political feelings were the annulment of his marriage and the significance of his imperial crown. They were central to the King's confidence in himself, in his dynasty and in his Kingship. To have any hope of winning a full measure of royal favour it was necessary for an ambitious servant of the Crown to play a decisive role in satisfying the King's wishes in these matters. As a new councillor, Cromwell was striving to make a place for himself and he was aware that his advice on these vital issues would make or break him.

Cromwell knew that the accepted policy for ending the King's matrimonial predicament was the traditional and safe one of obtaining a favourable papal verdict which would preserve the legitimacy of the Tudor dynasty both at home and abroad. Since the removal of the King's case to Rome in 1529 and the defeat of the King's wish to settle it in England, that policy had become almost wholly a matter of foreign diplomacy. As long as papal approval was sought and Charles V dominated the papacy, diplomacy was bound to remain the only practical means open to Henry whose ability to use military force was limited. Having neither standing nor employment in the field of diplomacy, Cromwell had little opportunity to take a lead in the long-standing negotiations and little incentive to join in the diplomacy which seemed to have exhausted the possibilities of the current situation in Europe. He could see no future for the King's policy or for his own career in European diplomacy. Not wishing to become associated with a failing policy of diplomacy, he stayed at the centre of power in the court and council and championed a domestic settlement of the King's case in which he could expect to take a decisive part.

A domestic settlement had already been mooted. In August 1530 Henry had declared that neither his case nor his person were under papal jurisdiction and that no Englishman could be tried in a foreign court.¹ Still vague in detail, there were suggestions that an annulment of the King's marriage might be pronounced by the court of the Archbishop of Canterbury or by convocation or by parliament.

29

Whether such moves were to be in defiance of the Pope in office and only in the King's particular case or would amount to a total rejection of papal authority was, however, still unclear.[2] The risks of such unilateral action were serious. Such action would isolate England and might invite and excuse open attack from catholic Christendom. Moreover it would not secure the acceptance by Christendom of the legitimacy of the succession. It was not surprising that Henry, despite his bold words, remained hesitant to forego the papal approval which both he and his father had always sought.

In the meantime Cromwell was caught up in Henry's exploration of the powers of his imperial crown. A determination to exact obedience from his clergy led the King to make charges of *praemunire* against a number of clerics who were suspected supporters of Catherine of Aragon. When the plan for charges in court failed through bad timing, a general charge of *praemunire* was brought against the whole body of the clergy. Henry counted upon the clergy following the example of Wolsey in seeking pardon and he was ready to pardon in exchange for a subsidy of £100,000 from Convocation. In recommending the dubious legal device and its use as a means of extortion there is no evidence of Cromwell's part. He was, however, among the King's legal advisers and knew of the *praemunire* proceedings.[3] The extension of a limited and particular measure into one of general application was characteristic of his method.

When early in 1531, after quibbling over the size and the timing of the collection of the required subsidy, Convocation agreed to pay the full amount, it had the temerity to give its own reasons for making the grant and to request a regal confirmation of clerical privileges and a definition of *praemunire*. Henry sensed provocation and countered by making his own self-assertive conditions. Convocation was required to recognise the King as sole protector and supreme head of the English Church and clergy and the royal right to spiritual jurisdiction and cure of souls. It was further required to sanction only those clerical privileges which did not detract from the royal prerogative and the law of the land and to accept the pardon of the clergy and the laity. Henry had somewhat overrreached himself in playing the Emperor Constantine. But despite his bumptious caesaropapism, the King showed his desire for the assent of Convocation.

Convocation kept its nerve, debated the royal claims at length and made the royal demands a matter of negotiation.[4] In the second week in February 1531 Cromwell and Audley discussed the matter with Archbishop Warham.[5] Their argument was that the Supreme Headship made no change in the King's position, that there was no intent to exceed traditional powers and practice in royal dealings with the English Church and that the King had no powers beyond those allowed by God. Meanwhile Lord Rochford put high-sounding statements of the King's supremacy before the clergy.

Convocation was tactfully deemed by its silence to have assented to the carefully worded proposition that Henry was Supreme Head of the English Church as far as the law of Christ allows. By dextrous emendation of the wording of the clauses on spiritual jurisdiction and cure of souls the King's claims were nullified. The purport of the wording accepted by the clergy can hardly have escaped the King and his lawyers. As far as words could go Henry's claims had been limited and trimmed. That the clerical amendments were accepted suggests that the parties concerned were satisfied with their interpretations of the settlement. The clergy as guardians of the law of Christ relied upon it to restrain the Supreme Head. For Henry the Supreme Headship was an acknowledgement of his imperial sway over the English Church which so long as he was prepared to recognise papal authority merely confirmed that he would not allow the English clergy to obey the Pope without royal assent. For Cromwell and the lawyers the recognition of the Supreme Headship was, as they argued, a formal acceptance of the powers of the Crown which existed in practice and which had already been made manifest in statutes.

There was some substance in the lawyers' argument, although it deliberately underplayed the novelty and importance of the title of the Headship which turned royal practices in ecclesiastical matters into rights. In his explanation of the Headship to Bishop Tunstall, Henry declared that 'in all those articles concerning the persons of priests, their laws, their acts and order of living, forasmuch as they be indeed all temporal, and concerning the present life only, in those we (as we be called) be indeed in this realm *caput*', but allowed that 'as to spiritual things, meaning by them the sacraments . . . forasmuch as they be no worldly nor temporal things, they have no worldly nor temporal Head'. By a narrowly restrictive definition of spiritual things Henry was able to avoid claiming sacerdotal powers.[6] In treating the Supreme Headship as a matter between himself and his clerical subjects he evaded laying stress upon the implications for the Church and the Papacy. The Headship was, however, neither simply a domestic affair nor a mere gesture to regularise the past. As Cromwell perceived, its significance lay in its provision for future innovation rather than in consolidation of historic practice. He was aware that, in the contest with the clergy over the reform of the English Church and with the Papacy over its jurisdiction, the King had changed the rules of the game to his own advantage.

The parliamentary session in the spring of 1531 was not as effective in promoting a domestic solution of the King's matrimonial problem as Cromwell might have hoped. Henry remained content merely to advertise in parliament the support of the universities for his case and to urge members to publicise it. It was Henry's first official approach to parliament on his great matter but it showed no change in the policy of obtaining a papal verdict and it was far from an invitation to parliament to take part in settling the matter.

For Cromwell it was a step in the right direction in that it recognised a parliamentary interest in the case. Similarly there was encouragement for him in the measures of reform put forward by the lawyers, led by Rastell, which called for an English translation of the Bible, reform of the canon law by parliament, free burial and intercession for the dead, examination of heretics by a council instead of by bishops, penalties for attacking recent statutes as contrary to clerical privilege and for a ban on recrimination between clergy and laity. Although the measures proved abortive, they were another indication of the initiative for reform which existed in the Commons and which Cromwell could exploit at a more propitious time.

Proceedings in Convocation raised fears in the Commons that the laity might also incur the charge of *praemunire* and be expected to buy a pardon. The bill to confirm the pardon did nothing to allay the apprehension of the Commons. Cromwell was suspected of having disclosed their fears to the King who declared to a deputation of the Commons that he was free to pardon the clergy without the aid of parliament. [7] His eagerness to provide statutory approval for acts of the King had met with a rebuff from Henry and Cromwell found it necessary to reassure the Commons that the laity could not be charged with *praemunire* since it involved the exercise of spiritual jurisdiction. The revised bill did not suggest that the mere exercise of spiritual jurisdiction was unauthorised by statute but that its use contrary to statute was illegal. Just as the Royal Headship indicated that ecclesiastical jurisdiction was subject to the royal prerogative so the bill confirmed that it was circumscribed by statute. It was an important affirmation of the authority of statute which suited Cromwell.

Established among the King's councillors Cromwell had shown his desire to keep the King in touch with parliament and the parliament in touch with the King's business. He had found a place for himself and for parliament in the conduct of the King's relations with the clergy and with convocation. But as Henry had made plain over the pardon of the clergy he regarded himself as free to act without resort to parliamentary legislation. Cromwell's legalistic approach might have looked pettifogging in the eyes of the Supreme Head and wearer of an imperial crown. When he had high claims to make, Henry was still more inclined to use obliging nobles and rely on the persuasion of their prestige than he was to employ his lawyers and rely upon their legal expertise. In his first year as a councillor Cromwell had made his mark but he had not won the King over to his legislative methods or to his preference for a unilateral domestic settlement of the royal matrimonial case.

Early in 1532, however, there were signs that the King and his councillors were considering more seriously the annulment of the royal marriage through the exercise of ecclesiastical jurisdiction in England. A domestic settlement was looking less like an outrageous threat and more like a possible course of action. Parliament met in January 1532 and Norfolk was employed to win the support of the nobility for Henry's claim to spiritual jurisdiction as Emperor. As no solid support was forthcoming, Henry used Norfolk and Wiltshire to cajole Warham into pronouncing the annulment. But the Archbishop proved obdurate and went on to declare that he would not be party to any statutes touching the powers of the papacy or of the Church. Meanwhile Cromwell and Audley were ready in the Commons with a bill whereby Convocation would be empowered to decide the King's case. The bill showed that Cromwell was ready to exclude papal jurisdiction and to use parliament to authorise a decision in convocation, if the Archbishop remained unwilling to give Henry the verdict that he wanted.[8] But Henry was not yet prepared to take action and the bill was not introduced.

The effort to secure a domestic settlement had failed. The King, however, took up a complaint in Convocation against paying annates to Rome in order to apply financial blackmail to the Pope. Cromwell could see little point in such a move and his doubts about its reception in parliament proved correct.[9] Henry by the unusual device of a division in the Commons forced an amended bill through. Cromwell used the bill, which made the payment of annates dependent on the King's discretion and an amicable composition with the Pope, to assert royal immunity to papal excommunication, interdict and the refusal to consecrate bishops. In safeguarding against a papal riposte, he spelled out the implications of the royal Supremacy for the Papacy by authorising the royal consecration of bishops. Unable to bring Henry to outright rejection of papal authority, he took his opportunities to whittle away the powers of the Pope.

While the significance of the royal Supremacy was becoming more obvious in the struggle with the Papacy, Cromwell took action to make its meaning plainer to the English clergy. Capitalising on support for reform in the Commons, he skilfully revamped the complaints which had been voiced in the Commons since 1529 and which had become the basis for an official programme of reform into a Supplication against the Ordinaries.[10] By using the support of the reformist element in the Commons to present the supplication as a petition, Cromwell planned to outflank the opposition to him in council by such men as Thomas More and Gardiner and to precipitate a clash between the King and the clergy over their respective rights.

The Supplication complained of the delay, partiality, inconvenience and extortion in litigation in church courts, of high fees for clerical services and for institution to benefices, of the preferment of infants to clerical office, of the employment of clerics in lay jobs and of the evil results of the excessive number of Holy Days. But the main emphasis, which revealed Cromwell's hand, was laid upon the malicious use of heresy charges by the clergy to discredit or destroy those who offended them and even more on the detrimental effect of the clerical right of legislation upon the interests of the King and the laity. The former of these two complaints had disturbed laymen since the notorious Hunne case some fifteen years previously. The assumption behind the grievance and the implications of its remedy challenged the integrity of the clergy and their role as sole judges and guardians of orthodoxy.

The complaint against clerical legislation had been made in the 1520's by Tyndale and Fish and it was made the principal grumble of the Supplication by Cromwell. In its suggestion that the laws made by convocation were contrary to equity, right and good conscience and in derogation of the King's prerogative it set the clergy against the royal authority and the law. Passed without the assent of the King and his lay subjects, couched in latin which was not understood by the laity, clerical legislation, it was declared, nevertheless imposed penalties, censures and expenses on laymen. The attack upon the legislative independence of the clergy raised fundamental issues concerning the relationship of the temporalty and spiritualty.

It was a well timed attack, since an unusual flurry of law making in convocation by the bishops in their effort to retain the initiative in reform seemed to provide evidence of clerical disregard for the royal prerogative and the rights of the laity. In engineering the Supplication Cromwell hoped to bring the question of the Supremacy before parliament and obtain legislation to remedy the grievances. His expectations were revealed in a draft bill putting forward the notion of a body politic of the three estates of the realm under the King's supreme legislative and jurisdictional authority which excluded all foreign power both spiritual and temporal.[11] Cromwell was ready to assert that Henry's Supreme Headship and his imperial crown provided the instruments by which the King could not only control his clergy but also by which he could settle his great matter through regulating canon law and excluding papal authority. Once again Cromwell made clear his antipapal intentions.

Henry did not respond by calling for parliamentary legislation as Cromwell might have anticipated. Bills were indeed put forward on minor matters of reform arising from the Supplication and an Act to restrain the citation of persons outside the diocese of their residence was eventually passed. But the important issue of the independent legislative power of convocation did not come before parliament. As over the pardon of the clergy in the previous year Henry was ready to exercise his Supreme Headship as a personal prerogative and deal directly with the clergy without the aid of parliament. He sent the Supplication to Convocation and called for an answer to be made by the clergy to himself as Supreme Head and not to the Commons.

The Answer of the Ordinaries, largely the work of Gardiner, was a deferential but uncompromising defence of clerical rights and the powers of convocation. If Henry had hoped to use the Supplication to harrass the uncooperative Warham, he had succeeded only in putting himself in the embarrassing position of being called upon to do his duty as Supreme Head and to protect his clergy from the unwarranted attack of the Commons. Henry would not allow the tables to be turned on him. Dismissing the answer as slight, he sent it to the Commons on the last day of April 1532 in the expectation of a reply which he claimed he would judge impartially. Cromwell, recognising that he could not wait upon parliament which was about to be prorogued, turned the King to Convocation with demands that it recognise that it had no authority to legislate without royal licence and that it submit all canons to a royal commission of sixteen clergy and of sixteen laymen, drawn from parliament, which would purge canon law of anything contrary to the law of the land and present the reformed canon law for royal assent.

If Henry's treatment of the Supplication and his angry riposte to the Answer of the Ordinaries had not followed the parliamentary lines which Cromwell had planned, the King's demands on Convocation had been used to further the main objective of the Supplication, the extinction of independent clerical legislation. It was evidence of Cromwell's influence that Henry had chosen this objective in his retaliatory demand on Convocation. When it came to intimidating the clergy into submission, it was Cromwell, if Foxe is right, who urged Henry to raise the vital question of the divided loyalty of the clergy.[12] The King's observation that the clergy were 'but half our subjects, yea and scarce our subjects' was made to a deputation of the Commons, but it had its impact on Convocation. Henry's request to the Commons to 'invent some order' to prevent his being 'thus deluded' by his spiritual subjects was far too belated to be seriously considered near the end of the session. Yet it was a gesture which kept Cromwell's hope of future parliamentary action alive. Cromwell had shown himself able to take advantage of the King's impulsive personal initiatives.

Henry needed no prompting from Cromwell in his determination to make the clergy submit to his demands. In the absence of its strongest leaders, Warham and Fisher, and with its numbers depleted in anticipation of dissolution, Convocation was bullied by Henry's deputation of nobles, supporters of Cromwell, into submission on 16th

May 1532.[13] The submission of the clergy meant that the legislative initiative in Convocation was now dependent on the King and that canon law was circumscribed by statute. The areas in which the Supreme Head was exercising autonomy were achieving definition. Like the other princes of Europe Henry was making sure that the clergy were his subjects. Because of his quarrel with Rome over his marital affairs, he was unable to negotiate a concordat which would have given him the substance of power over the church in his realm, while leaving the theory of papal supremacy intact. Henry's unilateral actions inevitably flouted the claims of the Papacy.

Cromwell's sponsorship of the Supplication against the Ordinaries had precipitated Henry into a royal assertion of supremacy and, in the terms of the commission, an assertion of the supremacy of statute over canon law. He had won a success for his policy of rejecting papal authority and demonstrating the self-sufficiency of the Supreme Headship. He had brought the initiative of the Commons to bear on the debate in the Council and had won a victory over his opponents. Thomas More retired. Gardiner was under a cloud of royal distrust for his part in the Answer of the Ordinaries. Cromwell's influence in the Council increased. His colleague Audley replaced More in the office of Lord Chancellor. By August Henry was prepared to associate his name with adumbrations of a plan to use parliament in a domestic settlement of his matrimonial case.[14] Cromwell's opportunity to use his influence came with the death of Warham at the end of August, 1532.

The archiepiscopal jurisdiction, an important element in a domestic settlement of the King's case, was now at Henry's disposal. Through an obedient archbishop Henry could make good his claim to spiritual jurisdiction. With the royal nomination, as Archbishop of Canterbury, of Thomas Cranmer, an established champion of the King's case, Cromwell could take for granted a favourable archiepiscopal verdict on the King's marriage. Parliament would not have to be used to override the opposition of a reluctant archbishop by supporting the expedient of a judicial pronouncement by Convocation in lieu of an archiepiscopal judgement. In September Cromwell and Audley were busy with plans for parliament to support and safeguard Cranmer's expected ruling.[15] In October the King gained the agreement of Francis I to a proposal for marrying Anne Boleyn without awaiting papal permission. In the same month Henry's decision to marry Anne Boleyn was anticipated by a papal brief forbidding the marriage. With the prospect of Cranmer's ecclesiastical, Cromwell's parliamentary and Francis I's diplomatic backing Henry was becoming more confident that he could now disregard the Pope and adopt a domestic settlement. In January 1533 he made the decisive move by marrying Anne Boleyn. On all reasonable calculations about the future he was now committed to Cromwell's advice and management of affairs.

The secrecy of his marriage betrayed Henry's lingering hope that some sudden change in European politics might yet enable him to gain papal approval. But the pregnancy of Anne Boleyn set a deadline for the legitimation of the marriage and the expected heir. Parliament was summoned for early February, 1533. Cromwell's proposals for it revealed his political vision.[16] Audley had suggested the necessary minimum of a statutory prohibition of an appeal to Rome against Cranmer's anticipated pronouncement on the King's particular case. From Cromwell's revision of six drafts there emerged a bill which in restraining appeals in causes testamentary, causes of matrimony and divorces, rights of tithes, oblations and obventions was meant to be a rejection of papal jurisdiction in England. The rejection was not based on arguments of expediency or on defensive apologetics, but on the bald assertion in a brief preamble of the historical and political nature of the English polity. The realm of England was an Empire. Its body politic embraced both the temporalty and spiritualty under one King and Supreme Head. The Church of England possessed a self-sufficient ecclesiastical jurisdiction. The preamble read like a précis of the assumptions which every patriotic and loyal subject was expected to take for granted. No purchase for doubt or argument remained in the confident declaration of the independence of the English body politic of all external authority.

In exploiting the situation Cromwell had taken the opportunity to go to extremes. In order to provide the King with a legal safeguard for his marriage to Anne Boleyn, he had all but severed England from Rome's jurisdiction and pronounced it an autonomous realm. The preamble of the Act of Appeals went beyond the practical effects of the Act but it was a significant declaration of intent and it heralded a campaign to realise all its implications. Through the weft of Henry's historical imperialism and ecclesiastical Headship Cromwell had woven the warp of the ideas of Marsilio of Padua and had made the English Emperor a new suit of clothes.

Cromwell took precautions to ensure the passage of the bill. He concerned himself with the by-elections for the coming session and drummed up royal supporters. He showed his bill to Henry and to selected clerics. Henry proffered amendments but left the final wording to Cromwell, who dropped the King's suggestions. But Cromwell took the advice of the clergy on the administrative clauses concerning the mechanism of appeal and adopted a more conciliatory tone towards ecclesiastical susceptibilities. In parliament the bill raised a few minor amendments and some perturbation about its financial results but there was no debate on the political theory behind the preamble. To all appearances the radical change in the relations of the English King and clergy with the Papacy had been accepted without a murmur. By early April the Act of Appeals was passed. The parliamentary measures were completed on time.

Over the Archbishop's role Cromwell was watchful. The reluctant Cranmer had been hurried back from the continent by Cromwell's agent, Stephen Vaughan, and had arrived in England in January. Papal bulls had been obtained to ensure the archiepiscopal authority by a traditional consecration of the Archbishop which took place on 30th March. Convocation was hustled into accepting the King's case on the invalidity of his marriage to Catherine of Aragon. Then on 10 May Cranmer began hearing the King's case in his court. The favourable verdict came on 23 May. Cromwell had kept himself informed on the progress of the hearing and on 28 May he was present at Lambeth to hear Cranmer pronounce the validity of Henry's marriage to Anne Boleyn in time for her coronation three days later.[17]

Cromwell in the Act of Appeals had with a great economy of means substantially eliminated the jurisdiction of Rome in England. In a single act he had provided for the settlement of the King's great matter in an English ecclesiastical court, and given substance to the Supreme Headship by furnishing the conceptual framework for an autonomous realm and a unitary body politic. He had demonstrated his ability to use parliament as a decisive instrument of policy. His management of the whole affair had vindicated his advocacy of a domestic settlement and had shown how far he excelled the King's other servants in political vision and acumen. He had become a man upon whom the King could rely. Towards the end of 1533 the publication of the *Articles devised by the whole consent of the King's most honourable council* which defended the King's moves and vilified the Pope made it plain that Cromwell's influence was supreme in council and that further action in parliament could be expected.[18]

The point of no return in the making of the Supremacy came in the parliamentary session of spring 1534. The submission of the clergy was recorded in a statute which also prohibited all appeals to Rome and directed appeals from archiepiscopal courts to the King in Chancery for final judgement by delegates. A second annates act forbade their payment to Rome and established the traditional royal *congé d'élire* as the sole means of appointing bishops. A Dispensations act prohibited the payment of Peter's pence and other exactions to Rome, put dispensations in the grant of the Archbishop of Canterbury and reserved the right of visitation of the monasteries for a royal commission. It was also the occasion for an exposure of the royal intention to abide by the Catholic Faith of Christendom. Finally a succession act endorsed with parliamentary authority the nullity of the King's first, and the validity of his second marriage, entailed the crown on the King's issue by Anne Boleyn, defined treasons with regard to the succession and provided an oath of obedience to the act, to be tendered to all subjects.[19]

The cumulative effect of the King's determination to control his clergy and of his final disregard for papal approval of his matrimonial policy had issued in a stream of legislation. Cromwell had responded to circumstances and defeated as they arose the machinations of the Pope and provided remedies for the grievances of the laity against the clergy. It was the immediate tangible advantage of each particular measure rather than the realisation of the Marsilian theory which Cromwell set out in the preamble of the Act of Appeals that seemed compelling. Under the pressure of events neither the King nor the parliament were prepared to entertain any grave doubts about their authority to act. Cromwell's success had been at the level of practical politics. It remained to establish the theory of Empire and to develop the implications of the Supremacy.

The advantage which Cromwell enjoyed over his opponents was that he had realised his view of the realm as an Empire in law. He had taken intellectual controversy out of the sphere of academic argument into the courts where it was a matter of life and death. Fisher and More did not have to be defeated in argument, merely convicted by the law. It was through the enforcement of the law that Cromwell was able to argue his case. It became clear, as it had to Thomas More, that the law was the law of a realm which was an Empire.

While the law gave Cromwell power over men's bodies, he was well aware of the need to capture their minds. The elaboration of the theories behind Cromwell's moves was the work of churchmen, such as Fox, Sampson, Gardiner and Starkey.[20] They rested their arguments upon biblical, patristic, scholastic and Erasmian sources. They conceived of a divine right kingship, based on scriptural precedent. The responsibility and authority of the King under God was a theme from the past which was extended to meet the requirements of a King and Supreme Head.

In practice as in theory the responsibilities of the King were heavy. The reformation of the Church and the maintenance of uniformity and true doctrine were, as Cromwell found, exacting tasks. The Church of England, as a constituent of the body politic, was an active institution affecting the lives of all subjects. It provided an ecclesiastical constitution for the body politic and gave it a religious purpose as Cromwell acknowledged, when he pictured the King bringing his subjects 'out of all blindness and ignorance into the true and perfect knowledge of Almighty God by his most holy word'.[21] The divine source and purpose of government was the accepted inspiration of action.

In the perspective of contemporary Europe Cromwell's making of the royal supremacy can be seen to be in line with the increasing control of the clergy by the continental princes. In England, however, peculiar circumstances led to a break with the Papacy and ensured that royal claims were antipapal. Antipapalism acquired a political and constitutional significance because Cromwell rested upon it the legitimacy of the Kingship and the succession, the legislative supremacy of parliament, and the existence of the realm as an Empire. Cromwell created the important association in English historical thinking between the rejection of Rome and the assertion of national autonomy. Protestant antipapalism was able to inherit the advantage of a patriotic appeal and of a constitutional form.

Cromwell's activities in the making of the Supremacy have been seen as a triumph of the laity. It must be remembered, however, that Cromwell envisaged the laity as bible-reading members of the Church of England. If he had made the clergy into subjects of the King, he had drafted the laity into church membership. Laicisation meant changes in the character of religion but it was seen as a means of banishing the secularisation which had overtaken the papal church. Cromwell maintained institutional religion and supported it with the authority of the King in parliament.

The Supremacy created a national sovereignty in the sense that it added the rejection of papal authority to that of every other foreign potentate. The Church of England was, however, regarded as part of the Catholic Church and General Councils were recognised as sources of doctrine. The national sovereignty, created by Cromwell, was still limited by reference to the doctrinal tradition of a universal church and by reference to the divine law. Cromwell worked within a religious framework and until that collapsed the significance of his actions for the development of the secular modern state, exercising national sovereignty, was not to be fully realised.

4 THE AUGMENTATION OF THE KING'S REVENUES

It was generally believed that Thomas Cromwell had won royal favour by a promise to make the King rich. It was a belief that reflected his preoccupation with and his achievements in royal finance. With his training by the Frescobaldi and his experience in commerce and money-lending he was not a man to underrate the importance of finance. His speech for the Commons in 1523 set the proposed war in its economic context. Soon after becoming a councillor, he put amongst his papers an advice on taxation. In 1534 he was said to have boasted that he would make Henry the richest prince in Christendom. In a letter to the King from the Tower in 1540, reviewing his services, he put first his intention and effort to enrich the King.[1] His remembrances showed him supervising all aspects of finance. He made his mark on government finance both in the provision of resources and in administration.

If Cromwell thought of matching Henry's income with that of such a prince of Christendom as Francis I, he would have had to have trebled it. Yet such was the scale of royal finance which Cromwell, it would seem, had in mind. But the experience of opposition to Henry VII's exploitation of landed revenues and to Wolsey's demand for loans and taxes made clear that enriching the King without impoverishing his subjects and straining their loyalty was a difficult problem. Cromwell did not flinch from maintaining and even increasing the burden on the laity but he achieved his most spectacular increase in royal revenues at the expense of the Church. He gave the break with Rome a financial significance by his taxation of the clergy and his appropriation of monastic wealth. By the diversion of ecclesiastical revenues and monastic capital to the Crown on an unprecedented scale he was able to surmount the limitations set by lay resistance to taxation and to give Henry the opportunity of doubling his revenues.

Cromwell was fortunate in being able to realise so many of the ecclesiastical assets of the realm. Political observers in the past, such as Fortescue and Dudley, had either ruled out or advised against the appropriation of Church lands. But opinion was changing. In 1516 Thomas More wrote in *Utopia* about the redistribution by King Utopus of both lay and clerical wealth. By the late 1520's More was hearing from Simon Fish proposals for a royal redistribution of clerical wealth in

41

England. He knew of clergy, wondering about the validity of their title to lands, of seven nobles, prepared to countenance the dispossession of the Church and of merchants in Lombard Street with similar sentiments. When in 1529 Henry took York Place in London from the Archbishopric of York, Wolsey feared that other clerics might surrender patrimonies which were not theirs to give. In 1531 and 1533 foreign observers anticipated sequestration of clerical revenues and lands by the King. St German blandly represented public opinion as favouring either total or partial confiscation of clerical riches.[2] Such ideas were nourished by late medieval heretical thinking about the impropriety of a wealthy church, by precedents from the past and by continental examples of the secularisation of church lands.

In the light of such a debate in the church, in the city and at court, it is not surprising that Cromwell was prepared to suggest in 1533 that in the event of war it would be necessary to seize half the temporal lands of the church. Such a move had come to look like the line of least public resistance in the emergency of war. By 1534, among Cromwell's papers was a plan for reorganising the finances of the church in order to provide a large surplus for royal use in peacetime.[3] Cromwell was not carried away by radical proposals. A thorough survey of the wealth of the Church, the *Valor Ecclesiasticus*, was compiled.[4] He began in 1535 in an area in which he had had experience under Wolsey by preparing to dissolve the lesser religious houses which had long proved the most vulnerable institutions in the church. The piecemeal realisation of monastic assets which followed was to proceed faster, perhaps, than Cromwell had anticipated.

Cromwell moved tentatively. The dissolution was begun as a financial precaution to support the King's new position in Europe. The demands for expenditure were growing but there was no overwhelming pressure in 1535 to undertake more than the dissolution of the lesser monasteries. But there was inflation in costs and threats in the political scene which made it prudent to continue to expand revenue. The appetite for monastic wealth grew by feeding.

The first dissolutions disturbed the vested interests of lay society in monasticism and stirred opposition in the Pilgrimage of Grace. But opposition subsided as it became clear that the fortunes of the laity could be improved by the dissolution. It was a change of ownership effected from above with no hint even in the Pilgrimage of Grace of the consequent social revolution, predicted by Thomas More. Cromwell's efforts to allay fears and the pace and timing of progressive dissolutions allowed expectations of advantage to grow among the laity and the terms of dissolution to seduce the religious.[5]

Like Fortescue's proposals for the endowment of the Crown, Cromwell's diversion of ecclesiastical wealth to the Crown was part of a wider political vision. In place of Fortescue's overmighty subject, Cromwell, echoing Tyndale and Fish, presented an overmighty church challenging the political power of the King and battening upon the wealth of the laity. Whereas Henry VII had resumed, as feudal lord, the lands alienated by the Crown to the nobility, Henry VIII, as patron, feudal lord and Supreme Head of the Church, resumed the lands, granted to monastic foundations. Cromwell represented the Dissolution as the recovery by the King of his own lands from their misuse by those to whom he had conditionally granted them. [6]

The Dissolution exploited the weakness of contemporary monasticism and the strength of monarchical government. Cromwell played a notable role in the long process by which lay powers all over Europe were appropriating to their use the riches of the Church. Even in the widest perspective his action remains impressive and in England the most decisive move in that historical process. However opportunistic the course of, and however fiscal the motive for, the dissolution might appear, it is clear that Cromwell had read the religious signs of the time. It was this percipience which made the dissolution not a desperate fiscal expedient but an act of calculated statesmanship.

The dissolution ultimately doubled the income of the Crown. Such an increase might have been expected to have solved the King's financial difficulties and to have removed the burden from his lay subjects. It did not, because it tempted Henry in the end to emulate his wealthier fellow sovereigns and to play his ambitious role in European politics. In Europe Henry was a poor King. Even the preservation of a defensive isolation against the threats of Valois and Hapsburg was as much as the King could, and his subjects were prepared to, afford. Cromwell's feat in augmenting the revenues of the King was doomed in a short time after his fall to prove inadequate.

The increase of the financial power of the monarchy was Cromwell's objective. But he did not isolate the King from the commonwealth of which he was head. Where Fortescue planned to make the King largely self-sufficient so that he would not impoverish his subjects by his demands, Cromwell moved beyond the idea of the King living of his own. He wished to make the King so rich that he could enrich all men. [7] His was the notion of distributive justice which his friend Elyot defined as 'the distribution of honour, money, benefits and things semblable'. [8] The increase in royal patronage was not lost upon the gentry and nobility. Requests for a share in the King's newly acquired wealth poured in upon Cromwell. He once remarked that the King was becoming greedy and that he and his fellow councillors would have to persuade him to use his riches for the common good. [9]

Cromwell's view of the common good was that the riches of the King should satisfy the political nation, reward services and provide the defence of the realm. In these ways the royal wealth would percolate through the commonwealth and enrich all men. Although his concern for poor relief and education were manifest, he did not share the belief that the goods of the Church belonged to the poor. For him the wealth of the King and the commonwealth could not be separated and a rich King symbolised the prosperity and strength of the realm.

In 'his treatment of the royal revenues he blurred the vague distinctions between seigneurial, personal, royal and public funds. When he came to list the royal revenues, he did not divide them into the ordinary revenues, deriving from the crown lands, feudal rights, customs and the profits of justice, which constituted the King's own income. His concern was to distinguish which revenues were certain, the regular fixed income, and which were casual, the variable receipts. The Yorkist notion that the King should live of his own and only in emergency call for parliamentary grants from his subjects did not influence Cromwell either in theory or in practice. He spent the King's personal reserves on military emergencies and justified the dissolution to the Lincolnshire rebels by pointing to the King's own expenditure on defence.[10]

When Cromwell called for parliamentary taxation, he did not simply plead the extraordinary needs of defence but argued that the provision of wise and politic government, of justice and of religious unity deserved the support of the King's subjects. He did not represent taxation as an extraordinary requirement of a crisis but as the consequence of normal governmental expenditure over the reign. In 1539 his propagandist, Morison, was in the Commons to develop this argument.[11] In parliamentary taxation Cromwell's view prevailed in the drafting of subsidy acts for a few decades. But the old distinction between extraordinary and ordinary revenue was not eradicated from the thinking of the financial officialdom or the commons. It was too useful a check upon taxation to be readily abandoned.

Besides advocating acceptance of parliamentary taxation as a regular means of financing royal government, Cromwell also attempted to relate the assessment of taxation more closely to the individual wealth of the King's subjects. Tenths and Fifteenths, virtually fixed district levies, had become the accepted parliamentary grant, but, as Cromwell stressed, they provided a 'small sum of money'.[12] Since the early fifteenth century the government had struggled to introduce the subsidy, assessed on each individual's land and moveables at rates and on conditions which varied with each subsidy act. The subsidy spread the load and tapped the wealth of different classes, but the Commons resented individual assessment and at the same time objected to voting a tax without a predictable yield. Attempts to make the subsidy palatable had failed. After the parliament of 1523 Cromwell himself had expressed the Commons' distaste, when he complained that a subsidy had been granted 'the like whereof was never granted in this realm'.[13] In the session of 1532, although ready to grant a Fifteenth, the Commons resisted the royal proposal for a subsidy and in the event made no grant.

In 1534, despite such a record of reluctance in the Commons, Cromwell called for a parliamentary grant. It proved the first successful call since 1523. Despite amendments by the Commons in their favour, he managed to secure a grant of a subsidy and a Fifteenth and Tenth, which, although collected with difficulty in an economic depression, yielded about £80,000. In 1540, while completing the Dissolution, he obtained assent to two subsidies and four Fifteenths and Tenths which were to produce well over £90,000.[14]

Cromwell deliberately persisted with the subsidy as a more flexible, equitable and profitable form of taxation. He studied past acts and produced his own complex bills. In 1536 he had thought about true assessing of the subsidy but he did not attempt as Wolsey had in 1522 a census of personal wealth on which to base assessments.[15] The mere rumour of assessments created opposition which prevented the full potential of the subsidy from being exploited. Resistance to taxation deterred Cromwell from following up Wolsey's experiments in taxation. The threefold increase in the landed revenue of the Crown relieved him of the necessity of undertaking a reform of parliamentary taxation. He extended parliamentary taxation to all Wales and made great efforts to enforce it in Ireland but in England the old exemptions which included Cumberland, Northumberland, Westmorland and the bishopric of Durham remained. Apart from his effort to treat parliamentary grants as a normal part of royal finance he was content to leave the taxation of the laity as it was. In permitting the postponement of taxation reform, the revenues, obtained by the Dissolution, were to prove a mixed blessing.

While there were still difficulties in the regular taxation of the laity, from the clergy Cromwell was able to obtain regular taxes. The break with Rome gave him the opportunity to reorganise clerical taxation on an up to date assessment, the *Valor Ecclesiasticus*. The old papal imposts, denied to Rome by the Annates act and an act of 1534 for the exoneration of papal exactions, were diverted to the King. First Fruits, a whole year's income on entry to all benefices, were collected annually from the 1st January 1535. The Tenth, formerly granted by Convocations to the King, was made a regular annual tax, payable every Christmas from 1535. Subsidies from the Convocations were authorised, although a subsidy from the clergy was not demanded until 1540. Some exemptions from clerical taxation were granted, but Cromwell's reorganisation made clerical taxation between two and three times heavier than it had been prior to the break with Rome. In 1535 First Fruits and Tenths produced some £46,000 and, although the yield declined with the progress of the Dissolution to £28,000 by 1540, the subsidy sustained the average yield of clerical taxation.[16] If Cromwell refrained from confiscating all the wealth of the Church, as some of his more radical advisers recommended, he profited the Crown by taxing what remained in clerical hands. Above all he had made ecclesiastical taxes a regular part of normal government revenue.

The significant increase in royal revenues came from the proceeds of the Dissolution, clerical taxation and parliamentary grants, but Cromwell exploited other sources. The growing number of penal statutes contributed to the profits of justice. Only clerics, like the Bishop of Norwich, however, could complain of exorbitant fines. Attainder brought in a random harvest and after the Pilgrimage of Grace Cromwell made special arrangements and appointed Tristram Teshe as receiver of all attainted lands in the North. The only Act of Restitution, made by Cromwell, restored the title but not the lands to the offender's son. As a variant from legal forfeiture he persuaded the sixth earl of Northumberland to make the King his heir in 1534. Although later evaded by legal devices, restraint of knighthood was exploited and its incidence widened by granting ex-monastic lands on condition of knight service with liability to wardship and licence for alienation. Cromwell's scheme for a court of Wards in 1540 showed his respect for the fiscal side of feudalism. His legal reforms in the Statute of Uses provided another way of making profit for the King from the process of inheritance.[17]

His opponents played upon Cromwell's efforts to gather clerical and lay taxes by stirring up rumours in the autumn of 1536, which helped to foment the Lincolnshire rising. It was said that he would confiscate parish plate, put a tax on christenings, marriages, burials and on horned cattle, levy a sumptuary tax on the consumption of geese, capons and white bread by persons of low degree and demand a sworn declaration of personal property by every man. Again in 1538 he was obliged to deny that he contemplated new exactions. Yet in 1539 he was assured that in Lincolnshire he was regarded as good to the poor in advising the King 'to take nothing but of them where it may well be spared'.[18] In practice Cromwell avoided the blatant fiscal devices which characterised European government finance and the experiments which had marked Wolsey's régime. He even abstained from raising loans or benevolences which had acquired a bad reputation, confirmed in 1529, when the King cancelled the repayment of royal borrowings. His resort to Church wealth enabled him to avoid such exactions.

As in his efforts to extend restraint of knighthood and to pass the Statute of Uses, Cromwell had met the resistance of the landholders, so in his attempts to increase the yield of customs he encountered the opposition of the merchants. Although well informed on the customs by two reports, he accomplished little. Opposition in parliament quashed proposals to increase the revenue from kerseys in 1531 and to improve trade by allowing foreign merchants to pay the same rates as native merchants in 1534 and 1535. In 1536 uniform rates were established throughout the realm, but the aim of adjusting rates to current values was not achieved so that the rates of 1507, rendered unrealistic by inflation, remained in force. In 1539 Cromwell used the opportunity of the crisis, caused by Charles V's threat of war, to evade mercantile opposition in parliament and to issue a proclamation, authorising the same rates for foreign as for English merchants, in the hope of increasing trade and winning support for peace from the merchants of the Netherlands. Although he represented the move as a sacrifice by the King for the good of the Commonwealth, he failed to induce the English merchants to accept the sacrifice and an act of 1540 largely nullified the effect of the proclamation by allowing concessionary rates for foreigners only on goods, transported by English ships.[19]

Despite Cromwell's efforts the customs revenue was lower during the 1530's than it had been in the 1520's.[20] He was unable to make up for the decline in the wool subsidies by raising the revenues from the export of cloth. He failed to adjust the rates to meet the rise in prices and to stimulate trade by concessionary rates to foreign merchants. The administration was inadequate for the task of ensuring the collection of customs. Cromwell was dependent on the goodwill of the merchants. He could not afford to destroy the cooperation of the merchants by expanding the customs revenue at their expense. His personal experience as a merchant, his ties with the London merchants and his appreciation of mercantile interest in parliament persuaded him to refrain from exploiting what was an obviously expandable source of revenue.

Although he had set a fatal example in debasing the Irish coinage, Cromwell did not allow a debasement of English coinage. When in 1523 he visualised a leather coinage, he showed that he was aware of the dangers of debasement. He punished false coiners and in accord with current orthodoxy he banned the export of bullion. In 1536 he attempted to suppress the exchange business. But licensed exchange transactions persisted to meet the needs of trade and in 1537, yielding to mercantile pressure, expressed by Richard Gresham, he freed exchange from all restrictions.[21] He found the profits of trade more convincing than the traditional bullionist doctrine.

If the choice of resources was of importance in the conduct of government finance so was the administration of funds. A financial administration, composed of agencies and departments in which the key offices were for life was neither easy to enter nor, because it was not centralised, to control. Entry depended on the death of office-holders and on royal favour. Control depended on strategic pluralism and personal dynamism. Cromwell was ready to seize whatever vacancies occurred and he was fortunate in acquiring three minor offices. In April, 1532, he became master of the King's Jewel House, in the following July, the clerk of the Hanaper and in April, 1533, Chancellor of the Exchequer.[22]

The bestowal on Cromwell for life of these offices with their modest income and patronage was a sign of royal favour. Such random appointments were no evidence of the King's intention to put Cromwell in charge of finances. They nevertheless gave Cromwell an official standing in three institutions, the Household, the Chancery and the Exchequer and he was able to exploit his offices to exert on royal finances all the force of his personality and of his position as a favoured councillor.

The clerkship of the Hanaper offered Cromwell least scope. Without involving himself in the performance of its limited routines, he learned through experienced clerks the workings of Chancery and controlled a useful revenue. He thought better of his plan of 1535 to expand Hanaper business with the task of accounting for First Fruits. From April, 1535, he made Ralph Sadler his deputy and shared the office and its emoluments with his trusted servant.

In the Exchequer Court Cromwell, as councillor, secretary, Lord Privy Seal and spokesman for the King, came to use his accumulation of authority in such a way as to give the chancellorship of the Exchequer an unprecedented influence and status among the Barons of the Exchequer to whom this minor office in the Upper Exchequer had always been subordinate. He used the new power which he personally conferred upon the chancellorship of the Exchequer to direct departmental appointments and to maintain the general efficiency of the institution. He projected a scheme to end delay in the delivery of cash, but it affected the profits of collectors and failed. Since the late fifteenth century it was accepted that the rigid traditionalism of the Exchequer made it incapable of satisfying the immediate cash demands of government and that it was not a suitable institution for the exploitation of royal estates.[23] Because of this prevalent view. Cromwell did not appreciate, as Paulet did later, the possibilities of the Exchequer as a centralising agency in the financial administration. Although he made no radical reforms and, apart from increasing parliamentary taxation, did nothing to increase the turnover of the Exchequer, he did make one contribution to its development by revealing the potential of its chancellorship.

It was in the Household, in the office of Master of the King's Jewel

House through which he controlled the royal reserves, that Cromwell was able to exert his personal authority in financial administration to its greatest effect. Close to the King, offices responded to the royal convenience. Secure in the King's confidence, Cromwell was able to improvise. Employing his own servants in his financial business, he used his access to the royal reserves in the Jewel House to finance his policies. He directed the surplus funds of other departments to the Jewel House. The annual turnover of his operations came to exceed that of the Exchequer and almost equal that of the Chamber. He disposed of the royal capital reserves and of miscellaneous revenues without apparent audit and often in advance of warrants. The Jewel House became a major spending office, financing not only the King's personal items of expenditure, for example the preparation of his tomb, but also military, naval and diplomatic projects and patronage. In this way Cromwell was able to command the spending power to support his executive actions as a minister. Up to 1536 he personally attended to the transactions of replenishing and expending the reserves of the King and his Jewel House, but from the beginning of that year, he made John Williams, formerly a clerk of the Jewel House, his deputy.

Cromwell extended his personal dominance in finance beyond the offices which he held. Scrapping his proposal to use the Chamber for the receipt of, and the Hanaper for the accounting of, clerical taxes, he appointed his man John Gostwick, with whom he had served Wolsey, as commissioner of First Fruits and Tenths. Leaving the collection of clerical taxes with the Church and their administration with the Exchequer, the commissioner accounted for the cash only to his master. Clerical taxes along with funds, which Cromwell diverted from other departments, amounted to an annual average revenue of £60,000 between 1536 and 1540. With his control of the Jewel House and of First Fruits and Tenths, Cromwell had come near to improvising an informal system of ministerial household finance which could last only as long as he remained in favour.

While Cromwell boldly relied on royal favour as sufficient warrant for his virtually personal management of large funds, the established bureaucrats sought legal authority for their actions. Ever since the death of Henry VII, when the King's personal supervision of the agencies, developed by royal initiative, had ceased, the bureaucrats had shown a desire to safeguard themselves by official definition of their responsibilities and functions. Detached from administration, Henry VIII had become its critic and judge. The fate of Empson and Dudley reminded bureaucrats of their vulnerability. The process of self-protection, pursued by officials, was evident in the Acts of 1513 and 1515 which, after noting the methods of Henry VII, proceeded to give statutory authority to the methods of the auditing agency of the General

Surveyors.[24] Bureaucrats such as Sir Brian Tuke, Treasurer of the Chamber since 1528, and William Paulet, Master of Wards, were anxious to clarify their responsibilities and obtain legal sanction for their activities, even if it meant restricting their initiative. A bureaucratic reaction to the experimental methods of Henry VII was making itself felt.

While Cromwell understood the bureaucratic caution of officials like Sir Brian Tuke, he was not a prey to it himself. He was prepared to intervene in and to supervise the whole financial administration, as his own ministerial initiative required, regardless of bureaucratic formalities. It suited him, however, to promote the bureaucratic formalisation of offices in which he neither had an official position nor a concern for their expansion. In 1535 he made the statutory arrangements for the office of General Surveyors permanent and he accepted that neither that office nor the Chamber should expand their activities. His use of the Jewel House reduced the importance of the Chamber as a spending department and his development of other sources of revenue made him ready to comply with the cautious Treasurer's wish for a more restricted role for the Chamber. In 1540 he was ready to give the administration of wardships, already bureaucratised by William Paulet, the formal framework of a Court of Wards. In these ways Cromwell satisfied the bureaucratic desire among officials of those financial agencies, which had flourished under Henry VII's personal supervision, for a reassuring, if restrictive, definition of their responsibilities and procedures.

It was, however, the erection of the Court of Augmentations to deal with the proceeds of the dissolution of the monasteries which proved to be the development of greatest consequence in the development of the financial administration under Cromwell. The scale and complexity of the handling of monastic wealth could not be met by existing institutions or by Cromwell's improvisations. The general predilection for courts as the solution to administrative problems left Cromwell little choice but to expand the bureaucracy and organise a new institution. That Audley and Rich were later credited with the creation of the Court of Augmentation suggests that there was support in officialdom for the method of piecemeal addition to the administration.[25]

Cromwell did his best to keep some control over the new court. As Vicegerent he managed the policy of dissolution and so influenced the administrative business of the court. On matters of mutual concern to the court and the Vicegerent, Cromwell's views usually prevailed. He exercised royal patronage to appoint his protégé, Richard Rich, as chancellor, and Thomas Pope, who shared his and Audley's favour, as Treasurer. Despite its departmental independence, the court proved ready to respond to Cromwell's directives in such matters as paying annuities and pensions, and surrendering plate to the Jewel House.

The Court of Augmentations was a response to new revenues, which indicated a return to an older pattern of financial administration, represented by the Court of the Duchy of Lancaster upon which it was modelled. The device of the Yorkists and Henry VII for dealing with new landed revenues through the Chamber was not adopted. The importance of the Court of Augmentations did not derive, however, so much from its institutional organisation as a department of state rather than a household department, as from the sheer magnitude of its revenues. It soon outclassed and displaced the Chamber as the chief source of money for the immediate needs of the King and his government. In the face of such overwhelming competition household finance declined.

While Cromwell's pragmatic reaction to the new ex-monastic revenues was conservative in its reliance on the precedent of the Duchy of Lancaster Court, its effect was to bring about a change from dependence on the Chamber to dependence upon the Court of Augmentations. The King's detachment from administration had prepared for such a change by removing the vitalising royal initiative from household finance and by causing the household bureaucracy to stabilise its position in the absence of the King's personal involvement. Cromwell's promotion of the Court of Augmentations suited the King's style of rule, satisfied bureaucratic opinion and provided for the management of ex-monastic wealth. The final scale of its operations made the court a major financial institution, altered the centre of gravity in the financial administration and changed the relative importance of its components.

The creation of the Court of Augmentations and the consequent restriction of Chamber finance, the prolongation of the statutory authority for the General Surveyors, a proposal for a Court of Wards and the demonstration of the potential of the office of Chancellor of the Exchequer were Cromwell's contributions to the development of the financial administration. The result of his activities has been seen as effecting a change from household finance or Chamber administration to a national system, based on bureaucratic courts, functioning as departments of state.[26] Such an analysis from hindsight may be a useful historical interpretation of the consequences of Cromwell's actions, but as an indication of his aims and motives its value is debatable.

Whatever the differences in status between household offices and departments of state of which Cromwell was aware, he did not classify them as representative of different systems. In his memorial of 1533 he did not give a departmental framework to his review of royal finances.[27] His reference to departments was incidental and did not divide them systematically into household and state departments. He treated the royal administration as a whole. He exploited the Jewel House, the commission of First Fruits and Tenths and the Court of Augmentations without any other apparent consideration than convenience. Whether he employed informal or bureaucratic methods or household or state departments was dictated by practical needs rather than by any self-conscious realisation that he was substituting one system for another, a national for a household system. Cromwell's Act of Precedence in 1539 placed officers of state and household officials in one list.[28]

In his conduct of royal finances Cromwell used his personal authority and informal influence as much as bureaucratic procedure. His personality tended to determine the competence of his offices. Over the whole financial administration his control was personal rather than institutionalised. Far from promoting bureaucratic centralisation, he added to the collection of financial offices and agencies which he held together by pluralism and cumulative authority. In Privy Council he dominated the formulation of spending policy which was not initiated at departmental level. His personal initiative and supervision was required to give coherence to spending policy, to revenue policy and to the business of administration.

Whether Cromwell would have proceeded to establish, as well as the Court of Wards, a Court of First Fruits and Tenths, which was to emerge in the bureaucratic reaction to his fall, is a matter for conjecture. His use of deputies in his financial offices suggests that he might have bowed to the need for delegation by creating further courts. There is little sign, however, of a set policy by Cromwell to create a consciously new style of administration, based upon courts. The Court of Augmentations was a necessity, because he chose to copy the existing Court of the Duchy of Lancaster rather than tackle any fundamental reorganisation. The Court of Wards was made possible by the work and ambition of William Paulet who created it and was its first master. Cromwell's decision to prolong rather than suppress the office of General Surveyors, which survived from Henry VII's administration, allowed for the creation of a Court of General Surveyors in 1542 but it cannot be regarded as evidence of active preparation to create such a court.

By the end of Cromwell's period of power it was clear that there was no future for the Chamber in government finance. The future development of the remaining collection of financial agencies, when his directing hand was gone, was, however, less obvious. After Cromwell's downfall the worsening financial position of the Crown, rather than any administrative trend or bureaucratic tradition, established by

Cromwell, determined the development of the financial administration.[29] His expansive piecemeal approach was reversed in the effort to consolidate and centralise. The bureaucrats who exercised most influence over the necessary adaptation to circumstances were Walter Mildmay who was too young to have served under Cromwell and the experienced William Paulet who was as old as Cromwell and beside whom Cromwell was a mere bird of passage in the bureaucracy.

Cromwell subjected the financial administration to the conflicting influences of his overriding personal initiative and of his gift for business organisation. On balance his ministerial initiative rather than his bureaucratic talent characterised his achievement. In contrast to Cromwell both John Heron, who preceded him, and William Paulet, who followed him, as influential figures in financial administration, were more bureaucrats than ministers at a time when servants of the Crown were both. Under Cromwell the emphasis lay on meeting governmental demands for increased funds rather than on bureaucratic preoccupations with economy and formality. For all his skill in improving the details of administrative practice, his handling of the financial administration was dominated by *ad hoc* responses to new revenues and to the vested interests of the bureaucrats rather than by any large scale planning of a fully institutionalised and centralised financial system. He was the effective finance minister rather than the supreme bureaucrat.

The establishment of the Court of Augmentations has been taken to indicate Cromwell's decision as a finance minister to adopt in 1536 a policy for the total suppression of the religious houses and to provide for the Crown a permanent endowment in order to avoid dependence on parliamentary grants. These are debatable conclusions. The creation of the court was justified by the scale of business resulting from the 1536 Dissolution Act. It may suggest a hopeful anticipation of wider dissolution but it is not a sure sign that Cromwell had decided on total suppression in 1536. As for a plan for permanent endowment of the Crown, it belonged to the notion of the King living of his own to which Cromwell did not subscribe. In practice royal need had always triumphed over the argument for an inalienable endowment of Crown lands. The 1536 Dissolution Act envisaged grants and lettings of ex-monastic lands. From the start ex-monastic assets had been sold and the disposal of lands was begun by Cromwell who was a commissioner for the sale of lands. The ex-monastic revenues were not regarded by Cromwell as an alternative to parliamentary taxation but as an addition. In the 1540 session in which he proposed the suppression of the last surviving religious order he demanded parliamentary grants.

The success of Cromwell's financial provision resulted from his opportunity to budget ahead of need.[30] He did not inherit a desperately weak financial situation. The rise in prices, the King's extravagance, especially in building, and the cessation of the French pension in 1534 were trying but not critical. The real threat to solvency came from defence expenditure. The ever present prospects of attack from Scotland, France and the Emperor had been aggravated by the break with Rome. Precautions on the Border in 1533 and 1539, rebellion in Ireland in 1534, the Pilgrimage of Grace in 1536 and the constant menace from Charles V, becoming intense in 1533, 1536 and 1539, imposed heavy strains. Fortunately Henry VIII was thrown onto the defensive and his enemies did not engage him in active warfare. Campaigning was confined to the suppression of rebellion in Ireland and England. In these circumstances Cromwell could provide. His fall spared him the insuperable problem of financing the King's renewed aggression which led to debasement of the coinage, debt and the destruction of royal credit.

The wealth which Cromwell amassed for the King was spent on the conduct of government, including patronage and the maintenance of the court, and above all on defence. Its dispersal brought benefit to the governmental and military centres, Calais, Carlisle, Dover, Ludlow, York, London and elsewhere. The leaders of lay society enjoyed their share. Mercantile affluence was not drained by heavier customs. Those who did not benefit were the regular clergy and the vagabonds who obtained no direct aid from the government. The unsatisfied claimants complained. The insatiable consciences of reformers, who demanded the banishment of ignorance and idleness from the commonwealth by royal largesse, were unappeased.

Although publicists, preoccupied with vagabondage, protested that Cromwell's desire to enrich the King so that he might enrich all men had not been realised, the political nation knew that it was more prosperous for the redistribution of the wealth of the Church by the King. Besides providing for the prime duties of government, defence and justice, and bringing the King's subjects 'into the true and perfect knowledge of Almighty God', Cromwell claimed to the King that he had taken measures for the commonwealth to increase 'such wealth in the same amongst the great number and multitude of your subjects as never was seen in this realm since Brutus' time'.[31] His financial policy had been a means to many ends. Making the King rich was never an end in itself for Cromwell.

5 LIMITATIONS AND OPPOSITION

Cromwell was the King's servant and in that relationship lay the source and limitation of his power. As the holder of high office and a councillor he was expected both to execute royal policy and by giving counsel to shape policy. For Cromwell the art of government lay in conceiving of policy in terms of its enforcement. A devotee of achieving the possible, he has appeared as an executive who was concerned above all with ways and means. Occupied with the drafting of legislation and the details of administration, his role as the agent who put policies into force seems so demanding and absorbing that it is tempting to regard him as the mere servant who obeyed the King and carried out the King's policies.

Yet Cromwell was recognised by contemporaries as a counsellor who was something more than a good lawyer who knew how to give legal form to the King's wishes. His opponents credited him with initiating policies and usurping the royal power. While evidence against a scapegoat is suspect, the choice of Cromwell as scapegoat is significant. Foreign observers and his rivals within the circle of government were convinced of his influence over matters of state. His papers reveal his consideration and selection of topics for action. In Privy Council and in Parliament the agenda reflected his choice of business. In the origination of policy by King and council he often took the initiative.

Although Cromwell was a policy maker of importance, it may be asked whether his initiative was confined to those areas in which the King, lacking a personal interest, delegated his authority. Henry expected officialdom to get on with its job. Cromwell was left to carry the burden, where policy was a settled matter of law and where established lines of policy, stock responses and precedents were available. He did not trouble the King with the formal functions of the administration. How the bureaucracy and its business was organised was left to Cromwell and the bureaucrats. The King was concerned with the efficiency of the service which he received and, it seems, was prepared to accept changes in the secretaryship and council and even the reorganisation of his household with approval.

The bulk of administrative business was activated from below. Cromwell dealt with a mass of requests for action and took the appropriate administrative course at his own discretion. In matters of social and economic regulation the initiative often came from parliament or interested parties. In these spheres, it seems that the King had little interest and allowed Cromwell and the council to devise the necessary bills and proclamations. While in finance the royal demands were the stimulus to action, the means by which money was raised and accounted for was not of great concern to Henry. In the day to day conduct of government Cromwell could use his own judgement as to what the King would approve and he was ready to take for granted the royal sanction.

In matters of high politics Henry, as Thomas Wolsey knew only too well, had set ideas which were not to be easily changed.[1] His sense of personal and royal honour made him watchful in his dealings with other princes. It was his prerogative to deal with foreign affairs. Cromwell, as Secretary, could exercise his influence by the way in which he presented news from abroad to the King and by negotiating with ambassadors, but he could not remove Henry's conviction that he knew how to handle foreign affairs rather better than Cromwell did. The King's reluctance to accept the consequences of the break with Rome and seriously cultivate protestant alliances prevailed until 1539, when he allowed Cromwell to arrange a matrimonial treaty with Cleves. It was a mistake which would contribute to Henry's sense of superiority.

Henry's views on his imperial right to control his clergy and on matters of doctrine were firmly rooted. Cromwell was able to exploit Henry's vision of himself as a new Constantine. On doctrinal questions he found it less easy to win the acquiescence of the Defender of the Faith for reform. The division in the episcopate over doctrine caused both traditionalists and innovators to turn to the King. Placed in the position of arbiter, Henry tended to consult his own conservative conscience rather than allow his Vicegerent to settle matters of faith. The balance of the religious parties meant that the official formulation of the faith rested ultimately with the King.[2]

The dynastic mode of politics gave a peculiar importance to the King's emotional attitudes to marriage. Where political calculations ended and personal considerations began in Henry's matrimonial manoeuvres, it was not always easy to discern. If his marriages reflected the intrigue of faction and the triumph of policies, they in their turn provided the opportunities for Henry's personal passions to encourage faction and promote policies. The King's complaints about Anne of Cleves' person left Cromwell in no doubt about the likely future of the marriage, should it ever depend on the King's personal feelings rather than upon political necessity.[3]

Over his servants Henry enjoyed the authority of his position. It was an advantage which he made good with his personality. He was sure enough of himself to choose strong men to serve him. He was not addicted to time servers, although he demanded ultimate obedience. Even Cranmer opposed Henry on occasion. Henry seems to have relished tussling with Stephen Gardiner and regarded him as a man whom he alone could manage. Cromwell had clashes with the King and was prepared to retire in a huff even in the presence of a foreign ambassador. The story of how the King struck Cromwell indicated the degree to which Cromwell was ready to provoke the King in argument. The exhibition of emotions by both King and minister was in keeping with the individual's code of social behaviour of the time and explains in part the compensating insistence upon the public formalities and upon the ideal of a counsellor, devoid of passion.[4] It also shows how difficult it was to persuade Henry against his wishes. The King might be manoeuvred and even panicked into action but he was not to be browbeaten.

When Cromwell gained a place in the Council, the King was already set upon asserting his control of the clergy and had threatened the possibility of a break with the Pope over his matrimonial plans. The King had taken over the conduct of the quarrel with Rome and had indicated the lengths to which he was prepared to go. Henry's threats became the substance of Cromwell's policy and events slowly forced the King to fulfil them through Cromwell.

In persuading the reluctant Henry to accept the break with Rome Cromwell was introducing not so much his own original policy as supporting the extreme measures which Henry had envisaged as a last resort in his determination to overcome all obstacles to his second marriage. Cromwell's growing hold upon royal favour indicated that he was carrying out a policy which was not contrary to Henry's wishes. Yet Cromwell's execution of the break with Rome constituted something more than the performance of tactical moves to realise the royal strategy. While he stayed within the broad limits of the King's aims, he transformed the basis of royal policy. He not only gave precision to Henry's general requirements but he also gave them a justification which lifted them out of the sphere of temporary political advantage and placed them in a more permanent constitutional and ideological setting.[5] He retained enough of the King's ideas and objectives to satisfy Henry that the policy was his own. In achieving the King's goals he went beyond those originally contemplated by the King.

Cromwell's elaboration of the imperial theme put Henry's insular historic claims into the context of the extremist continental imperialism of Marsilio of Padua. Henry's imperial crown became more than the token of a personal authority; it was established as the symbol of an independent body politic, of a realm which was an Empire. The *Ecclesia Anglicana* acknowledged Henry's Headship, but was given by

Cromwell a different relationship with the temporalty and with the Catholic Church.[6] The settlement of the King's particular and personal matrimonial case, was given general significance in the rejection of papal jurisdiction. The King's resort to biblical authority, concerning his marriage to a brother's widow, was developed by Cromwell's evangelical interests into a wider reliance on the authority of the very lively word of God in the formulation of religious doctrine and the practice and the vindication of the King's ecclesiastical role. The intellectual, religious and political content of the King's policy came to owe more to Cromwell than it did to Henry. The responsibility for the policies which eventuated in the Henrician Reformation must be shared between the King and Cromwell. Yet the more significant contribution would seem to have come from Cromwell.

Even in the King's matrimonial affairs Cromwell played an important role. He engineered the means by which Henry disposed of Catherine and married Anne Boleyn. His support was vital to the plot which destroyed Anne Boleyn.[7] He used the Seymour marriage to gain a marriage alliance with the Seymours for his own son. He was the leading advocate of the marriage with Anne of Cleves. In matters which engaged Henry's closest personal attention, Cromwell was able to infuse his own aims, as he did in working for a protestant alliance in Europe through the Cleves marriage.

In policy making Cromwell remained in appearance the King's obedient servant and acted in the royal name. He was not able to block openly the royal will or maintain policies in opposition to the King's wishes. His scope lay in the elaboration, transformation and generalisation of Henry's intentions. His initiative in these directions arose partly from his own sympathies and intellectual force and partly from the demands made by the legislative methods which he adopted. His use of legislation had a profound effect upon the formulation of his policy. Making public law called for a justification of measures which would be broadly acceptable to the political nation in Parliament. It required a basis in law which would convince lawyers of its legality. It demanded general legal application to the whole body politic. It necessitated a shift from the personal dynastic level of the King's outlook to a level of political thinking in which there was a concept of a body politic and a territorial jurisdiction over a realm which was conceived of as an empire. Cromwell's version of royal policy was realised at a different level from that in which the King matured his ideas. His policy achieved in public law an intellectual and legal independence of the King.

In the transformation of policies centred on the interests of the Kingship into those centred on the body politic, of claims resting on royal titles into those resting on statute, the nature of Cromwell's policies can be detected. The terms of political thinking had been altered to meet the needs of legislative and judicial machinery. The legislation concerning the break with Rome was in its coherence, in the exploitation of its consequences and in its justification largely Cromwell's work. It was a selection and new arrangement of elements from the past. Its novelty lay in the fact that the arrangements for the break with Rome had led to the theoretical and constitutional realisation of an alternative authority in the imperial realm. Its peculiarity lay in the denial of universal authority to any human authority. Cromwell's inventiveness lay in establishing different relationships between existing institutions and authorities and in altering the assumptions on which those relationships rested.

In such ways Cromwell was able to find considerable freedom inside the limitations laid upon him by the King. Within those limitations he concocted and executed policies which embraced but transcended the King's aims and which may be seen to have been shaped by Cromwell's grasp of concepts, inspired by his own evangelical enthusiasm and formulated by his own legal expertise. His contribution to policy was so decisive that he may justly be said to have had a policy of his own. His greatest achievements were necessarily carried out within the bounds of royal favour. The limitations imposed by Henry's authority could not always be exploited successfully by Cromwell. He had to accept rebuffs and to withdraw as gracefully as he could. The loss of royal favour proved ultimately fatal. Henry, as Cromwell and all other royal servants knew, was the ruler. Yet in his heyday Cromwell had found room even within the interstices of Henry's most obsessive political preoccupations to inject his own transforming ideas.

In his administrative capacity Cromwell had to deal with the vested interests of an old and sophisticated central bureaucracy. As the act of 1536 showed the bureaucrats knew how to look after their own interests in the face of a powerful minister who was trying to adapt the bureaucracy to new business and make it more responsive to his own needs.[8] Supported by the King, he was able to dominate officialdom, upsetting the old balance of departments and altering the importance of established offices. He accelerated the process by which the bureaucracy continuously adapted itself to changing circumstances. Although he responded quickly and forcefully, his alterations remained in the bureaucratic tradition of piecemeal change.

Cromwell did not create the bureaucracy, he joined it and learned from its ways. His use of statutory authorisation, his readiness to define functions and his concern with precedence and precedents were part of those ways. He adopted the well tried forms of court and commission. Despite the changes, the appearance of continuity was preserved. In all these activities he was acceptable to the bureaucrats. Moreover he created the opportunities for employment and advancement for a generation who were educated to serve the state. It was a boom time for ambitious young men who sought Cromwell's favour. His patronage gave Cromwell a hold over the bureaucracy.

Under a King who judged by the results rather than by the methods of administration, however, Cromwell was more concerned with efficiency than restrictive formalities and cumbersome procedures against fraud. The laxity in his financial administration became apparent later in the mid-century period of retrenchment.[9] In the reform of the Household he showed himself capable of enforcing economy and checking corruption but elsewhere in the administration he was less successful and, perhaps, less interested. His own success in gathering the fruits of office did not set an example of restraint in enjoying the spoils of power. The bad reputation which he had won in the dissolution under Wolsey was not erased. In an age when public servants were expected to reimburse themselves by unofficial gifts and fees, Cromwell was accused by Paulet of bribery. Yet it must be remembered that in the giving of gifts the initiative came from below. Cromwell did not have to solicit gifts: they were thrust upon him. The refusal to accept them would have caused more consternation than the acceptance of them.

While in detail Cromwell, by reforming the clerical side of Chancery, by improving on the methods of the Court of the Duchy of Lancaster in the Court of Augmentations and by reorganising the Household, increased efficiency, in general he did not create a more centralised or a notably less corrupt administration. His success in doubling the King's revenues removed the urgency of making minor economies and of establishing strict checks at every level of the administration. Financial circumstances, the convention of unofficial remuneration and the vested interests of officialdom persuaded Cromwell to accept a measure of laxity.

Although Cromwell's heyday might appear to have been a golden age for both dutiful and corrupt bureaucrats, there was a considerable unease in the bureaucracy over Cromwell's methods of government. His officials were not convinced that he had created a bureaucratic government. The attack in his attainder on his high-handed and personal methods revealed the resentment of the bureaucrats for a minister who appeared to be usurping the role of the King and abusing royal authority by overriding the procedures and conventions of the administration. It was significant that the men he had trained, Rich, Wriothesley and Paget were the men who gave evidence against him. The protest in 1540 against his conduct of the administration was an attempt to safeguard the bureaucracy against the actions of a minister in bureaucrat's clothing. Much of Cromwell's power derived from his command of the bureaucracy. His failure to keep its loyalty contributed to his downfall.[10]

In his great days Cromwell largely overcame the limitations, imposed by the personality and authority of the King, and the restrictions upon his initiative, posed by bureaucratic tradition. His success placed the responsibility for the conduct of affairs upon him. His policies divided public opinion, as they divided the factions at court. The opposition in the country grew. Late in 1536 rioting broke out in Lincolnshire and was followed by an organised demonstration and show of force, the Pilgrimage of Grace, during the winter in Yorkshire. Cromwell had precipitated what appeared to be a grave threat to his person and his policies.

The King's reaction to any popular expression of discontent that smacked of rebellion protected Cromwell from popular demands for his dismissal. Henry would not allow parliament to dictate to him on his choice of counsellors and he was prepared to resist any dictation from those whom he regarded as rebels. The Pilgrimage was a protest at change from above. Its conservatism prevented a demonstration of opposition from becoming outright revolt. In resentment at the interference of central government the local ruling class exercised their leadership of the community but they were aware that their ultimate interest lay in maintaining law and order and the hierarchy of authority under the Crown.[11]

The Pilgrimage made Cromwell more careful in his methods but it did not deflect him from his policies. The common aim of the Pilgrims to halt the dissolution was not achieved. Yet the popular grounds of opposition to Cromwell had been established by the Pilgrimage and those grounds persisted and were expressed again in the successful attack by his enemies in 1540. The social, political and religious resentment of the Pilgrims created the picture of Cromwell as a base-born, evil counsellor who fostered heresy.

Cromwell's elevation from the dust was an affront to the assumptions of degree society and excited anticipation of his fall. It was against the hierarchical nature of things for the base-born to rule. The wheel of fortune could be expected to turn. Cromwell's birth was a social and a political disqualification. The Pilgrimage of Grace urged the King to rid himself of low born counsellors and restore the nobles to their natural place in his counsel. Lord Darcy expressed the aristocratic prejudice, when he claimed that Cromwell intended to execute all nobles. In 1540 his attainder stressed Cromwell's disdain of the nobility in order to represent him as a subverter of hierarchical government and society.[12]

In practice Cromwell supported the hierarchical order and

participated in it by accepting titles, marrying his son into the Seymour family, and by living according to his rank. He sustained hierarchy both as a divine order and the necessary means of rule. His Act of Precedence in 1539 characteristically gave legal expression to his acceptance of hierarchy.[13] His attitude to the nobility was determined by political rather than social prejudice, although he, no doubt, shared that disdain of the nobility which was fashionable in humanist circles and voiced by Thomas More. Nevertheless he distributed patronage to the aristocracy and promoted the fortunes of those who like himself were to be elevated to the peerage. But, while he was prepared to use the nobility in the King's interest, he was not ready to allow considerations of status to override the political and legal necessity of obedience.

Under provocation Cromwell justified his high estate with the argument, popular among humanist intellectuals who aspired to the active life, that public virtue rather than noble birth was the essential constituent of nobility. Morison was allowed to use it in counter attacking the slur on base-born councillors in the Pilgrimage of Grace. The point of the argument lay not in any implication about the equality of men or of opportunity but in defining the qualifications for and the nature of nobility. Cromwell was no egalitarian. To his protestant-minded friends, like Shaxton, he spoke of his vocation, ascribing his place in government and society to the divine purpose. The ironic words of his last speech that his base degree was 'not unknown to many of you' were an admission of the futility of the humanist argument against the prejudice in favour of noble birth. It was in divine vocation that he found his ultimate justification, when on the scaffold he claimed to have been called to high estate.[14]

In the light of assumptions about the divine pattern of society Cromwell's career called for a supernatural explanation. While Cromwell acknowledged a vocation from God, Reginald Pole declared him to be an emissary of Satan. Less sophisticated minds detected a magical power at work. It was said that Cromwell possessed King Solomon's ring. He was alluded to as 'the Crum' in the popular prophecies of disaster which expressed the fatalistic pessimism of those who suffered the rule of men whom they mistrusted. The powerless endowed Cromwell with a sinister magical aura and saw him as a man predestined by a malign fate to bring ruin upon the land. As his response to the prophecies of the Maid of Kent showed, he did not underrate the effect of such expressions of popular opposition, which, because of their irrationality, were so difficult to refute.[15]

If Cromwell's career inevitably ruffled the feathers of hierarchy, the doctrines by which he sought to govern were no less disturbing. His claim to enforce the law and demand obedience to the King 'without respect of persons' made no concessions to the distinctions and privileges of degree. His reduction of all the complex loyalties within society to the simple relationship of King and subject made manifest his determination to treat all as equal before the royal authority. He wanted no half-subjects. He insisted that the greatest must submit to the meanest when they acted with the royal authority.[16] The demand for universal obedience to the King and the enforcement of one law cut across the multiple loyalties and privileges and the particularism of traditional society. His relentless execution of royal justice was a negation of hierarchy with its respect for persons and degrees.

The assumptions of society were challenged by Cromwell's advancement of mean men in the provinces as much as by their promotion in central government. New men disturbed the patterns of goodlordship. The numerous commissioners emphasised the royal interference in local affairs. The demand by the Pilgrimage of Grace for a parliament at York revealed the dissatisfaction with the representation of local interests. There was a complaint that local men were being displaced in parliament by the servants of the King. The way in which the aristocracy had joined the commons in the Pilgrimage indicated the frustration of those who felt entitled to be the natural leaders of their community in the locality and the patrons of its representatives in parliament.[17]

The Pilgrimage of Grace revealed the dilemma of the nobility. Their demand to counsel the King was a recognition of the new concentration of power in the Council and Court and an expression of their resentment at being excluded from the centre.[18] Yet their resistance to the interference of central government showed their desire to halt the process of concentrating power at the royal centre. They saw upstart officials in royal government and aspiring gentry in the provinces, who for the sake of advancement sacrificed local to royal interests, creating a new network of power which was replacing their influence in county affairs. Yet they were loath to abandon the old ways of goodlordship in the countryside and become a court aristocracy. Adapting to strong central direction proved easier and more rewarding for the gentry than for the nobility for whom it meant fundamental changes in their whole way of life and in their assumptions about their role.

The charge of heresy, attached to Cromwell by the Pilgrimage of Grace, was the equivalent in religious terms of the accusation of the disruption of the political and social order. Old associations between heresy and sedition prompted some to call him a Lollard. Cromwell's alleged heresy had its political dimension in the substitution of the royal Headship for the papal supremacy. It involved him in intellectual controversy over the issues of authority and unity. Although he deployed his intellectual arguments, the issues could not be resolved by arguments alone. It required the aid of the law. Fisher and More were executed and those who wished to escape the penalties of the law had, like Pole, to remain in exile or change their minds, like Gardiner. The dissolution of the monasteries, authorised by statute, was the particular instance of law enforcement which united opposition in the Pilgrimage of Grace. Cromwell had strained respect for the law to breaking point and provoked disorder.

While papal authority, the unity of the Church and points of doctrine were matters for the far-sighted and educated few, the traditional practices of religion were more widely understood and cherished. The dissolution of the monasteries was seen as an attack on 'good religion'. By his suppression of holy days, pilgrimage and superstition, Cromwell was striking not only at the personal expressions of piety but at the public religiosity of the community. 'Good religion' gave society its ritual opportunities to sense its solidarity and its acceptance of the beliefs which bound it together. It was natural and appropriate that a demonstration by a community should take on the title and trappings of a Pilgrimage of Grace.[19]

Besides the communal and personal resentments which Cromwell's disruption of traditional religious ways caused among the laity, he had to face the reactions of those clergy who believed that he was undermining the status and privileges of their profession. The religious orders failed to organise effective resistance and present a united front. They played only a secondary role in the Pilgrimage of Grace and relied on the leadership of the laity. The religious houses treated in individual isolation with the royal commissioners. They fell one by one. From the outwardly impressive monastic establishment Cromwell met only rare and sporadic obstruction. The regular clergy received no support from the secular clergy. The Church did not prove to be a monolithic institution.

The secular clergy were in a stronger position than the regular orders. The ecclesiastical administration was necessary to the government. With Warham's archiepiscopal leadership and More's intellectual and official support, the clergy put up a struggle before submitting to royal demands for obedience. Even as subjects of the King, the traditionalists defended their professional position and clung to their old ways. Neither Acts of Parliament, oaths, commissions nor injunctions affected the practices of all the parish priesthood in many areas. Despite Cranmer's compliance, the episcopate remained divided over the Vicegerent's policies. In 1539 Gardiner was able to rally the traditionalists and to engineer in the Six Articles Act a check to doctrinal innovation and a defence of the clerical profession, which preserved for the clergy their celibate status, the power of auricular confession and the performance of the miracle of the Mass.[20]

In 1540 Cromwell was convicted of heresy by Parliament and

declared to be a supporter of the Lutheran views of Barnes. That his enemies represented him as a sacramentary was a demonstration of their obsession with what they saw as his dangerous extremism. To them his middle way was the highroad to heretical perdition. They recognised only his destructive capacity. The accusation of heresy, made in 1536, proved four years later to be an important factor in his undoing. Under Gardiner the traditionalists appeared to have won in 1540 a rearguard action which halted their retreat.

Alongside the political, social and religious opposition to Cromwell can be detected the motives of economic interest. The economic consequences of his policies, being more obviously calculable than the repercussions of his measures on religion or politics, could be appreciated by all manner of men. Robert Aske feared that the Dissolution would impoverish the North. The aristocracy saw the Statute of Uses as an attack upon their family fortunes. The presence of subsidy commissioners contributed to the outbreak of the Lincolnshire riots. Rising prices alarmed the tradesmen of London. The causes of vagabondage frightened the poor, worried the municipal authorities and stirred the consciences of reformers. Cromwell was beset with a variety of economic grievances.

Cromwell was well aware of the effect of economic grievances in stirring opposition. His measures were usually framed to take account of the interests involved. While stripping the religious orders of their wealth, he made the terms of surrender sufficiently acceptable to individuals to lessen their economic resentment. Despite all the rumours of extortionate novel exactions, he made no unprecedented demands upon lay taxpayers. He responded to demands for price regulation and, when his policies interfered with business, gave way in such matters as customs and exchange control. If he could not meet the expectations of reformers in his measures of poor relief, he did something to organise charity in the parishes. The tussle in parliament to enact the Statute of Uses was of the King's and not of Cromwell's choosing.[21] In general Cromwell tried to avoid exacerbating economic grievances.

While inflation was beginning to cause problems, the economy in general was healthy in the 1530's. The harvests were satisfactory or very good throughout the whole decade. The cloth trade and its dependent industry was sufficiently buoyant to avoid the disaster of a slump. The movement to enclosure had slackened. Builders found work constructing fortifications, harbour works and palaces and in demolishing religious houses. No great epidemic attacked the population. The economic grievances, faced by Cromwell, were based on exaggerations of interested parties and reformers rather than on the deep seated needs of an economy that was severely out of joint. The avoidance of large scale war enabled Cromwell in a period of inflation to keep the government solvent and the currency sound. His fall was precipitated neither by an economic crisis nor by the bankruptcy of the government. In 1540 he could confidently boast of the prosperous reign of Henry VIII.[22]

The interests of all the various groups in the country who were opposed to Cromwell were ultimately brought to bear upon the politics of the Court, where they were resolved into the policies and principles, which divided those who struggled for power. It was at the centre of affairs in political conflict that the fate of Cromwell and his policies was decided. His antagonists might be driven by personal motives of revenge but they also represented however indirectly the broad themes of opposition to Cromwell in the country at large. His attainder showed the animus against a low-born heretic councillor of the King which had been voiced in the Pilgrimage of Grace. Cromwell's end was determined by the King, but the disfavour of his humble subjects seemed to echo the conscience of the King. To George Cavendish who knew the intrigues of high politics at first hand the fall of Wolsey and of Cromwell suggested the comment that 'the inclination and natural disposition of Englishmen is, and always has been, to desire alteration of officers'. Behind the fickle favour of princes he detected the fickle opinion of the people.[23]

6   THE CHURCH OF
        ENGLAND

By the end of 1534 the recognition in law of the Church of England under a royal Supreme Head had been achieved by Cromwell's legislation. The conflict between the spiritualty and the temporalty had been resolved, at least in theory, and in practice the clergy were now treated as the subjects of the King. Under its Supreme Head the Church of England, it was officially held, had been restored to its historic independence of all foreign potentates. It still remained, however, to enforce the statutes which removed the authority of Rome and to formulate and administer the policies of the Supremacy. Cromwell had given constitutional meaning to Henry's Supreme Headship and he was anxious to influence the exercise of the royal power over the Church.

The King viewed the Supremacy, which had been acknowledged by the clergy before it had been declared by parliament, as an attribute of his imperial heritage and a personal prerogative. He had prevailed upon both convocations to accept his Headship and his control of ecclesiastical legislation in 1531 and 1532. In 1533 he regarded Archbishop Cranmer as his most principal minister of his ecclesiastical jurisdiction. Henry showed a proprietary interest in his Church. Over the Supplication against the Ordinaries he had posed as an arbiter, 'indifferent', between convocation and parliament. The fear that the King might play off the prelates against the laity and might allow his clergy to use his quasi-papal powers as a protection for their interests alarmed the lawyers, like Cromwell. As Audley later expressed it, it was the fear that 'you bishops would enter in with the king and by means of his supremacy order the laity as ye listed'. [1]

Cromwell wished to apply the Headship as a legal power, circumscribed by statute. Such was the intention of translating Henry's imperial longings into Marsilian terms and the reiteration in statute of the declarations of convocation regarding the Supremacy and its powers. Cromwell stressed the Marsilian doctrines of the supremacy of the lay community, the King in parliament in English terms, over the government of the Church and he emphasised the union of the royal capacities of Kingship and Headship under one law. To achieve his aims he required, like the King, an ecclesiastical *alter ego*. He found it in the creation of the office of Vicegerent early in 1535[2] The ease with which he assumed by royal commission the quasi-papal reformatory powers and jurisdiction of the Supremacy was largely due to the compliance, however reluctant, of Archbishop Cranmer without which the conflict of spiritualty and temporalty might have continued.

Where Wolsey as Chancellor and Legate united the powers of two separate authorities, royal and papal, in his person, Cromwell as councillor and Vicegerent expressed the authority of one King and Supreme Head. While ecclesiastics continued to serve in royal administration, a layman now supervised the administration of the Church. Cromwell's commission to reform empowered him to appoint commissions for particular purposes, to undertake visitations, to discipline the clergy, to require notice of vacancies and to receive any revenue arising, to call convocations, chapters and synods, to control the election of bishops, to issue injunctions and to exercise ecclesiastical jurisdiction over any person. To meet such responsibilities Cromwell set up an office and appointed Petre as his deputy to organise the business of the Vicegerency.

Under Wolsey Cromwell had dealt with litigation in church courts, with patronage, with the dissolution of religious houses and with Wolsey's clerical rights and properties during his master's disgrace. As a layman, he was quite used to ordering ecclesiastical affairs. In royal service he had continued to exercise an interest in clerical patronage and the licensing of preaching. His legislation demonstrated his grasp of the administration of the Church and his interest in and ability to achieve reform. The Vicegerent as successor to the Cardinal legate was well prepared for his task. It was significant of his unique suitability that upon his fall the Vicegerency lapsed.

The aims of the Vicegerent were expressed in the statement that the Ten Articles were 'holily provided, decreed and established by common assent and public authority for the weal, commodity and profit of all this realm'. They were reiterated in the injunctions of 1536 which were set forth 'to the glory of Almighty God, to the King's Highness honour, the public weal of this his realm and the increase of virtue of the same'. In a body politic, where the division between the temporalty and the spiritualty was nominal only, the reformation of the church and of the commonwealth were one and the same thing. Cromwell was not simply announcing the subordination of spiritual to the temporal interest but affirming their interdependence in the realisation of a Christian commonwealth. He recognised that Providence played a role in politics and affected the welfare of the commonwealth. 'For undoubtedly I take God to be not only your Grace's protector but also a marvellous favourer', he wrote to the King.[3]

While accepting the theory of a nominal distinction between the temporal and spiritual powers, in practice Cromwell preserved the

Church of England as a distinct institution. His anti-clericalism did not reject in principle a church and a clergy. Since he argued that the Church of England had long existed, he stressed its historic continuity and preserved its tradition as far as was compatible with the Supremacy.[4] The provinces of Canterbury and York, united in their recognition of the Supreme Head, survived. The church courts continued to function. The Vicegerency was exercised in legatine fashion through visitations and injunctions. The suspension of episcopal jurisdiction in 1535 was a normal legality of a general visitation rather than a novel assertion of episcopal dependence on the Supreme Head. As Vicegerent Cromwell acted as an ecclesiastical statesman and administrator. In parliament the Vicegerent had his place on the King's right hand, first among the Lords Spiritual.

Cromwell had every reason to cultivate the traditional cooperation between the King and the clergy. The church provided a valuable nation-wide bureaucracy which proved its efficiency in the compilation of the *Valor Ecclesiasticus*. He continued the employment of churchmen, such as Rowland Lee and Nicholas Heath, to serve the King at home and abroad. The parish was pressed into service to administer poor relief. The church courts and pulpits provided the means of coercion and indoctrination, required to maintain the morals and beliefs of a Christian commonwealth. The Church contributed to the royal revenues. While Cromwell complained about clerics in lay jobs in private employment, he had no qualms about using them in the royal service.[5]

Just as Cromwell used prelates in royal government so he expected laymen to continue to serve the church, as he had done for Wolsey. He set sheriffs to watch bishops and justices of the peace to enforce injunctions. He regulated the church through circular letters, proclamations and statutes.[6] *Adiaphora*, the things necessary to good politic order in religion, were the concern of the clergy and the laity who were obliged as loyal subjects to work together to implement the royal reformation. Cromwell's activities increased lay concern with the church but whether they led to any further secularisation of the church depended on the religious convictions of those involved, whether they were clerics or laymen.

The suppression of abuses in the Church proved difficult. The King's prejudices, the vested interests of clergy and patrons and the practical problems of change obstructed Cromwell's efforts. He limited but failed to abolish benefit of clergy. He was unable to end all sanctuary rights. He was obliged to insist on the payment of the detested tithes. Despite the pressure of common lawyers for the transference of cases of probate and testaments, of tithes and of defamation from church to common law courts, he preserved the ecclesiastical jurisdiction intact. The attempts of canonists to reform the canon law by activating the royal commission, set up at the time of the submission of the clergy in 1532 and later confirmed by statute, met with no response from the Vicegerent. The King refused to treat clerical marriage as a matter among the *adiaphora* and allow it. Cromwell condemned pluralism and simony but the spread of lay patronage as a result of the dissolution of the monasteries made their eradication even more difficult. [7]

While the old abuses of clerical privilege and ecclesiastical administration tended to persist, the old beliefs and practices proved tenacious. Yet Cromwell's activities encouraged the elements of change in the religious climate. The reduction of Holy Days and pilgrimages, the destruction of religious houses, images and shrines limited the communal and personal expression of traditional faith. [8] The condemnation of so much, that had been taken for granted, as superstition prompted the reconsideration of convention and a reappraisal of what was necessary for salvation. Cromwell did not create the doubts and criticisms in matters of religion but by his efforts to enforce the law and the injunctions he made them the subject of urgent personal decisions which affected not only salvation in the next but also conduct in this world. The denial of papal authority posed the question of obedience. Cromwell created a situation in which protestant views might seem more satisfying and appropriate.

The most obviously effective of the Vicegerent's reforms was the dissolution of the monasteries. Despite the fears of pessimists that the spoils would go to the wealthy and that the great abbeys would follow the lesser to destruction, the dissolution began in an atmosphere of reform which raised the hopes of optimists. Granted that monastic reform was necessary, Cromwell's measures could be justified. The scheme in 1536 was to dissolve the small houses with an income of less than £200 per annum, to transfer their inmates to better disciplined larger houses or to offer them other employment or pensions to the superiors, and to maintain the hospitality and tillage of the dissolved houses. A poor relief act in 1536 compensated for any reduction in monastic alms giving. Injunctions, issued to the surviving houses, called for strict adherence to monastic rules. [9]

The evidence, obtained by visitation, of immorality in the monasteries was exaggerated and emotive but it impressed the Commons and provided justification of the acknowledged need for reform. In choosing to attack the monasteries for their immorality, Cromwell hoped to rally the support of all those who were against sin. He was attacking abuses, not monastic ideals. There were no official moves to raise doctrinal objections to monasticism. Exemptions were granted, where a case could be made for survival of a house. The limited dissolution was accepted by the ruling circles at court. There was little sympathy for the contemplative life among the humanist intellectuals and among the secular clergy. Only in the Pilgrimage of Grace was the dissolution accepted as a cause for organised opposition.

Those idealists who were more concerned with the reform of the commonwealth than with the reform of monasticism welcomed the opportunity to put the wealth of monasteries to better use. The unthriftiness of the monks was stressed to suggest their waste of resources. Cromwell's act appeared to be in the tradition of Wolsey's dissolution. Hopes were high that monastic revenues would be used to endow education and relieve the poor.[10] Whatever encouragement Cromwell may have given to these hopes, he did not give any official commitment over the disposal of the proceeds of the dissolution.

Not until 1539 was a gesture made to put the ex-monastic wealth to better use, when an act was passed to set up new bishoprics. The act gave effect to a reform, mooted in Wolsey's day, but Cromwell moved to limit the number of sees which Henry was prepared to create.[11] The act also contained a declaration of intent to alleviate poverty and endow education. It did not satisfy the champions of welfare in the commonwealth. Their bitterness revealed the depth of their convictions. For Cromwell the ex-monastic funds were better used in augmenting the royal revenues to make the King stronger than his enemies. In a dangerous world he put security before welfare.

How necessary it was to strengthen the King was demonstrated by the Pilgrimage of Grace. A regional community mobilised in order to protect its spiritual and economic interests which appeared to be threatened by the dissolution. The Pilgrimage of Grace did not, however, confine itself to opposing the suppression of the lesser houses. Its demands amounted to an attack upon the King's conduct of government. Henry felt compelled to assert his authority. Fortunately for the King the opposition disintegrated and he was able to get the upper hand by the beginning of 1537.

The suppression of the Pilgrimage of Grace created the conditions for further dissolution of religious houses. The cost of countering the Pilgrimage provided an inducement to acquire more monastic wealth and in its aftermath new methods of dissolution were discovered. Forfeiture of monastic property by conviction of the head of a house for treason and voluntary surrender were methods which secured the King's title to the proceeds. The low morale of the religious orders was evident and to those who predicted that the greater houses would follow the lesser it looked as if their predictions were about to be vindicated.

In March 1538 Cromwell thought it necessary to avert panic measures by the religious to evade the consequences of impending suppression by denying any intention of further dissolution. With the dissolution act of 1536 executed and with the prospect of further easy pickings, the time had come for the government to decide whether to proceed to total suppression of the religious orders. If the King was hesitant, his hesitation was soon overcome and the decision to extinguish the religious orders was made.

From Cromwell's actions it was clear that he now aimed not to reform and discipline but to discredit and expose monasticism. Monastic shrines, relics and images were condemned as superstitious and fraudulent. The surrender of houses was accompanied by confessions of the idleness and vanity of life in the cloister. Except where abbots were executed for treason, the pretence of voluntary surrender was maintained, although Cromwell's commissioners were busy inducing surrender with both stick and carrot. From the parliament of 1539 Cromwell obtained an act confirming past and future surrenders. In the next year the last religious order in England was suppressed.[12]

By removing their material means of existence Cromwell destroyed the religious orders. He had directed the impetus for monastic reform and for the better use of their resources into a drive for the extinction of the religious life. The dissolution undermined the beliefs exemplified in monasticism. Latimer concluded that the end of the monasteries implied the end of purgatory. Whatever the religious contributed to the spiritual and social life of England disappeared with them. The ecclesiastical presence was reduced. The religious orders no longer played a part in the church, the universities or local society. The abbots no longer sat in parliament or held royal office. The dissolution emphasised the shift away from institutionalised contemplative religion to the active pastoral role of the secular clergy among the laity.

In the eyes of the Vicegerent the secular clergy were expected to do those things which 'appertain to good congruence and honesty with profit to the commonwealth'. Through his injunctions in 1536 and 1538 he did much to stress the pastoral and educational role of the clergy and to forward the required changes in their training and outlook. Convocation had already considered measures to provide a more learned clergy to match a more literate laity. Erasmian reformers pleaded for an understanding of faith rather than a reliance upon ritual. Cromwell wanted a parish clergy who were competent to read and expound the Scriptures and to teach the laity to comprehend their beliefs. While ornaments and images were to remain as the 'books of unlearned men', priests were urged to show their flocks where they could consult written or printed expositions of the faith. The Creed and the Lord's prayer were to be taught by priests to parents and children. None 'ought to presume to come to God's board without perfect knowledge of the same'. The vernacular was encouraged so that all might know 'the very lively word of God that every Christian is bound to know, to embrace, believe and follow, if he wish to be saved'.[13]

Access to the biblical truths had to be accompanied by an authoritative declaration of those things which were necessary for salvation and those things that were 'meet and convenient to be kept for a decent and politic order'. For the formulation of the things necessary to salvation Cromwell first looked to the theologians, supported by royal acquiescence. Later he turned to parliament for confirmation of doctrine and practice. For the determination of things meet for a politic order he relied upon the authority of his commission or on statute.

In doctrine and practice Cromwell proclaimed the need for moderation and the middle way. The avoidance of extremes was not only an Erasmian virtue but it was also sound political sense. Even before the Pilgrimage of Grace showed the necessity of caution, he urged the bishops not to burden their flocks with 'over many novelties' which might provoke contention. The revelation of the truth was to be 'little by little'.[14] In a time of controversy the middle way promoted conciliation and allowed for temporary alliances and for many shades of churchmanship between papalist and extreme heretic.

The moderation of the middle way was made self-evident by condemning those to either side as extremists. Yet Cromwell pursued his campaign against superstition and papistry with a zeal which appeared to be worthy of an extremist. The execution of Fisher and More, the destruction of the monasteries and the imperialist doctrines of Marsilio of Padua did not convey an impression of moderation to Europe. The need to enforce uniformity prompted Cromwell to seek statutory sanctions against offenders in doctrine and practice in 1539, when to his surprise the Six Articles Act emerged to promote persecution for heresy by the bishops. The tolerance which Cromwell had previously shown was condemned as partisan in 1540. While Cromwell was not a fanatic, he was an enthusiast who calculated the limits to which he could go and accepted those limits as the dictates of moderation. It was significant of the impression left by his religious attitudes that his opponents could seriously charge him with being a sacramentary.

Across the broad middle ground Cromwell looked to the Bible as his guide. In the scriptures were to be found the justification of the Supremacy and the source of the doctrine which it was the duty of the Supremacy to declare. From the start of his Vicegerency Cromwell agreed with Cranmer on the need to produce an authorised translation into English of the Bible. The Archbishop's efforts to gain the support of the episcopate in producing a translation failed. Cromwell obtained royal approval for Coverdale's translation in 1535, which, it appears, he had encouraged, and for the Matthew Bible in 1537.[15] But the execution of the Vicegerent's plan to place an English Bible in each parish church depended upon the availability of an official translation at a reasonable price.

Cromwell undertook to publish an authorised version. With Coverdale's aid a suitably revised translation was completed. When the printing of the massive work in Paris was thwarted by heresy proceedings, Cromwell arranged for the printing to be completed in England. By the spring of 1539 the Great Bible, appointed to the use of the churches, was ready for sale to the parishes. Through his business and financial acumen, his contacts with the Lutheran Coverdale and with printers, and his evangelical convictions he had overcome the difficulties of publishing an English Bible.[16]

Cromwell had triumphed over determined opposition. In England the long association of the vernacular scriptures with the Lollards identified open access to an English Bible with heresy. The teaching authority of the Church was challenged by the Lutheran claim for the prior authority of the Word of God. The application of humanist scholarship to the translation of the Bible undermined the long standing interpretations, based on the Vulgate. Uninstructed reading of the Bible led to heretical misinterpretations. Cromwell's championship of an English Bible was seen as an attack upon the bases of traditional orthodoxy. For him it was the source of true doctrine. As the frontispiece of the Great Bible showed the Word of God descended through the King to the Archbishop and Vicegerent and through them to the clergy and laity. In the 1538 injunctions the clergy were directed to recant such of their previous teaching as had 'no ground of scripture'.[17] The word of God was the necessary vindication of the doctrine declared by the Supreme Head.

In the declaration of the biblical truths the Vicegerent played his part. Cromwell was fortunate that in England there was no repository of orthodoxy like the Sorbonne in France and that the few trained theologians in the episcopate were incined to protestant notions. In June and July 1536 Cromwell used his authority as Vicegerent to preside, in place of Cranmer, over Convocation which was preparing a doctrinal statement. The Ten Articles which emerged leaned to Lutheranism. They were largely the work of Cromwell's trusted Bishop Fox.[18] But the Articles to which Cromwell had subscribed left unsaid so much upon the most important doctrinal issues that they could not be regarded as a final and sufficient formulation of faith.

In 1537 Cromwell presided over a commission to clarify the Ten Articles. His casual introduction of the Scottish divine, Alexander Alesius, to address the commission proved a mistake. Although Alesius was a follower of the moderate Melanchthon, his expulsion from his native land and from the university of Cambridge suggests that his behaviour was not as moderate as his theology. Cranmer was not amused and Alesius was excluded from further proceedings. When the commission produced the so-called Bishop's Book, the King did not confirm it with his authority. Progress towards an agreed statement of doctrine was slow. During the next year Cromwell was in close touch with Cranmer through his chaplain, Malet, over the Archbishop's consideration of a more obviously Lutheran service book.[19]

By 1538 the need for an authoritative statement of doctrine and practice had become urgent. As a proclamation in November showed, Cromwell was defending evangelical religion against the reaction to extreme heresy. Henry had become alarmed at the presence of Anabaptists. Diversity of opinion was threatening the unity and concord of the body politic and the commonwealth. There was still no agreement about the terms on which a uniformity of faith could be achieved. Cromwell decided to settle the terms by the authority of parliament.[20]

Early in May 1539 Audley announced to parliament the King's determination to abolish diversity of opinion in matters of religion. To that end a committee of two archbishops and six bishops over which Cromwell presided was set up. Before the committee could present its findings, Cromwell's opponents persuaded the King to allow six articles on religion to be debated in the Lords. The King's intervention resulted in the Six Articles Act which was a more conservative declaration of doctrine and practice than Cromwell may have hoped to obtain from the committee. The Vicegerent accepted the check and continued to proclaim his faith in the middle way, defined by the truths of the Bible.

Up to the Six Articles Act there had been no formulation of faith which had the support of the King and parliament. Cromwell had dropped Thomas More's campaign against heresy and had discouraged the unpopular clerical initiative in heresy charges. Heretics were in danger only when the King wished or needed to demonstrate his orthodoxy. Cromwell attempted to dissociate himself from heresy trials as he did in the case of Frith. In the proceedings against Lambert the King made Cromwell play a leading role and gave the trial conspicuous publicity. Under Cromwell, as under Wolsey, there had been a period of tolerance. Even in February 1539 Cromwell obtained a general pardon for heretical offences up to that time. His treatment of heresy justified the suspicion that he favoured heretics.[21]

In assessing Cromwell's own religious attitudes it must be remembered that his critical and activist temperament made him susceptible to reforming movements. In his early life he may have sensed something of the political hostility to the Papacy which was prevalent in the cities of Northern Italy. Later he became aware of the Erasmian criticism of institutionalised religion. The Lutheran reformation did not develop until he was in his thirties. While in Wolsey's service he showed his sympathies with his master's Erasmian attitudes. He acquired a knowledge of Erasmus' latin version of the New Testament and gained an interest in evangelical religion from his contacts with Miles Coverdale. His complaints about Wolsey's treatment of lay servants and about the Cardinal's idle chaplains revealed that he shared in the grudge against the clergy and showed why he was so interested in the grievances which were put forward in the Commons in 1529.[22] By the time of Wolsey's fall he was deeply critical of the Church.

At this stage, however, despite his disposition to change and his interest in ideas of reform, Cromwell did not cast off the heritage of traditional religion. He was moved by the services in the Chapel of Wolsey's college at Oxford. In his depression at Wolsey's fall he had turned to his primer and the conventional consolations of religion. His will in 1529 with its invocation of intercession by the saints and its provision for prayers for his soul by the most notably spiritual of the religious orders, the friars of London, was the sort of orthodox will which could be expected of a man who had amongst his possessions an *agnus dei* and numerous religious pictures.[23] Admittedly it was no time to flaunt heresy in a will, but to all appearances Cromwell was behaving as a man with the traditional religious responses.

Yet in private Cromwell may have been prepared to entertain radical notions which as yet did not affect his public observances. In 1530 he had wished that Luther had never been born. It was a sign, perhaps, not of his rejection of Luther but of how deeply Luther's ideas troubled him. The controversy between Tyndale and Thomas More had advertised the points at issue between orthodoxy and Lutheran heresy. When in 1531, his friend, Stephen Vaughan, assumed that Cromwell would be ready to recommend Tyndale to the King, it would appear as if Cromwell had given Vaughan the impression that he sided with Tyndale.[24] But Cromwell, like the King, may have been favourable only to some of Tyndale's political recommendations without accepting his Lutheran religious doctrine.

Vaughan's expectations of Cromwell's support for a notorious Lutheran may well have been founded upon Cromwell's interest in Biblical studies. Knowing Erasmus' latin New Testament by heart, Cromwell had developed a mastery of the Scriptures which in 1532 impressed his old colleague from Wolsey's day, Dr Oliver, the canonist. It was a mastery which was to enable him later to deal with the biblical arguments of men of such different persuasions as Fisher and Shaxton.[25] By the early 1530's it was clear that what had begun as an Erasmian interest in the Scriptures as a source of Christian faith and behaviour was becoming a Lutheran acceptance of the authority of the

Bible as the word of God. It was his evangelical enthusiasm which made his protestant friends believe that he shared all their convictions.

While he was in the service of the King, he found that the political situation was such as to confirm the drift of his thinking and to offer the opportunity for its realisation. Lutherans appeared as his natural allies. The break with Rome pointed to the adoption of a protestant position. In private it appears that Cromwell was prepared to bring his religion into line with his political actions. In 1539 he confessed that he personally would adopt Lutheranism were it not for the necessity of believing what the King believed.[26]

By 1536 his policies had convinced the protesters in the Pilgrimage of Grace that Cromwell was a heretic. His secretary, Richard Morison, had no doubt that religious beliefs motivated his master's actions. Gardiner became convinced that Cromwell was a heretic. There was little disagreement between his friends and his enemies that he was a man inspired by religious faith. Cromwell felt that he had been called by providence to high estate.[27] The changes which he brought about seemed to have the coherence which a religious belief imposed.

However ready Cromwell may have been to become a Lutheran, it was a step which he did not take. Like Cranmer, he remained an eclectic protestant sympathiser. Ultimately he could not divide his religion from his politics. England was an Empire and it was the faith of the Church of England which had to be accepted. He wanted to verify the tradition of the insular Chuch by the truth of the Bible. When he came to reject the authority of Rome or the views of the sacramentaries of Calais he turned for support to the wisdom and learning of the English clergy.[28] Although he felt the force of the Scriptures, he retained a respect for the tradition of the Church of England.

Cromwell had approached Lutheranism through the intellectual attitudes of Erasmus rather than through any experience of inspired conversion. It was by learning and study that he expected men to arrive at the truth. Like Cranmer, he did not accept that man's reason had been totally impaired by the Fall. His Lutheran leanings never amounted to a total acceptance of Lutheranism. His position did not fit the denominational categories. Despite the pull of his personal convictions towards Lutheranism, he remained in the last resort closer to Erasmus. He could not dispense with the authority and tradition of the Catholic Church as it was manifested in the Church of England.

On the scaffold he declared, 'I die in the Catholic faith, not doubting in any article of my faith, no nor in any sacrament of the Church'. His faith was the doctrine of the Church of England. His reference to the sacraments was in rejection of the charge of being a sacramentary. That both Hall and Foxe printed Cromwell's last speech and that Pole doubted its authenticity suggests that it was no gesture of reconciliation with Rome. Cromwell's last prayer, which Hall called 'godly and learned', was printed by Foxe who evidently found it worthy of the man whom he described as 'a mighty wall and defence of the Church'.[29]

The compromise which Cromwell achieved between his hopes of reformation and the demands of the King produced a Church of England that contained many of the elements of later Anglicanism. Cromwell did not sever the link with the historic Catholic Church and the Catholic faith but he made clear their basis in the Scriptures. His attack on superstition had lessened dependence on ritual and increased dependence on the Word. His distinction between *adiaphora* and the essentials of faith broadened the middle way. The destruction of the religious orders made the pastoral and teaching function of the secular clergy the chief expression of the spiritual guidance of the Church. As a layman he had fashioned a church for the laity and for the benefit of the commonwealth. The memorial of his endeavour lay not only in the statute book but also in the Bible in the parish church, open to the clergy and the laity to read in their native tongue.

7 THE GOVERNANCE OF THE REALM

The royal authority which Cromwell wielded on behalf of the King was grounded in the law through which it was applied to the governance of the realm. Since it was the necessity of a legalistic mode of government that there should be precedents, Cromwell presented himself as the champion of the historic rights of the English Kingship. Legality which sometimes covered both the spirit and the letter of the law was his working rule and his technical solution to the problem of exercising authority on behalf of the King. When Cromwell gave instructions for the 'Abbot of Reading to be sent down to be tried and executed at Reading', he spoke as a lawyer confident in his knowledge of the case.[1] He did not take into account any further considerations. He relied on the law.

The legal traditions of the Kingship supplied the framework of Cromwell's government. Just as Henry VII had exploited the financial rights of feudal monarchy, so Cromwell utilised the tenurial and judicial rights of the Crown. The old propositions that all land was held of the King and that all jurisdiction derived from, and could be resumed by, the King formed the basis of the strong Kingship which Cromwell strove to establish. The acquisition of monastic lands and the imposition of the English law of tenure in Wales and Ireland rested ultimately on the King's title to land by right of conquest. The retraction of liberties and franchises was founded on the traditional acceptance of the King as the fount of justice. Cromwell strove to apply the jurisdiction of the royal courts throughout the King's dominions. In Ireland and Wales he promoted the English tongue, the language of the courts.

Cromwell's emphasis upon the tenurial and judicial aspects of the historic Kingship preserved the continuity of legal thinking. Even the Supreme Headship was asserted to be traditional and Cromwell found a reference to it in Bracton.[2] Those who speculated upon the adoption of civil law and the merits of absolutism made no impression upon the conduct or inspiration of domestic rule. Cromwell worked within the assumptions of the Common Law and contained the monarchical authority in the framework of its legal rights. It was in the capacity of a professional legal adviser to the King that he faced the difficulties of the governance of the realm.

The success of the early Tudors in striking down distrusted nobles had created a governmental problem. In destroying great nobles the monarchy removed the most cohesive force in local society and the prop of its authority. Both Henry VII and his son had been obliged on occasion to restore magnates to local influence in order to re-establish peace and order. The removal of a great lord created a local power vacuum. The same result occurred, when magnates proved weak or were incapacitated. Action to fill the vacuum had to be taken by the King. With his desire to assert the royal authority Cromwell was ready to exploit such opportunities. He had the political motive to respond to such situations and the expertise to turn his response into a more durable legal gain for the King by legislation in the English and Irish parliaments and by strengthening the bureaucratic organisation and jurisdictions of the regional councils.

The spread of royal power did not mean the extinction of local influence. Cromwell had to redistribute such influence in the King's best interests. The imposition of royal justice was not the assertion of an impartial justice in the place of local corruption. Cromwell exercised the law on behalf of the King's supporters and against his opponents. Patronage went to the King's men. Cromwell outplayed the magnates at their own game on behalf of the King. His methods promoted direct reference to the Crown and consequently greater royal intervention in local affairs.[3] They ensured that the royal interest was taken into account by local men in their struggle for ascendancy. To take the King's part was shown to be both honourable and rewarding.

The methods and apparatus of local government which Cromwell used were inherited by him. Wolsey and the King had employed regional councils under royal figure-heads, as in Wales under Mary Tudor and in the North of England and in Ireland under the Lord Lieutenancy of the Duke of Richmond, Henry's bastard. The means of breaking the local sway of great lords by deprivation of office and transfer of royal patronage to rival neighbours or imported nobles, bishops and officials were well known. Royal intervention in local power struggles with the object of winning the victor's gratitude had long been practised. If Cromwell did little that was new, he practised with success and developed the old devices.

Cromwell improved his inherited political repertoire by insisting on constructive action to secure the royal gains. Regional councils under strict supervision were given a sounder institutional structure and a greater competence. They were more securely founded upon a balance of power in local society which was stabilised by the judicious use of the royal patronage. Bureaucratic administration and litigation were promoted in place of the rough and tumble of local family struggles. A broader spectrum of local expectations were focused upon the Crown by encouraging the gentry to look directly to the King for favour. A devolution of the administration of justice paradoxically served the interests of central authority by a more effective enforcement of royal jurisdiction. Although regional councils drew business away from the central courts at Westminster, such decentralisation extended royal justice more widely through the realm. The assertion of royal jurisdiction in the regions was inspired by an insistence upon a uniform legal order for the King's subjects. The traditional aim of securing obedience to the King was reinforced by the need to win acceptance from all subjects of the Supreme Head.

The councils at Ludlow, York and Dublin were the chief institutional bases of Cromwell's regional government. He confirmed the tendency, already noticeable in the council in the Marches of Wales, of the local council to become an instrument of central control rather than of feudal and dynastic devolution. Similarly he furthered the development, already marked in the councils of the North and Ireland, which led to the councils acting on their authority as conciliar institutions rather than on that of Lord Lieutenants. By abolishing or comprehending rival jurisdictions he made the local councils the supreme administrative and judicial expression of royal authority in its area. When in 1539 the need to organise the defences of the South-West prompted Cromwell to fill the gap, left by the destruction of Courtenay influence, he created a council of the West, based on the instructions issued to the Council of the North. It was apparent that he had taken the opportunity to develop a conciliar policy to meet the problems of regional government.[4]

The policy of multiplying regional councils failed with the fall of Cromwell. The traditional reliance of the King on loyal magnates was not to be easily changed. John Russell evaded the attempt by Cromwell to institutionalise his family influence in a council of the West. The personal relations of the King and the nobles remained an important element in provincial government. The Lancashire territory of the Stanleys remained under their sway and was excluded from the jurisdiction of the Council of the North. In East Anglia the Howards preserved the quasi-palatine powers, conferred on them by Edward IV.[5] Cromwell's success in asserting royal control through bureaucratic regional councils was limited to those regions, where the Crown had already established councils and had shown a long-standing interest in local politics. Only in those areas where the nobility proved incapable of control or were of suspect loyalty did the regional council come to be accepted as an alternative to rule through the nobility.

Those regions were the North of England, the Irish Pale and the Marches of Wales, where in the past conditions had especially favoured royal reliance on the power of certain nobility. The King's dilemma had been that the nobles who commanded the following to keep the peace in frontier zones were those most tempted to abuse their power and strategic position to menace the throne. Recent history made Henry VIII especially suspicious of Northern, Welsh Marcher and Irish lords. The situation, when Cromwell came to power was that in the North an incompetent and heirless, Percy, the Earl of Northumberland, still merited Henry's deep distrust, that in the Irish Pale royal authority was dependent upon the Geraldine Earl of Kildare, who had recently resumed the deputyship, and that in Wales, after the execution of the greatest Marcher lord, the Duke of Buckingham, in 1521 and the greatest Welsh magnate, Rhys ap Griffith, in 1531, the King was in command, but frustrated by the legacy of feudal rule, native custom and English legislation which distinguished the Welsh from his English subjects. As the complexities of this situation developed Cromwell took his opportunities to deploy the powers of the Crown and to establish a more direct royal authority over each area.

In the North of England Cromwell worked to replace the faltering influence of the nobility with that of the Crown. He set out to cultivate those northern gentry who for some time had shown a readiness to turn to the service of the Crown. With their support he could manipulate local feuds and ambitions so as to undermine the power of the greater lords and render the gentry more dependent upon the backing of the King. His intervention put the substance of power into the hands of men such as Sir Thomas Wharton, chief officer of the Percy lands, whom he wooed over to the King's service. Cromwell skilfully exploited opportunities for profit and advancement in favour of those gentry who looked to royal patronage.[6]

In the north-west Cromwell moved against William, Lord Dacre. He kept himself informed of Dacre's doings through the Cumbrian gentleman, Sir John Leyburn. He played upon Sir William Musgrave's feud with the Dacres and the hostility of Dacre's rivals, the Cliffords, to fix a charge of treason upon Dacre. Perhaps Cromwell had engineered his attack too blatantly, for against all expectation Dacre was acquitted by his peers in 1534. Nevertheless Dacre's control in the West March was broken and the loyal Cliffords moved in to fill the gap. The impasse created by the feud between the Dacres and the Cliffords, which had made it impossible to employ either without offending the other, was thus broken. It was not until the Pilgrimage of Grace gave an excuse for change that the still loyal Cliffords were ousted from real power in the

West March, although they retained the empty title of Warden. In 1537 Cromwell was told that the cry, 'A Dacre, a Dacre' and 'A Clifford, a Clifford' had been replaced by 'A King, a King'. [7]

In the north-east the Percy influence had been waning under the unthrifty sixth earl. Wolsey had already plotted to gain control of the Percy lands for the King. Cromwell's plan, made possible by the rift between the heirless earl and his brothers, was to induce the earl to settle his debts, bought up by the Crown, by making the King his heir. In January 1536 the earl agreed and an act of parliament confirmed the deal. In the summer of 1537 the earl died and the Percy inheritance lay at the King's disposal. In the Percy lands along with the ex-monastic lands Henry now possessed sources of patronage in the North with which to win and hold adherents. Norfolk, Lord Lieutenant of the North and suppressor of the Pilgrimage of Grace, hoped to succeed to the former leading role of the Percies in the North. Cromwell thwarted Norfolk's ambitions and persuaded the King to give power to his protégés among the gentry in order to retain direct control in the North. The result was that all the Marches were put under the effective command of those gentry whom Norfolk regarded as 'mean men'. [8]

The transference of control of the Border from nobles upon whom the King was dependent to gentry who were dependent on the Crown was the important result of Cromwell's intervention in northern politics. After the failure of the Pilgrimage of Grace, Cromwell stabilised the new balance in the royal favour and asserted royal jurisdiction throughout the North. Since the summer of 1535 he had been investigating liberties and franchises and considering the powers of a council for the North. In 1536 he reduced the liberties and franchises through the dissolution of the monasteries and an act of parliament. The Palatinate of Durham retained only a nominally independent jurisdiction. In 1537 he took the opportunity, given by the failure of the Pilgrimage of Grace, to reorganise the Council of the North as the supreme executive and judicial body between the Trent and the Tweed, including even the Border Wardenries. Thus the Marches were temporarily brought under a council which derived its authority from a royal commission. [9]

In the immediate situation following the Pilgrimage of Grace the council was reorganised to serve the Lord Lieutenant, Norfolk, in restoring order. But Cromwell soon took advantage of the Duke's hope of returning to court to allow the Lieutenancy to lapse and to reconstitute the council as a permanent institution. In June, 1538, Cromwell replaced Tunstall, the Bishop of Durham, as Lord President of the Council of the North with his own vigorous protégé, Robert Holgate, Bishop of Llandaff. But Cromwell did not pack the council with his own followers as Wolsey had done. He brought in the nobles,

including the earls of Cumberland and Northumberland and Lord
Dacre of Gilsland, and those gentry, ambitious to serve the King, such
as the Bowes and Eures, so that no rival influence, capable of
challenging the council, was excluded. In the council both nobles and
gentry found themselves subject to the advice of lawyers and to the
authority of the Lord President.[10]

Cromwell's achievement in taking a firm grip on the North owed
paradoxically much to the Pilgrimage of Grace, the most threatening
demonstration of opposition to his policies. In its aftermath he had been
able to reorganise the Council of the North and deflate the influence of
the Percies and Cliffords. But even before the Pilgrimage of Grace he
had shown his intention of exploiting the division and incompetence of
the Percies and the feuds of the nobles of the North-West. He had used
the emergence of a gentry, prepared to look to the Crown rather than to
their local lords for patronage, to supply him with the 'mean men'
whom he placed in office. The peace with Scotland enabled his 'mean
men' to govern the Border instead of the military nobility whose
leadership would have been necessary in war. In the North Cromwell
had nearly met with disaster but in the event he had exploited the
conditions which he found there to the King's advantage.

In Ireland Tudor government had swayed between trust in the earls
of Kildare and reliance upon an English Deputy and Dublin
officialdom. While Cromwell was rising in royal favour, the King was
replacing an English Deputy, Sir William Skeffington by the Earl of
Kildare. Like his father, Henry had come to recognise the cost and
difficulty of ruling Ireland and he resorted in 1532 to reemploying as
Deputy, Garret Og, 9th Earl of Kildare, whose family had been
dominant in Ireland for nearly a century. His creation of the Duke of
Richmond as Lord Lieutenant of Ireland in 1529 and his appointment
of an English Deputy had failed to provide an effective alternative to the
influence of the Geraldine connection in Ireland.

In December, 1532 Kildare was partially incapacitated by a wound
and his control of affairs began to wane. Cromwell began to intrigue
with Kildare's rivals, the Butlers, and with the discontented New
English officials of the council in Dublin. In August, 1533, a leading
member of the Dublin officialdom, John Alen, who had been promoted
by Wolsey, came to England to report on the deteriorating situation and
urge that an experienced English Deputy be appointed. His advice
suited Cromwell who was convinced that the sort of government which
he wanted in Ireland could only be achieved through the New English
bureaucrats of the Dublin council.[11]

Kildare got wind of the moves against him and tried to strengthen his
position. But his transfer of royal artillery from Dublin castle to his own
stronghold at Maynooth was taken by Cromwell as evidence of

treasonable intentions. Kildare was called to court. Cromwell bided his time. A false move could have precipitated Kildare into rebellion. Finally in April 1534 Kildare came before the King. Under suspicion of treason he was sent to the Tower where he died in December 1534. With a new régime in Ireland to be established, Cromwell asserted his authority over Irish affairs in council during the spring of 1534.[12]

In taking control of Irish affairs Cromwell was involved not only in the power struggle in Ireland, precipitated by Kildare's fall, but also in its repercussions in England. Through their Irish lands and family connections with the Butlers both Norfolk and his Boleyn ally, Wiltshire, had an interest in Irish politics and wielded patronage in favour of many of the leading Anglo-Irish families of the Pale. Kildare had played into Cromwell's hands and Norfolk did likewise, when in a pique he withdrew from the council's discussions of Irish affairs in April 1534. The main props in the Pale and in England of the Anglo-Irish ascendancy had been withdrawn, but its supporters in Ireland had still to be broken or won. Under cover of purging Geraldine supporters, Cromwell set about placing his men in the Dublin officialdom and cultivating support among the New English and such Anglo-Irish rivals of the Geraldines as would serve him.[13]

By late May 1534, the Butlers, opponents of Kildare and of the Boleyn influence, had been won to acknowledge both the restoration of Skeffington as Deputy and the Royal Supremacy. But in June, Kildare's son 'silken' Thomas proclaimed rebellion and called upon the Emperor and the Pope for aid. Confidently anticipating a speedy suppression of the Geraldine revolt, Cromwell issued ordinances for the government of Ireland which envisaged enactment by the Irish parliament of measures to reject papal authority, to accept the royal supremacy and to attaint Kildare.[14] He equipped a powerful army and despatched Sir William Skeffington as Deputy at its head.

Skeffington did not break the revolt until March 1535. In April Cromwell was considering a bill asserting the King's title to the lands of Ireland by right of conquest. In July he discussed his plans with John Alen and Gerald Aylmer of the Dublin council and then with Audley's aid began to prepare legislation for an Irish parliament in January, 1536. Skeffington's death in December delayed parliament until May, 1536, when it assembled under the new Deputy, Lord Grey, a New English noble.

Subdued by the suppression of the Geraldine revolt and fearing implication as Geraldine sympathisers, the Lords and Commons passed all the important measures, required by Cromwell, on the supremacy, on the rejection of papal authority, on the English succession and on the attaint of Kildare. Not until the September session was there any serious opposition. It arose over measures for the dissolution of the monasteries which menaced the land holdings and the business of the Anglo-Irish families, especially of those in the legal profession in the Pale establishment. Cromwell did his best to manage the Irish parliament. He appointed a commission to handle elections and even to supervise the last session in September 1537. But by his compromise over taxes and customs, agreed by May 1537 with the lawyer, Sir Patrick Barnewall, leader of the Anglo-Irish, he was able to isolate the belated opposition of the clerical proctors and the spiritual lords and obtain the passage of a dissolution act. Monastic lands offered him the prospect of winning Anglo-Irish support by patronage and contributed to his wider policy of imposing the English law of tenure on the old disintegrating pattern of land holding in the Pale.[15]

When he followed up the surrender of 'silken' Thomas by executing him and five of his uncles in February, 1537, Cromwell made it plain by destroying the only Anglo-Irish dynasty, capable of exercising vice-regal sway in Ireland, that the Geraldine ascendancy was at an end and that henceforth the deputy would be an agent of the King. Malcontent Irish lords used the surviving child heir, Gerald Fitzgerald, as a figure-head of Geraldine revolt. The Anglo-Irish, having won financial concessions and royal patronage, came to recognise that conciliation was the only policy for the future. The New English who had served Wolsey were reinforced by Cromwell's nominees. Well entrenched in the administration, they recognised Cromwell as their patron. Finally Cromwell extinguished the influence in Ireland of Norfolk and Wiltshire by the Absentees act of 1537 which transferred their Irish lands to the Crown and created a virtual royal monopoly over the patronage exercised from England.

The Church in Ireland was caught in the web of patronage. The English King had long had a say in the nomination of bishops. In 1536 Cromwell obtained the appointment as Archbishop of Dublin of George Browne, a man who could be relied upon to support official policy. By the beginning of 1539 eight bishops and two archbishops had subscribed to the oath of supremacy. At the same time the dissolution of the monasteries began in earnest with much local support and by 1540 most of the houses in the Pale had surrendered. Cromwell's plan to bring the Church in Ireland into conformity with the Church of England appeared to have made much progress. But at the level of belief and practice in religion little impression was made and Archbishop Browne's efforts at reform were received with hostility.[16] The superficial compliance with which Cromwell's ecclesiastical policies had been met arose from political and business considerations. Religious reaction to his policy had yet to develop and inspire resistance. For the moment the Royal Supremacy appeared to have been established.

Despite constant policing campaigns by Lord Grey, Cromwell was more concerned with the legal subordination of Ireland than with its military conquest for which he could not afford to provide adequate forces. Although he had dropped the proposed bill to assert the King's right of conquest, he contrived through the dissolution of monasteries, the Absentees act and by indentures with the Irish Lords to assert the royal title to lands in and beyond the Pale. Through the Dublin council, commissions, the judiciary and parliament he sought to strengthen the legal and constitutional framework of government in Ireland. His aim to check the assimilation of a demoralised and depopulated Pale into gaelic Ireland was apparent in an act for the adoption in Ireland of English ways and language. He started the recolonisation of the Pale in the key posts of the administration. By grants from the newly acquired crown lands he gave the New English inducements to permanent settlement.

Cromwell's determination to extend the recognition of royal authority in Ireland proved costly. Despite his efforts to keep military forces at a minimum, they were a financial burden. The suppression of the Geraldine rebellion cost the King some £40,000. Although the yield of Irish revenues and ecclesiastical taxes increased and the dissolution and other confiscations provided further resources, Ireland remained a liability. He appointed Sir William Brabazon, one of his ablest men as vice-treasurer, and set up commissions to effect economies, collect taxes and end corruption. But a report of 1539 revealed financial chaos. Cromwell himself was accused of bribery and corruption in his handling of Irish affairs.[17] His disposal of patronage was open to such charges and he, no doubt, paid himself and his agents well for all their trouble.

If in six years Cromwell was not successful in making Ireland a peaceful or profitable dominion of the King, it was not surprising, in view of the conditions in the Pale and in Ireland at large. He did, however, destroy the long established Kildare hegemony and put in its place the foundations for a régime under royal control. The danger that Ireland might be used by the King's continental enemies was eliminated. Although the Deputy Lord Grey through his Irish connections and through lack of adequate forces proved an inadequate Deputy, nevertheless the basis of a royal government in Ireland had been established by Cromwell. He secured a firm hold upon the administration through his chosen agents by making the New English and the leading Anglo-Irish gentry dependent upon the King's patronage. He prepared the way for their acknowledgement of Henry's title to the Kingship of Ireland by the Irish parliament in 1541. It was the deputy and council who called upon Henry in December 1540 to assume the Kingship.

When in 1533 Cromwell decided that he must look into the state of Wales, it was evident that the old order was crumbling. Henry VII's local experiments in removing statutory disabilities imposed on the Welsh by Henry IV, his readiness to bring Welsh offenders before English courts, his restrictions on the jurisdiction of Marcher lords and abolition of serfdom in royal lordships established a trend towards treating Welsh and English subjects upon an equal footing. After the execution of the Duke of Buckingham in 1521, royal influence over the Marcher lordships became preponderant. The execution of Rhys ap Griffith in 1531 demonstrated Henry's VIII's power over the Welsh magnates. But in the marcher lordships the aggrieved tenantry were forcing reforms upon their lords, as they did upon the Earl of Worcester in 1532. Moreover the multiplicity of Marcher jurisdictions and the Welsh customs to protect kin were being exploited by law-breakers to evade trial and arrest.[18] Disorder and violence flourished along the Border. In such conditions there were opportunities for the King's enemies to spread discontent and win support against royal policies.

Cromwell responded to the call from the English Border gentry to establish law and order. The well-established Council in the Marches of Wales which Henry VII had revived with an expanded jurisdiction was the obvious instrument for quelling border turbulence. Ambitious Border gentlemen, like Sir Edward Croft, looking to crown patronage, called Cromwell's attention to the need for strong action by the council. In May 1534 Cromwell replaced the lax John Voysey, bishop of Exeter, as Lord President by an old servant of Wolsey and of his own, Rowland Lee, who was raised to the episcopate as Bishop of Coventry and Lichfield. Lee acted the strong man with ruthless conscientiousness and little love for the Welsh. There was a spate of legislation to make the escape of the Welsh law-breakers harder and their capture easier.[19] But these measures only dealt with the symptoms of the situation in Wales.

The way to tackle the causes of disorder in Wales lay in winning the support of the Welsh gentry by assimilating them to their English counterparts and opening to them opportunities for reward in the service of the King. The Welsh gentry were ready to respond. It was not a policy which was liked by Rowland Lee and the English Border gentry who did not trust the Welsh. But it suited Cromwell's aim of extending royal justice through the realm and of treating all residents of the realm as subjects of the King. No great magnates remained to lead resistance to change. The King was the greatest lord in the Principality and in the Marcher lordships. In the circumstances Cromwell could look forward to extending the English style of government to all Wales without the exercise of force.

As in Ireland, it was the enforcement of ecclesiastical measures which helped to bring the problems of government under consideration. The reformation of the Church and the reorganisation of border government went hand in hand. The unfounded story that Cromwell's attention was drawn to Wales through the interest in ecclesiastical lands there of his sister's Welsh relations has symbolic significance in that it suggests that the desire to enforce the Royal Supremacy was an important element in Cromwell's regional policies. Cromwell was ready to impose uniformity on the ecclesiastical and secular order in Wales. In the last session of the 1529 parliament in 1536, he launched an ambitious scheme to bring the government of Wales into line with that of the rest of England.[20]

The general principle of a uniform system of royal justice was set forth in 'an act for recontinuing of certain Liberties and Franchises heretofore taken from the Crown'. Wales was dealt with in an 'act for laws and justice to be ministered in Wales in like forms as it is in this Realm'[21] The act reaffirmed the union of England and Wales which had been accepted in English law since the reign of Edward I and declared that all those born in Wales should enjoy the same rights and liberties as the King's English subjects. It created five new counties. Monmouth, Brecon, Montgomery, Radnor and Denbigh, which covered the area of the old Marcher Lordships and set up an Exchequer and Chancery at Brecknock and Denbigh. It allowed for the administration of English law and such Welsh customs as the King, council and justices should regard as expedient and necessary. It required that all court proceedings should be in English and that all officials should speak English. Representation in parliament of the new shires and boroughs was granted. Commissions were set up to determine the new boundaries of shire and hundred and to recommend what local customs should have the force of law. The rights of certain magnates and Marcher lordships were safe-guarded. The whole act or any of its provisions were, however, subject to suspension or abrogation by the King within three years.

The plan for the government of Wales which put the Marcher lordships on the same footing as the principality was deliberately tentative and revocable. Its realisation depended on the King's will and the findings of the commissions concerning Welsh opinion. It gave room for manoeuvre in the event of Welsh resistance. But there was no resistance from Wales even during the Pilgrimage of Grace and the Irish rebellions. Far from treating the act as a deprivation of native customs and laws most of the Welsh political nation regarded it as an emancipation from oppressive customs and jurisdictions and from legal disabilities. The English speaking Welsh gentry appeared to welcome the new opportunities open to them not only in Wales but also in the wider realm of England.[22] Cromwell had succeeded in gaining the support of the Welsh gentry whose opinion he was prepared to test in the commissions under the act. The implementation of the act and the confirmation of its policy were not completed by 1540 at Cromwell's death. Yet what had been achieved by the assimilation of Wales to the English system of government proved more successful and durable than the temporary ascendancy which had been gained in Ireland.

In the privy council as the King's secretary Cromwell dealt with Calais and the Channel Islands. His main concerns in Calais were defence, victualling and religious uniformity. A tacit understanding with France not to fight over the Channel Islands was enshrined in a papal bull of 1483 which declared their immunity from attack. The cost of military preparedness, so heavy in Calais, was thus eased in the Channel Islands. The islands, moreover, accepted the royal supremacy and the withdrawal of the religious orders to France without demur and, although they were under mediocre governors or their proxies, they caused Cromwell little trouble. In Calais, however, religious beliefs, threatening political loyalties, had been allowed to spread by the ambiguous behaviour of the Governor, Lord Lisle. They were a constant source of disquiet to Cromwell. He had trouble with papists, with sacramentaries and with the more sophisticated teachings of Adam Damplip whose doctrines were approved by Cranmer. In 1540 intent upon raising a scare of popery, Cromwell accused Lord Lisle of papalist intrigue and recalled him to imprisonment in the Tower. That Cromwell made Lisle a scapegoat reveals his discontent with the governor's conduct of affairs in Calais. The maintenance of a foothold on the continent through a dangerous period was, however, the result of the general military preparedness of the realm rather than of competent rule in Calais.[23]

In the governance of the realm Cromwell personified the supervisory role of the privy council. He acted as universal policeman, investigating personally a vast number of infringements of the law. Through his legislation he made the obedience to the King a wider and a more direct obligation of the subject. Many intermediate and rival loyalties were weakened or removed by his moves against liberties and franchises, against papal authority and against local custom. His emphasis upon one law stressed the one obedience to the King.

Cromwell's understanding of the problems of law enforcement went as deep as his appreciation of the importance of a uniform law and strict adherence to its forms. He cultivated local opinion and the interests which would support the law. He exploited his opportunities to keep the workings of the conciliar, common law and ecclesiastical courts under review. His patronage permeated local officialdom not only in the regional councils but also among the wardens, sheriffs and justices of the peace. The development of the jurisdiction of the Chancery and the Court of Requests which Wolsey had encouraged was further strengthened by the specialisation of the judicial work of the council in

Star Chamber where the elements of a separate court emerged. Active central government increased the effectiveness of local government.

Cromwell's manipulation of local dynastic ambitions and his attempts to diffuse local power among the gentry enjoyed temporary success under a strong King. His efforts to further institutionalise and strengthen the procedural application of royal power at local level through regional councils provided a more permanent basis for the increase of central control. His achievement lay not in massive innovation but in the development of the existing system and methods. His inspiration he found not in the doctrines of absolutism but in what he held to be the historic rights of the Kingship.

8 THE CHARACTER OF GOVERNMENT

The statements of Cromwell's arch enemies, Pole and Gardiner, might be expected to be hostile to him. To counter Cromwell's charge of a papal tyranny, Pole represented the assumption of the royal supremacy as a tyrannical act and brought papalist invective up to date by accusing Cromwell of machiavellianism. Gardiner only went so far as to suggest that Cromwell argued for despotic rule, he did not accuse him of having established it. Just as it was natural for Pole with his Italian background to point to Machiavelli as the source of the despotic notions which he ascribed to Cromwell, so it was to be expected that Gardiner, a canonist, believed that Cromwell sought the support of Roman law.

Pole's reconstruction of Cromwell's justification of despotism was admittedly a literary device. Gardiner's story of how he had been called on to expound the tag, *quod principi placuit legis habet vigorem*, in support, as he supposed, of Cromwell's argument for despotism, and of how he had answered that the King should make the laws his will, was clearly the recollection of an embarrassing moment. Gardiner, afraid of being led on by Cromwell, had played safe. The seriousness with which he had taken the debate into which he had been unexpectedly drawn revealed his insecurity. What would he have said about More's *Utopia* or Starkey's proposal for an elective monarchy? Henry had remarked that Tyndale's *Obedience of the Christian Man* was a book for kings to read and Cromwell had pointed to the example of the Sultan without expecting to be regarded as disciples of Luther or Mahomet.[1]

The very predominance of the conviction that English government was not despotic in theory or practice made possible speculative political discussion at court. It also led Pole and Gardiner to believe that they could damage Cromwell by accusations of despotic action or intent. It is difficult to believe that only his enemies penetrated Cromwell's real political designs. Had he been so assertive an advocate of despotism as they suggest, it is strange that his views were not more widely appreciated and reported.

Cromwell created no tradition of absolutist thinking in England. Pole's belief that the rejection of Rome demonstrated that a tyranny had been established in England was countered by the widely held opinion that Cromwell had contributed to the freedom of English men by removing them from subjection to Rome. Cromwell was regarded as the champion of liberty from foreign domination. The Supremacy of the King over the Church did not affect the way in which the Kingship was viewed in the conduct of temporal government. Many of the laity saw the King as a reformer abolishing the oppressions, perpetrated by the clergy. The functioning of government continued to fit the established belief that the English constitution was a mixed polity.

A practical expression of the mixed polity was legislation by the King in parliament. The mutual assent of the King, Lords and Commons to the laws united the powers, derived from God and from the people, in the authority of an institution which was both a High Court and a representative assembly. Since parliament met more frequently than in the recent past and passed voluminous and important legislation during Cromwell's ascendancy, it may be concluded that Cromwell did not disregard or suppress this important element in the mixed polity. Even, when Cromwell had found parliament a momentarily regrettable necessity, he had treated it as a necessity. But it may be argued that he abused parliament by making a mockery of its representative character through electoral interference, by stifling its initiative through management, and above all by seeking to use its legislative authority to legalise despotism.

In his use of patronage in the Commons, Cromwell rallied to the Crown patrons whose influence would have otherwise been dispersed in local and social rivalries. He did no more than organise the current patronage system which controlled elections. That the King was entitled to seek support in parliament was accepted and appeals by Cromwell to support the King elicited the enthusiastic responses which ruling parties were later to attract.[2] Patronage has never been excluded from electoral practice, although patrons have changed. But, if Cromwell's methods at elections were nothing out of the ordinary, might it not be argued that the electoral process of the time failed to produce a representative assembly?

A minority electorate under oligarchic patronage sent an elite to the Commons. The Lords Spiritual and Temporal were not even elected. When by the Dissolution Cromwell removed the abbots from parliament, he did nothing to diminish the elected representatives. While in the Commons Cromwell increased the number of members by arranging for twenty-four members from Wales and two from Calais to attend.[3] Despite the electoral system and the composition of parliament, it is evident that Cromwell, like his contemporaries, persisted in regarding parliament as a representative assembly.

Edward Hall, a member of the Commons during Cromwell's time, wrote of 'the body of the realm in the High Court of Parliament assembled'. The head and members of an organic community were represented, not an electorate conceived of in numerical terms. Cromwell's provision of members for Wales was lavish for the size of the population, but Cromwell was not thinking in numbers. The random pattern of borough representation and the exclusion of the Palatinate of Durham from county representation made clear that representation did not rest on a numerical equation. Counting heads was a useful, but seldom used technique in electoral and parliamentary procedures. The vagueness of electoral procedure and qualifications demonstrated that the numerate vision of politics had little significance for ideas of representation. In the Dispensations Act Cromwell alluded to 'Your royal majesty and your Lords spiritual and temporal and Commons representing the whole state of your realm in this your most high court'.[4] Cromwell did nothing which diminished in contemporary eyes the standing of parliament as a representative body.

The management of parliament has never been regarded as incompatible with its representative function. It has been the necessity of every government with a programme and a belief that it is the duty of government to govern. Cromwell controlled parliament less surely than a modern majority party. While in power, he had the parliamentary task of obtaining the assent of the King, Lords and Commons. Business had to be expedited and opposition overcome. He would have been no more of a parliamentarian had he allowed opposition to triumph more frequently or business to drag on longer. For all Cromwell's management, parliament by its proposal, amendment or rejection of bills showed a considerable initiative in shaping legislation. Its initiative was chronicled by Edward Hall with evident relish.[5]

If the commons remained unruly and difficult to handle, despite all of Cromwell's devices of management, it might be argued that he had good reason to attempt to dispense with parliament by vesting its legislative power in the Crown. Such an attempt to legalise despotism has been detected in the bill on proclamations in 1539.[6] It is difficult to see why he should wish in 1539 to reverse his usual practice of pursuing his policies through parliamentary legislation, when he still had a large programme of legislation in hand and had secured a tractable parliament. But it has been held that such was the purpose of his original bill on proclamations which, it is alleged, proposed to make proclamation the equal of statute and empower the King to rule by edict.

The origins of the Statute of Proclamations do not indicate the formation of a despotic design. As early as 1531 Cromwell had sought and received reassurance from the Chief Justice not only of the validity of an informer action in the Court of Exchequer in a case, involving a breach of a proclamation, but also of the lawfulness of the royal right to issue in emergency proclamations which should be of 'as good effect as any law made by parliament or otherwise'. In this context the Chief Justice was presumably using the term, 'good effect' with reference to enforcement and not to suggest any equality of legal status between proclamation and statute. Certainly Cromwell did not take the Chief Justice's statement to mean that he could treat proclamations as the equal of statute. His use of proclamations showed a constant resort to statutory authority to support proclamations. Of seventy-two known proclamations in the 1530's a mere fraction lacked statutory authority for their regulations and of that fraction three were later confirmed by statute. While religion began to come within the purview of proclamation in this period, the majority of proclamations were concerned with the traditional subject of economic and social regulation. In a time of inflation the chief use of proclamation was in fixing prices, often in response to the demands of trading interests.[7] There was no sign of rule by edict.

Vagueness over the jurisdiction of courts and over the legality of penalties in cases of offences against proclamations made it difficult to enforce their regulations. Cromwell was driven to fix the prices of wine and meat by statute. It proved an insufficiently flexible method of controlling prices which changed with inflation and fluctuating supplies. To overcome this deficiency Cromwell devised acts which allowed for the delegation to a conciliar committee of the power to issue proclamations which would give effect to their decisions and which would allow for the suspension or modification of relevant statutes. Such proclamations under statutory authority gained full legal force for their prescribed penalties and could be enforced by informer action in the courts of common law. The use of statute to make proclamations effective was a device which Cromwell had learned from experience and was ready to employ again in 1539.

When parliament was not in session or refused to pass an act, Cromwell acted with the emergency powers of the Crown to provide the necessary regulation of economic affairs. Failing to obtain an act against regrating and engrossing, he issued a punitive proclamation against these offences. If statutes proved unworkable, as in the setting of cloth standards and in maintaining exchange control, he suspended them by proclamation. It was not surprising in 1539, when faced with the threat of religious disorder and of foreign invasion, that he should have wished to obtain parliamentary support for the enforcement of the emergency powers of the Crown and should have induced the Council to put before parliament a measure to ensure 'that proclamations made by the King shall be obeyed'.[8]

The original bill on proclamations emerged from a decade of

discussion in Council and of experiments with statute by Cromwell and the Council. It was intended to deal with the long standing problems of enforcement. It asserted that statute and proclamation had the same force at law. The obvious needs of the government, however, raised legal problems over which, as the Chief Justice admitted in 1531, there was disagreement among lawyers. Stricter enforcement of regulations affecting economic interests and religious beliefs was not generally welcomed as the complaints in the preamble of the bill recognised.[9] The bill on proclamations could not expect a straightforward passage in the parliament.

The Commons had no wish to make a rod for their own backs and were concerned with confirming the traditional limits of the penalties which proclamations could impose and safeguarding the existing laws. Their proviso appeared in the second clause of the final act, which guarded the life and property of all subjects and the property of all bodies politic or corporate from being taken away by virtue of the act. All existing laws and lawful customs were protected from infringement, breaking or subversion by proclamation. Future legislation was not, however, so protected. The Lords had other safeguards in mind. They provided for the issue of proclamations by the King and the whole council. To make it practicable the procedure had to be amended to allow for a majority of the council to act. They set up a special court to deal with offenders against proclamations. In this way the Lords restricted the means of enforcing proclamations. The special court was to prove a clumsy device which failed to work satisfactorily.

Faced with an amended bill which restricted penalties and introduced a new court, Cromwell by an astute amendment tried to make the best of a bad job. He added to the clause, which permitted the penalties, as declared in the act, an amendment which allowed the forfeitures, pains and penalties declared by every proclamation, which 'hereafter shall be set forth by the authority of the same' act. The final act as a result gave Cromwell the choice of issuing proclamations which were specifically under the authority of the act and proclamations which did not cite the act.[10] Proclamations, claiming the authority of the act, could specify penalties regardless of the restrictions of the act from which they were excepted. They could be enforced by the special court set up by the act. They could contravene statutes which were passed subsequently to the act and provide for informer action in the courts of common law. Under the statute Cromwell had found a way of strengthening the emergency power of proclamation and avoiding some of the restrictions which had been incorporated in the bill during the parliamentary debates.

Because of his fall in 1540, it is not possible to know how Cromwell would have used the Proclamations Act of 1539. Judged by his actions up to his fall it seems that Cromwell wished to be able to impose heavy penalties by proclamation, to keep the emergency powers of regulation flexible and responsive to the immediate situation and to ensure the enforcement of proclamations. In pursuit of these objectives he had not relied upon an independent legislative power, based on the prerogative of the Crown, but had shown a readiness to seek statutory authority. He had accepted that proclamations were subordinate to statute in the long run and that they were temporary measures to meet passing dangers. To bolster up these aims and assumptions with statutory authority he had framed the original bill on proclamations in 1539 and his amendments to the final bill were designed to preserve the same aims and assumptions. It was over the practice of proclamations rather than the theory of their legal nature that the Lords and Commons differed from Cromwell. The difference was not between a minister trying to persuade parliament to legalise arbitrary legislative powers for the Crown and a parliament determined to thwart a bid to make it acquiesce in despotism.

Yet, while in the session of 1539 the informed debate had been over the limits of a shared legal tradition concerning proclamations, there had been misunderstanding and suspicion about both the intentions behind the act and the effects of the act. It seems that the Commons were perturbed by a rumour of taxation by proclamation. There had been references to the powers of the French King and the Emperor to deal with heresy by decree. The French ambassador had gained the impression that the act on proclamations conferred upon the King arbitrary powers of legislation. Another unfounded story, which may have arisen at the time of the debates in 1539 or at the time of the repeal of the act in 1547, was to the effect that the King had tried to make proclamation the equal of statute but had been defeated in his purpose by the Commons. While the story never became part of the received history of the chroniclers, it persisted as part of the parliamentary gossip which contributed to the growing mythology of the Commons. Versions of the story served in special pleading, when it was required to enhance the prestige of the Commons. They kept alive up to the reign of James I the idea that the Act of Proclamations had high constitutional significance as a victory over attempted despotism.

The search for some contemporary evidence of a constitutional conflict between the Crown and the Commons has led to the close consideration of the Act itself in order to divine its intentions. It has been argued that the preamble betrays the despotic aims of Cromwell. But the preamble not only accepted the distinction between proclamations and ordinary law but also acknowledged that proclamations were emergency measures, taken when parliament was not in session, and were valid for a limited time. The intention, expressed in the preamble, of preference for a resort to ordinary law rather than to an extension of the liberty and supremacy of regal power was a declaration in conformity with Cromwell's usual practice rather than a threat of prerogative action which would have sounded hollow, following an admission of the impotence of government to enforce proclamations. Its propagandist purpose was not to make high claims but to demonstrate the scandal of a situation in which the highest authority was being flouted. The preamble fails to reveal anything which is inconsistent with the final act which is supposed to have defeated its aims.[11]

Even if his bill on proclamations concealed no despotic design, it must be noted that Cromwell seemed determined to preserve for proclamations the use of heavy penalties. In his discussion with the judges in 1531 it was agreed that if money should be conveyed out of the realm then 'proclamation should be made grounded upon the said statute adding thereunto politically certain things for putting the King's subjects and other in more terror and fear'.[12] It might be concluded that with the backing of the law and of the judges Cromwell was prepared to conduct a reign of terror in order to make subjects obey the King.

Deterrence is now fashionably odious but legal authorities, like Sir John Fortescue, believed it to be an important function of the law. Cromwell's humanist friend, Elyot, wrote, '. . . . condemnation or punishment is either to reduce him that erreth into the train of virtue or to preserve a multitude from damage, by putting men in fear, that be prone to offend, dreading the sharp correction that they behold another to suffer'. Cromwell acted in accord with the enlightened opinion of his day, when he declared, 'Yet in case prayer and gentle entreaty cannot pull and allure you away from the doing of wrong and injury, both to the King and his subjects, I will not fail to advance to the uttermost of my power Justice and to see punished with extremity the interrupters thereof to the example of other.' He had no consciousness that acting *in terrorem* was tyrannical or in any way reprehensible.[13] He did not abuse the doctrine of deterrence and he administered the penalties of the law with a serious regard for the due process of the law.

If Cromwell gave a lawful trial and even clemency to offenders, what of the methods by which he brought them to trial? The informer was a recognised agent of the law. Torture was an accepted means of investigation by Council. Cromwell extended informer action at common law. He did not use torture excessively. The lurid Spanish story of Cromwell, having a knotted cord round Mark Smeaton's head tightened, is not in character with the methods of Cromwell or of English torture. He had a reputation as an interrogator and investigator and the King referred to his 'circumspect manner, desirous and attentive mind in trying out the truth'.[14]

Cromwell has been accused of trapping his 'victims' by his use of spies. In foreign diplomacy espionage was taken for granted and every Englishman abroad was expected to report intelligence as Cromwell's friend, Stephen Vaughan, did. Even ambassadors were watched, as Wyatt watched Gardiner in France and as he was himself watched later by Bonner in Spain. While Cromwell's management of foreign intelligence has been accepted his domestic use of espionage has attracted less patriotic admiration. Yet at home Cromwell lacked any developed information services or police forces. Commissions and officials reported to him, but he did not put into action more ambitious plans, like that to bind the gentry to carry out regular searches for papists or for the creation of sergeants of the Commonwealth to detect and prosecute offenders against certain statutes.[15] He had to rely on such official sources as there were and cultivate the flow of information from unofficial sources.

In special cases Cromwell used 'espials' but most of his information on offenders came from voluntary informants. Those, who reported to him from the households of great nobles, abbeys, taverns and from wherever talk could be easily overheard, must not be taken to be spies, placed and employed by Cromwell. The vast majority were self-appointed agents, acting for Cromwell in hope of reward, out of a sense of duty or out of malice. His reliance on such voluntary initiative is demonstrated by the fact that reports of offences were for the most part random, and unrelated to the incidence of offences. From Lancashire, where there was little inclination to obey legislation on ecclesiastical matters and offences were numerous, reports were few and unsystematic. Cromwell was not the master of an organised network of spies throughout the land, but the inevitable recipient of all that informers were prepared to tell.[16]

It might be argued, however, that in his legislation on treason Cromwell increased the crimes against the state and made government more oppressive. Cromwell was not inhibited by the assumption, later perpetuated by Coke and Hale, that any addition to the Treason Statute of 1352 was tantamount to a violation of fundamental law. His laws did, however, take into account expert legal advice and precedent and were framed to provide the due process of law for offenders. While Henry VIII made poisoning a treason, Cromwell confined his legislation to the traditional purposes of protecting the King, his family and his authority. Henry's matrimonial career and his claim to the Supremacy over the Church made it necessary to guard, as the treason laws had always done, the succession and the titles of the King.

Cromwell's changes were justifiable extensions of, not random additions to, the law of treason. Treating the forgery of the sign manual of the King, like that of his great seal, as treason was a response to administrative practice. The increasing diffusion of rumour and printed propaganda amongst a more literate public made it prudent to establish clearly that words could be treasonable. Even under the act of 1352, judges in the fifteenth century had accepted words as treason by construction. By the early sixteenth century judges, influenced by humanist respect for texts, preferred strict verbal interpretation of statutes to the loose constructions, based on the general intent of acts. There was a professional interest in extending statutory sanction to treason by words and making the law more certain.[17]

Although the King had been pressing for further protection by treason legislation since 1530, practical considerations had delayed action until 1534, when Cromwell had to secure acceptance of the succession and obedience to the Supremacy. Together the treason act of 1534 and the succession acts of 1534 and 1536 provided a powerful deterrent against treason by overt acts and by writings and words. Treason now clearly included verbal, written and printed attacks upon the throne. Rights of sanctuary for traitors were finally extinguished in 1534. The oath, required by the succession act of 1534, provided a selective sanction for use against opponents, such as Thomas More.[18] Cromwell cannot be accused of over-reacting in his treason legislation. The threat to the King had grown.

The new treason laws caused little opposition. The debate in the Commons over the 1534 act concerned the requirement of proving malicious intent in treason by words and not the legality of the offence of treason by words itself. By insisting on the due process of law and by personal investigation of cases, Cromwell did what he could to guard against any injustice arising from ill-founded accusations. Admittedly he did not reform the due process of law which was heavily weighted against the defendant. But that accusations of treason had to be proved in the courts, before a conviction was made, can be seen from the fact that the number of cases vastly exceeded the number of convictions.[19]

While Cromwell attempted to safeguard the monarchy by his treason legislation and the prosecution of traitors in the courts of common law by due regard for the process of the law, he frequently responded to the threat of treason with the more formidable act of attainder. Supported by the judicial argument that conviction by act of attainder only was legal, because no lesser court could challenge the verdict of the High Court of Parliament, he used acts of attainder not as the confirmation of verdicts, reached by due process of law in the courts, but as the sole means of securing conviction. He had precedents but they belonged to different circumstances, where the offender could not be brought to trial. He secured the lethal effect of attaint for treason by imposing the death penalty in the act. He applied attainder to those guilty of misprision of treason and even to unnamed confederates in order to deal with the accomplices of traitors. He used single acts to convict large numbers of offenders, as many as fifty-three in an act of 1539.[20]

That Cromwell found the act of attainder a useful instrument is shown by the fact that the majority of such acts in Henry VIII's reign were passed in Cromwell's period of power. He employed it to suppress opposition, as in the case of the Maid of Kent and her backers, in faction strife, as in the attaint of Thomas, Lord Howard, in 1536, and to destroy the Geraldine power in Ireland and the Courtenay and Pole influence in the West country and the court. His development of the act of attainder exploited a parliamentary procedure which had been fashioned in the strife of the fifteenth century and applied it to the conflict, arising from the break with Rome. It was typical of Cromwell to find in the judicial, as in the legislative sphere, a role for the authority of statute.

If Cromwell's use of acts of attainder appears to be an exercise of political power to crush opposition, it must be recalled that the High Court of Parliament was the highest court in the land and that it was the most public court in that it was an institution representative of the whole body of the realm. Cromwell's presentation of bills of attainder in petitionary form may have been for the propagandist purpose of suggesting popular outrage and initiative behind the attack on traitors, but it calls attention to the fact that opponents of his policies were not arbitrarily or secretly dispatched and that their conviction required the approval of King, Lords and Commons. It was notable that parliament opposed the inclusion of Thomas More for misprision of treason in a bill of 1534 and that his name was removed. Admittedly More was caught later by retrospective legislation and finally condemned by parliament after his trial.[21] Parliament did, however, consider and amend acts of attainder, but usually to provide protection against the side effects of forfeiture.

Acts of attainder provided a more convenient and certain alternative to trials in the various courts, especially when the evidence for the prosecution was unimpressive. Lord Dacre had been acquitted unexpectedly by his peers. In the trial of Thomas More, which achieved notoriety in Europe, both the prosecution and the defence had stretched legality to the utmost. More eventually had to admit the conflict between his own concept of the dual nature of authority and Cromwell's concept of a unitary authority. The trial furnished an illustration of the incompatibility of two views of law and demonstrated that the prime antagonists from their different standpoints both condemned arbitrary tyranny.

While Cromwell made an example of traitors, he encouraged the sort of men with whom he had discussed in the Commons as early as 1523 'how a commonwealth might be edified'. He was interested in the welter of proposals, put forward by activists of every kind for the cure of social and economic ills and the promotion of truth in religion. Humanist evangelical piety and optimism, protestant dedication and pessimism, mercantile ambitions and agrarian interests combined to inspire a public awareness of the common weal. The edification of the commonwealth comprehended the improvement of education and of poor relief, the increase of trade and the regulation of prices, industry and agriculture, the acceptance of the moral responsibilities of degree society and the elimination of ecclesiastical abuses. It expressed a pervasive mood of reform which Cromwell shared.[22]

His role in Wolsey's educational schemes, his study of the law, his interest in the Bible and his membership of the Commons linked Cromwell with reformers of varied motives. While in power he possessed the patronage to attract the theorists and pamphleteers who were concerned with the principles and practical measures behind the edification of the commonwealth. There was Thomas Starkey who, having enjoyed the patronage of Wolsey and Pole, came home to roost under Cromwell's wing. A less speculative intellectual was William Marshall who worked up a scheme for poor relief and translated Marsilio's *Defensor Pacis*. Ready to defend policy was Richard Morison who quoted from Machiavelli but sympathised with Luther. While he showed enthusiasm for the ideas and measures of such men, Cromwell revealed the successful activist's critical discipline which allowed only utilitarian outlets to enthusiasm, when it came to political action.[23]

The support which Cromwell derived from the commonwealth school of thought was important not so much for the detailed recommendations, incorporated in his measures, as for the sense of moral and public duty, for the critical attitudes towards social, economic and religious conduct and for the belief in the efficacy and benignity of royal intervention. Cromwell gave a wider significance to local and individual initiatives by the idea of one law and one body politic. His programme for each session, selected from the projects which he accumulated in his office, made parliament more aware of its role in edifying the commonwealth and reformers more conscious of parliament as the instrument of reform, as they showed by their growing habit of presenting their proposals in the form of draft bills.

While the concern for the commonwealth stimulated consciences and intellects with the contrast between norms and reality and promoted coercive intervention, it did not excite a desire for fundamental change in the economic or social order. Cromwell's measures were shaped to meet current needs but for the most part they belonged to the traditional lines and devices of policy. The Apparel Act of 1534, confirming hierarchical values, had many precedents. His acts to increase trade and native shipping and safeguard vital supplies, such as metals, flax and horses derived from long established governmental strategy.[24]

The trading and financial interests of London in the City Companies had organised to put their case in parliament. The patronage which he enjoyed in the City and his close acquaintance with merchants, such as Richard Gresham, laid Cromwell open to informal pressures. His commercial experience enabled him to weigh the practical results of the schemes of projectors, like Clement Armstrong, and of the monopolistic companies, like the Merchant Adventurers. He was prepared to fix prices for wine and meat and to favour Richard Gresham's plan for an Exchange in London but he resisted proposals to ban the export of unfinished cloths.[25] Political caution marked his approach to commercial and financial measures. He was not ready to jeopardise the prosperity of existing trades by adopting the economic planning of theorists.

In agriculture, the dominant economic activity in the country, the loss of tillage by enclosure for conversion to pasture was held to be the cause of dearth and unemployment. Wolsey had tried to stop such enclosure by a commission to discover enclosers and by their prosecution in the courts. Cromwell devised a new approach by limiting the size of flocks and of farms in the hands of one sheepmaster. It was a novel way of attempting to halt enclosure and to preserve the existing balance between tillage and pasture. Because it cut across powerful incentives and sought to weaken the prosperity of pasture farming it proved no more effective than previous measures, despite Cromwell's confidence in it.[26]

In dealing with vagabondage Cromwell had before him a plan, devised by his adviser William Marshall, which was based upon the latest humanist thinking on poor relief in Europe. In his act of 1536 Cromwell dropped Marshall's proposal for an administrative officialdom and made the parish responsible for the regular collection of alms and for arrangements to relieve its own impotent poor and to set sturdy beggars to work. Although the act hindered the mobility of labour and continued to rely on voluntary charity through an ecclesiastical agency, it was more positive than the act of 1531 in that it moved beyond the merely punitive treatment of able bodied unemployed by its recognition of the need to provide work for them.[27] Despite Cromwell's organisation of charity in the parish, his constructive treatment of the able bodied mendicant and his encouragement of education to prevent idleness, his reputation in the relief of poverty suffered from the indignation at his failure to devote the proceeds of monastic dissolution to the benefit of the poor.

Cromwell's efforts to promote the common weal were impressive in the responsive and purposive efficiency with which he collected, sifted and prepared for legislation various proposals for reform. It could not be expected that a busy politician would provide an original or a more penetrative analysis than the intellectuals and men of affairs whom he consulted. His measures were intended to stabilise rather than revolutionize the existing order. If in number and effect they disappointed reformers, it was, perhaps, because the actual practice of reform seldom matches the expectations of reformers. His preoccupation with the social symptoms and political repercussions of the ills of the commonwealth rather than with their fundamental causes was natural to a politician. Yet Cromwell deserves a high place among those who have not only taken thought but have also taken action to edify a commonwealth.

If the rational calculation and appreciation of the practical possibilities of human action which characterised Cromwell's measures suggest the inspiration of a secular idealism, it must be remembered that he infused such idealism with his evangelical hopes. His actions may have been prompted by considerations of utility and efficiency and recommended by necessity but they were acts of positive law in which God permitted man to use his imperfect natural reason. Cromwell did not forget the divine framework of the universe. His praise of the prosperity of the King's reign was coupled with praise of the royal revelation of the truths of the Bible.[28]

It was Machiavelli who left out the divine context of politics. Cromwell's conduct of politics may be susceptible to interpretation in machiavellian terms but his conscious justification of his conduct was not that of the Florentine. None of Cromwell's intellectual entourage, despite some familiarity with Machiavelli's work, justified statecraft on machiavellian grounds. Although Cromwell was tempted to shock Reginald Pole with a douche of Italian political realism, it was Pole rather than Cromwell who appreciated more fully the import of Machiavelli's work and was among the first to condemn him. In 1540 no one followed Pole's lead in accusing Cromwell of machiavellian atheism or amorality. Cromwell was attacked as a heretic for his religious beliefs. The book which Cromwell promoted and with which he was personally associated by the depiction of his portrait and coat of arms in the frontispiece was the English Bible not *The Prince*.[29]

The nature of the government which Cromwell cultivated in England was neither machiavellian nor despotic. By insisting on the superiority of parliamentary legislation over all other positive law, including the canon law, he counterbalanced the extension of royal authority over the

Church and the royal claims to imperial autonomy and divine right. He enhanced the claims and authority of both Crown and Parliament, but by channelling the lawful expression of sovereignty through the King in Parliament he maintained the balance of the mixed polity. The balance was expounded in the Dispensations Act, when it described the laws of England as 'such as have been devised, made and ordained within the realm, for the wealth of the same, or to such other as, by sufferance of your grace and your progenitors, the people of this your realm have taken at their free liberty, by their own consent to be used amongst them, and have bound themselves by long use and custom to the observance of the same, ... as to the accustomed and ancient laws of this realm, originally established as laws of the same, by the said sufferance, consents, and custom, and none otherwise'.[30]

Cromwell's view of an historic mixed polity may have been idealised but it was from the lawyers' analysis that the political nation judged the nature and working of the government. Cromwell perpetuated the ambiguities and contradictions of the mixed polity. Without establishing a trend towards despotism or towards a parliamentary monarchy, he preserved the poise of a mixed polity which was based on the practical need for the cooperation of King, Lords and Commons and which was institutionalised to the satisfaction of contemporaries in the King in Parliament.

9 THE APPARATUS OF POWER

As Cromwell grew in royal favour there emerged a different pattern of ministerial power from that which Wolsey had established. Whereas Wolsey had made a great office of state, the Chancellorship, into his centre of power, Cromwell converted a household office, the King's secretaryship, into his centre of power. Following Wolsey's fall, Henry had appointed the Cardinal's former secretary, Stephen Gardiner, to act as his secretary and had discovered through his closer involvement in affairs that his secretary was his right hand.' During 1533 Henry, feeling the loss of Gardiner, who was on a diplomatic errand to France, employed Cromwell. The employment of Cromwell, already a leading councillor, as stop-gap secretary revealed that the office had become important in the eyes of both the King and Cromwell.

Wolsey's suspicions in 1521 of the influence of Richard Pace, then Henry's secretary, had indicated the potential of an office which had been gaining in importance for some time. But it was a potential which could only be realised by a man possessed of established power and the King's trust. Gardiner had standing in the government but he had lost Henry's full confidence. By serving as secretary in Gardiner's absences abroad, Cromwell proved that he had the abilities and the royal trust to make the secretaryship his base of ministerial power. In April 1534 he replaced Gardiner and his victory over his rival made him the King's new right hand.[2]

The secretaryship provided regular and confidential access to the King. It made Cromwell mediator between the King and the administration and the suitors to the King. He interpreted to Henry the business of both council and parliament and handled patronage. He plied the King with drafts and digests which he edited for the royal information and approval. He made himself the King's chief executive officer and the source of the royal initiative in the administration. Untrammelled by any defined commission, the secretaryship acquired a scope as large as the royal trust in its holder.

As secretary Cromwell supervised the activities of English embassies abroad and foreign diplomats in England. Along with the traditional duties of the secretary in matters of foreign policy, he dealt with the affairs of English merchants overseas and with the administration in

Ireland, the Channel Islands and Calais. He helped to carry the royal responsibility for the defence of the realm. He supervised the workings of the councils of the North and in the Marches of Wales. He further extended the scope of his office by bringing to it his coverage of the financial and ecclesiastical business of the Crown and his wide-ranging control of domestic administration.[3] The secretaryship, close to the King, was ripe for expansion and Cromwell made it the centre of his multifarious activities in all spheres of government.

With Cromwell as secretary the King could enjoy the advantage of having a confidential servant who was his chief minister and of reposing his trust in a secretary who was for the first time a layman of undivided loyalties. The stories of how Henry boxed Cromwell's ears and of how he claimed to have taught his secretaries their business confirm that the King had the sense that he was in personal control and had an intimate knowledge of government, while being freed from the donkey work and able to delegate much of his initiative.[4] Careful to act in the King's name, Cromwell tried to make it appear that in all important matters he was executing the King's express commands. It was a situation that suited both the King and his secretary. Henry believed that he knew what his right hand was doing.

With the elevation of the secretaryship by Cromwell a household office was once again being exploited to tap the initiative of the prerogative and provide a powerful agency in government. Its expanding role affected the standing of the secretaryship. In 1539 a statute ranked it last among the eleven top offices of state and household.[5] Such precedence hardly reflected the real structure of power but it went some way to acknowledging the change in the secretaryship from a confidential clerkship to the King to an office of acknowledged status in the officialdom of the realm. Cromwell's use of the secretaryship enhanced its role and status.

The secretaryship lost some of its standing in officialdom and of its expanded competence, when Cromwell handed over his office in 1540 to two of his followers who shared the work and were given official remuneration. Cromwell had managed single-handed with only a share in the profits of the signet office. His departure meant a more formal and bureaucratic role for the secretaryship. Although the importance of the secretaryship under Cromwell had rested upon his qualities and his accumulation of power and although its importance in the near future remained to a large extent dependent upon the relationship between the King and his secretaries, nevertheless, the secretaryship retained its potential as a ministerial office and its administrative functions were extended. From the secretaryship Cromwell had fashioned an office which could be made the centre of government by a trusted servant of the Crown. When under Elizabeth I a strong monarch and a trusted secretary once again cooperated the value for personal monarchy of Cromwell's experiment was confirmed.

Soon after Cromwell had gained the secretaryship, he reached out with his sense of strategic pluralism for further control of the administration. Early in October, 1534, on the convenient resignation of the Master of the Rolls, Cromwell cut across the tradition of appointing a chancery-trained cleric and cut out the obvious successor by taking the office for himself. It was a profitable post and provided him with an official residence, the Rolls House. In his tenure of the Mastership he elevated its administrative importance in the Chancery and asserted its control over the secretariat which he reorganised to improve its methods of business. While he increased the administrative role of the Mastership at the expense of the Chancellor, Audley, he left the bulk of the tedious judicial business of Chancery to him, although he served on judicial commissions as Master of the Rolls.[6]

In July, 1536, Cromwell resigned the Mastership of the Rolls. The fall of Anne Boleyn had put within his grasp a more important office, that of Lord Privy Seal, fourth in precedence amongst the great offices of state, which he took from the earl of Wiltshire. Its secretariat and seal gave Cromwell further official cover for his handling of the administration. With his barony and the dignity of the Lord Privy Seal, he acquired in 1536 a social standing and an official rank and title more in keeping with his ministerial control of affairs.[7] In the pageantry of public life he could now be seen to stand high. The activities in which he was engaged as secretary were now carried on for the most part in the name of the Lord Privy Seal. The scope of the office was expanded to serve Cromwell's dominant role in government.

Cromwell's use of offices reveals his ability to exploit their undefined potentialities. Yet while he made the Master of the Rolls more important within the Chancery, he did not make the Chancery more important. It was already apparent under Thomas More that the Chancery was losing its initiative in government. It was about to lose much judicial business to the regional councils. It is, perhaps, significant of the limitations of the office of Master of the Rolls that he relinquished it after two years. Despite speculation that Cromwell would become Chancellor, it appears that, with the signet office and Privy Seal office in his hands, the largely formal administrative functions of the Great Seal of Chancery did not attract him.

Perhaps the increasingly judicial function of the Chancellorship deterred Cromwell who despite his legalistic outlook was not prepared to have his time consumed by judicial duties. He did not take the opportunities for a personal judicial role either in the Court of Requests which was nominally under his purview as Lord Privy Seal, or in the Chancery as Master of the Rolls. It was the less defined judicial powers of a councillor which he preferred to deploy in his role as investigator, arbiter and prosecutor in political and police matters affecting the peace and order of the state. His influence over jurisdiction derived from his allocation of suits to the appropriate courts and from his readiness to create commissions to try particular cases. The suits which poured in upon him enabled him to pass cases to the courts and keep an eye upon their progress. [8]

Cromwell's use of the secretaryship and of the Lord Privy Seal's office as the bases of ministerial dominance proved to be expansive and experimental. He developed their business methods and organised them with administrative skill but their roles remained largely a function of his personal power. Their working depended much upon his unremitting personal supervision and initiative and his employment of his personal staff. His methods tended to blur the distinction between the official and the personal both in initiative and in staffing. He furthered the use of signed directives at the expense of the traditional use of seals. It was convenient, when he held both the signet and the privy seal. His papers were those of a hard working minister rather than the records of a bureaucrat, serving an institution. Perhaps the fact that literacy could be taken for granted among the ruling class made for greater informality in communication within the administration and outside it. [9]

Cromwell applied his administrative skills beyond his own offices in his reform of the Household. The conduct of the Household attracted criticism which reflected immediately upon the personal reputation of the King. It was, therefore, a matter of great political importance. Limiting the establishment and expenditure of the Household had been a perennial problem of monarchy. Cromwell's reform of the Household ranks high among his services to the King.

Having provided for Henry a more lavish Household, Cromwell took care in 1539 to stabilise the establishment and to bring expenditure under the continuous supervision and strict control of the Board of Green Cloth. The reorganisation of the Household proved to be one of the more durable of his administrative feats. [10] It was a straightforward task compared with the organisation of departments which were involved in active administration of the realm. The demands of policy and power made it less easy to preserve the limitations of bureaucratic procedure in other departments. The reform of the Household provides a model of Cromwell's bureaucratic skill. He was, however, an administrator who appreciated the value and the weaknesses of bureaucracy. He had the power to make and to break the rules.

In his approach to office Cromwell, wishing to know from what basis he started, appeared to be all for definition and formality. He sketched the financial organisation about 1531, laid down rules for the signet office in 1534 and in a statute of 1536 he confirmed the traditional role of the secretariats of the signet and privy seal offices. In this way he grasped the system, reassured his staff and demonstrated the efficiency of a new broom. The act of 1536, initially aimed at laxity and corruption, emerged as a confirmation of traditional ways and official fees.[11] It looks as if the new Lord Privy Seal had given way to the bureaucrats. But Cromwell was merely informing himself about the rules, he had no intention of tying his hands. The financial pattern, the organisation of the signet office and that of the office of Lord Privy Seal which he had clarified and defined upon assuming control tended to lapse and to give way to his personal methods and improvisations. He looked at the bureaucracy from above as a minister rather than from below as a departmental bureaucrat. For a minister, success and efficiency often depended upon the ability to make short cuts and waive procedures, while for the bureaucrat they lay in rigid adherence to routine official practice.

Cromwell's need to have latitude to manoeuvre and his desire to organise for effective and rapid action conflicted with the bureaucrats' need for known procedures and desire to organise for security, authorisation and precedent. While Cromwell was secure in royal favour, he could carry the bureaucrats with him. But when his authority wavered, the bureaucrats denounced his irregularities and strove to re-establish authorised formality in administration. Many of the charges against him in 1540 were bureaucratic complaints about his personal methods, about his misuse of authority and failure to abide by the rules. Bureaucrats like Paget, Rich, Throgmorton and Wriothesley betrayed him. After his fall even his trusted John Gostwick revealed his irregularities. Cromwell's confession that he had meddled in so many matters that he was not able to answer for them all was not that of a bureaucrat who could rely upon records and routine to vindicate his actions.[12] It was a revelation of a personal dominance rather than of bureaucratic system. His confession showed that an effective minister and a skilful administrator were something different from a good bureaucrat. The difference was made plain, when Cromwell fell, while the bureaucrats survived. The distinction between bureaucrat and minister was the ability to retain office in time of change.

In fulfilling the duty of a councillor to advise the King, Cromwell proved a powerful minister. With royal favour, control of finance, command of the administration and leadership in parliamentary affairs he was in a strong position among councillors. His initiative in selecting the agenda and in formulating legislation gradually secured his influence over council business. He was recognised as the King's principal councillor and as 'chief of the council'. Unlike Wolsey, he preferred to work through council and use its collective authority and formal unanimity as a cover for his policies. Anxious to avoid being saddled with sole responsibility for the break with Rome, he emphasised the solidarity of the council. In 1533 a defence of policy was entitled *Articles devised by the whole consent of the King's most honourable council.*[13]

Whenever the Council had become a centre of active government, it had tended for the sake of efficiency to become in practice a small body with a permanent core of the officials, essential to its administrative functions. Such was the sort of council, recommended by Sir John Fortescue in the fifteenth century and envisaged by Wolsey in the Eltham Ordinances. It was the sort of council promoted by Cromwell who needed effective administrative action to execute his policies. Continuity of action and of policy was achieved by the regular attendance of a small group of advisers and officials. Under Cromwell's leadership a council with a limited and stable membership emerged by the mid 1530's. It came to be distinguished by the name of Privy Council. If the Privy Council took on institutional form and authority, its procedure remained, it would appear, at the discretion of its creator.

The predominance of his political initiative led Cromwell to treat the Privy Council as primarily an administrative board. He encouraged moves to lighten the burden of time-consuming judicial work in the Privy Council. The regional councils took some of the load and at the centre the judicial sessions in the Star Chamber were becoming a separate conciliar activity. The developments in Star Chamber resulted partly from Wolsey's expansion of judicial business and partly from the move towards formalising proceedings, when Wolsey's personal dominance ceased. During the general assertion of institutional routines which followed the removal of Cromwell's control of conciliar affairs there emerged an independent Court of Star Chamber.

In creating the Privy Council Cromwell strengthened his administrative, but made more precarious his political power. In limiting the membership of Privy Council he had not only offended the excluded nobility but had also narrowed his opportunities for building up support for his policies. Although Cromwell attempted to establish a largely *ex officio* membership, he was unable to exclude, except on temporary duties elsewhere, all his opponents because of rights of office and because of the King's jealously guarded right to choose his councillors. Time and tradition did not allow Cromwell to name all his fellow councillors and secure a powerful faction in the Privy Council. As well as differences of policy and personality, there remained the tension between the noble and the merely professional advisers for hostile noble councillors, like Norfolk, to exploit. When Cromwell lost the King's favour, the noble councillors, led by Norfolk, asserted their old claim to be the leading councillors of the King. In 1540 they arrested Cromwell in a session of the Privy Council.[14]

With their existence no longer guaranteed by Cromwell's ascendancy the councillors sought to perpetuate the corporate identity of the Privy Council, which Cromwell had thrust upon them, by further formalising procedure. In August, 1540, they appointed a clerk and started an official record of their agreed decisions. A move towards a procedural sophistication to ensure an institutional survival of the Privy Council had begun. A further consequence of Cromwell's fall was the full revelation of the political capacity of the Privy Council which had been partially masked by Cromwell's dominance. With its collective expertise and unanimous voice the Privy Council offered the King an alternative to a great minister as a means of conducting his personal rule. Ironically, after Cromwell's fall the King was less ready to accept the formal unanimity of the Privy Council and played upon individuals and factions within it.[15]

At Cromwell's fall, his personal supervision, the linkages of his pluralism, the support of his personal staff and the drive of his overriding cumulative authority and strong personality ceased. Having killed their scapegoat, the bureaucrats hastened to protect themselves from the wrath of the King, as John Gostwick did, by formalising the legacy of Cromwell's personal régime. Agencies, such as the Jewel House, inflated by Cromwell's power, shrank to their former dimensions. Others attained institutional form, like the Court of First Fruits and Tenths. In such offices as the secretaryship and that of the Lord Privy Seal there was a renewal of emphasis upon bureaucratic routines.[16] As in the past there was a bureaucratic reaction to the exploitation of the royal prerogative in administrative experimentation. After the death of Henry VII the collective influence of officialdom, animated by a profession's instinct for security, had slowly bureaucratised and legalised the results of royal initiative. On the downfall of Cromwell the bureaucratic reaction was more rapid in establishing formal relationships within the bureaucracy. Officialdom digested Cromwell's personal régime.

Cromwell's immersion in administration gave the appearance of a bureaucracy, generating policy, and of a government functioning without a King. But neither Cromwell nor those who attainted him for 'usurping' the Kingly Estate believed that government could work without a King. Cromwell's removal made clear the distinction between the initiative of royal government and the limited reflexes of the royal administration. Cromwell had fashioned the means of his ministerial rule and the bureaucrats formalised them to serve the personal rule of the King. From Cromwell's action and the bureaucrats' reaction there was created not a government which could run without a King, but an administration which made the continuance of the personal rule of the monarch an effective possibility. The changes in administration had not altered the monarchical character of the government. Privy Councillors remained individually responsible to the King and secretaries, dependent on royal trust.

The important governmental changes of Cromwell's régime had been his adaptation of the secretaryship and his creation of the Privy Council. That both these developments were paralleled in the continental monarchies, and that both became durable features of English government, suggests that Cromwell had shown perspicacity in meeting the needs of monarchical government in this period. In providing secretaries of a wide competence and a council of a more stable and professional composition, close to the King, Cromwell's legacy enabled the monarch to delegate without alienating power and to meet the increasing burden of business and court life, while remaining an effective ruler.

In the development of parliament Cromwell's period of power has been regarded as of decisive importance. His use of parliament, it has been held, assured the perpetuation of the institution and of the tradition which produced a parliamentary rather than an absolutist monarchy. The duration of and the scale and importance of the legislation of the parliament which met in 1529 and was dissolved in 1536 were both extraordinary and suggest that the so called Reformation Parliament must constitute a landmark in the history of parliament. Under Cromwell's guidance parliament had acted as an engine of reform in ecclesiastical, economic, social, legal, administrative and financial matters. It had shown how a commonwealth might be edified.

Between November, 1529, and July, 1540, parliament had been in session twelve times. Such frequency could be expected to keep an institution in working order. The nature of the legislation was such as to rouse political and religious interest and stir the social consciences of members. Cromwell may be said to have strengthened the parliamentary habits of the political nation and of the government. His legislation could be expected to lead to further parliaments, required for its repeal or amendment, as did his ecclesiastical legislation in the changing religious situations of the sixteenth century. His practice of accumulating measures for future legislation and his view of taxation as a continuous requirement of peacetime government revealed his acceptance of parliament as a regular part of government.[17]

In matters of procedure and privilege neither Cromwell nor parliament made any advances which would have allowed parliament to regulate more fully its existence or composition. The means by which parliament could control the government were not enlarged. No novel means of blocking legislation were practised. There were numerous attainders, launched from above, but no impeachments, engineered from below. The appropriation of taxation was not attempted. The King's benign attitude to such claims for privilege as were made by the Commons in his reign indicated that there was no suspicion of an ambition to increase parliamentary powers at the expense of the Crown. The general doctrine which could be construed as requiring the continuance of parliament was that, enunciated by Sir John Fortescue, which required that no new impost or law should be made by a King without the assent of his people. In the circumstances the continuance of parliament seemed to depend rather upon its readiness to assent than upon its determination to withhold consent.

If parliament was strengthened during Cromwell's period of power, it was from above. This is not to deny that there were powerful pressures from below that sustained parliament. The demand among the gentry for seats in the Commons which had begun to appear in the fifteenth century remained strong. Parliamentary service had a role in determining the social prestige and political importance of the local gentry which those increasingly powerful members of the political nation would have been loath to sacrifice. Elections gave the nobility a chance to exercise their patronage which they valued. All kinds of reformer and suitor looked to parliament for the redress of grievances. There was a general expectation, admitted by Henry VII, that parliament would be called for great, urgent and necessary causes. It may be argued that the summons of parliament in 1529 was a response to such an expectation rather than to any very clear decision on policy by the King.[18] Cromwell exploited an established parliamentary tradition and allowed it an expression which was beyond normal expectations.

The activities of the Reformation Parliament have been held to have increased the importance of the Commons at the expense of the Lords. It seems unlikely that Cromwell made a deliberate choice as to whether to introduce legislation in the Commons or in the Lords on the grounds that the Commons were more sympathetic to his policies than the Lords. He encountered opposition in both the Commons and the Lords and he had to win the assent of both to his measures. If he used the Commons as his base during the Reformation Parliament it was because he sat there and had acquired his experience of parliamentary procedure in the Commons. The decisive factor for the future importance of the Commons was not so much the role, given to it by Cromwell, as the growing quality of its members and their increasing influence in society.[19] His increase of numbers in the Commons and his decrease of numbers in the Lords was not conceived in terms of making the Nether House more powerful because it was more representative. Parliament as a whole was representative and Cromwell had no intention of upsetting the old order of precedence in parliament.

The immediate result of Cromwell's activities in parliament would seem to have been the elevation of its central figure, the King. Henry had all the personal qualities to make his presence felt in parliament. In 1543 Henry declared, 'And further we be informed by our judges that we at no time stand so highly in our estate royal as in time of parliament, wherein we as head and you as members are conjoined and knit together into one body politic . . . . .'.[20] In his statement Henry touched upon one of the reasons for crediting Cromwell with a part in the perpetuation of parliament in English monarchical government. The King had evidently been reassured by Cromwell's use of parliament that it enhanced rather than detracted from his royal estate. Cromwell had made parliament acceptable to a King who was notably sensitive to any challenge to his estate royal.

Having satisfied the head of the value of parliament as a means of expressing royal authority, Cromwell had to persuade the members of the body politic that parliament was the most effective and acceptable mode of exercising sovereign power in a lawful way. His sustained use of legislation in pursuit of policy and his renewal of the royal initiative in legislation proved the usefulness of parliament in the practical business of government but above all it impressed the political nation with the legality of the King's actions. While enactments in parliament had long been established as the way of affirming what was lawful, they assumed a particular significance in the light of the claim to imperial autonomy. The assumption that the realm of England was an Empire was associated in the mind of the King with his historic imperial crown. It was Cromwell's achievement to associate it with parliamentary legislation.

It was not so much by frequent sessions or by any changes in composition, procedure or privilege, that Cromwell gave parliament its hold upon the mind of the King and the political nation as by the occasion on which he asserted the competence of statute. He used the opportunity of the conflict with papal authority to settle in favour of statute the conflict with foreign jurisdictions. The employment of statute to secure the break with Rome ensured that parliament was indispensable to the lawful conduct of a government which did not recognise papal authority. In making statute the law upon which the legality of the body politic depended, Cromwell made parliament a necessary part of lawful government.

The success with which Cromwell made the King in parliament the legal basis of imperial autonomy depended to a large extent upon the already high status of statute in English law. Statute was held to be the most authoritative law in the land, taking no account of the authority of the Holy Roman Emperor and limiting the exercise of the authority of the Pope. Its intrusions into ecclesiastical matters were not challenged even by the Cardinal and Legate, Wolsey, who surrendered to them. The creative force of statute which gave it its superiority over the prerogative and the common law was recognised in the fifteenth century by the term *novel ley*. The old and experienced legal expert, Christopher St German, finding it difficult to assign plausible limits to the competence of statue, declared that it should conform to the law of reason and then went on to admit that statute could declare the law of reason. In 1532 the submission of the clergy subordinated canon law to statute.[21] The short step to the sovereignty of statute had been taken.

The potential of the competence of statute was illuminated by Thomas More's supposition that 'parliament would make a law that God should not be God'. For most practical purposes, however, the statutes did not challenge the hierarchy of the laws. While the distinction between human and divine law was not denied, the declaratory function of statute and its apparent ability to fix the effective limits of its competence gave statute the benefit of any doubts about its relationship to higher laws. The political situation did not encourage speculation about the legality of parliamentary acts. Men, like Gardiner, preferred to avoid the problems and accept that whatsoever was laid down in statute was legal and not to be further questioned. There was a greater emphasis upon the duty of obedience than upon the validity of the law among the political pamphleteers.[22] Since the acceptance and enforcement of the royal policy towards Rome depended upon the sovereignty of statute, it could be expected that it would be upon personal and patriotic loyalties rather than upon fine points of theory that respect for the acts of parliament would be based.

Within five years of Cromwell's fall the general admission of the sovereignty of parliament was described as 'the thirteenth article of our creed added of late, that whatsoever the parliament doth must needs be well done, and the parliament, or any proclamation out of parliament time, cannot err'. Henry Brinklow's comment on the thirteenth article of his countrymen's creed was made in protest at the sovereignty of parliament which appeared to him to be like the old papal tyranny writ large. Yet he made his appeal for reform to parliament. He called upon godly members of parliament to remedy the ungodly use of legitimate power. Although a victim of its legislation, he looked to parliament because he recognised no higher power on earth.[23]

Brinklow's thirteenth article was a tribute to Cromwell's parliamentary achievement. The development of parliament was, of course, conditioned by broad social, religious, governmental and intellectual trends of the time. But it was Cromwell who advocated the choice of parliamentary methods and applied them to the situation. His expertise in legislation and management made parliament the effective vehicle of change. His use of parliament satisfied the King that parliament was the appropriate instrument of royal policy and his subjects that it was the lawful engine of reform. He realised the potential of the existing parliamentary tradition and made explicit the capacity which was already implicit in parliament's past actions. However limited his choice was by the historic situation, Cromwell made the crucial choice to act through parliament. In so doing he gave his own peculiar twist to the great process of change. In the long run it was the role of parliament in great, necessary and urgent causes which determined its importance and survival.

10   THE MANIPULATION OF POWER

In order to keep his hold upon power Cromwell had not only to satisfy the King but also to win enough support from below to enable him to carry out the royal policies. He had to control the incentives and rewards of the King's patronage. He had to deal with the manoeuvres of hostile faction. To obtain the legislation which he required it was necessary for him to manage parliament. In justification of his measures he was obliged to direct a campaign of propaganda and to watch over the formation of opinion by education. The difficulties of the government in paying for services and in applying military force led to a certain sophistication in the manipulation of persons, institutions and opinion.

Cromwell's influence on the disposal of offices grew until by 1534 he was reported to have all the great offices of state in his gift. In 1540 he was still able to appoint his successors to the secretaryship, an office peculiarly subject to the King's personal choice. From beyond the ranks of officeholders he won acknowledgement of his control of patronage by satisfying suitors of every rank and description. Even the Duchess of Norfolk called upon him to persuade her husband to treat her better and the King to grant her favours. By 1536 the volume of suits required the special attention of one of his chaplains, Anthony Bellasis.[1]

Cromwell extended and directed royal patronage. Commissions multiplied. Offices in the central bureaucracy increased. More seats in the Commons were provided. In the provinces regional councils became centres of a wider royal patronage. Cromwell's intervention to exercise royal patronage at the expense of local systems of patronage led to an increasing centralisation of the determination of appointments, rewards and favours at the court. He extended his interest to the humblest posts and called upon established patrons to nominate his men. Borough patrons and authorities were charged with returning to the Commons the members whom he chose. For his extensive patronage within the City of London he thanked the accommodating officials who had allowed him to make so many appointments. The more successful he proved in securing places and favour the more the demand from below for his support grew.[2]

The break with Rome secured the ecclesiastical patronage of the

Crown and made episcopal appointments a royal monopoly. As Vicegerent, Cromwell obtained official control of the clerical patronage in which he had shown an interest since Wolsey's day. He took a prebend at Salisbury and a deanery at Wells for himself and made his trusted servant Rowland Lee a bishop.[3] The dissolution of the monasteries decreased ecclesiastical patronage but it vastly increased the King's capacity to reward the laity. The exchange of lands between the King and the bishops which was to the King's advantage also strengthened the resources of the Crown patronage to the benefit of the laity.

Cromwell feathered his nest with the official and unofficial proceeds of patronage. Besides acquiring broad lands and great offices, he held a host of minor posts, such as The Chancellorship of the University of Cambridge, the deanery of Wells, the wardenship of the Royal Forests North of Trent and the recordership of Bristol. His nepotism benefited his son, his nephew, Richard Cromwell, and his niece's husband, John Price. Yet Cromwell knew that patronage was held to be justified and even honourable provided that it was earned by service. He toiled for his own rewards and did not encourage parasites. Men whom he had known in Wolsey's service, like Gostwick and Brabazon, profited by his patronage, not because of old acquaintance but because of their abilities and service. Under Cromwell patronage remained a functional part of government and did not degenerate into favouritism.

Yet Cromwell's control of patronage had its limitations. Henry had his way with his favours as Cromwell discovered, when he admitted that he was unable to damage Cranmer's reputation with the King. It was difficult to regulate access to the King, who in assertive or affable mood, was not to be kept at a distance from suitors of any rank or persuasion. Those who attended the court or held a place in the royal Household took their opportunities. Courtiers served as stalking horses for more powerful men, as Cromwell learned, when at the beginning in his royal service, Sir John Wallop complained of him to the King. He used Sir Nicholas Carew in bringing down Anne Boleyn. He found it necessary to purge the Privy Chamber of supporters of his opponents, where they had created a rival source of counsel and a centre of court intrigue. The political aim of his reform of the Household was to extend his patronage within the Household and so deny rivals influence through the Privy Chamber.[4]

Patronage alone was an imperfect means of securing loyalty, when religious convictions, personal feuds and dynastic ambitions and honour were involved. Cromwell was not disposing of patronage to an organised party. Even in the administration the practice of holding offices for life and the limited field of trained men hindered the choice which he could make. Although he often promoted men of humble birth to ensure their dependence upon him, such men were, like himself, career men whose ultimate loyalty was to the King. It was patent that Cromwell exercised goodlordship by the King's favour. Yet Cromwell did attract certain personal loyalties. For those who could divine principles in his policies, he was a leader. He had a following of his own.

Intellectuals, like Starkey and Morison, served him because they were committed to his policies. Churchmen, like Cranmer, gave him their friendship for the same reason. Reformers, such as Coverdale and Taverner maintained relations with him from abroad because of his evangelical leanings. The projectors of schemes to edify the Commonwealth hopefully presented them to him. If he had a local following to compare with those of the provincial nobles, it was to be found in London among the leading merchants, officials in city government and more widely among the military forces of the city who felt honoured to be led on parade by him. Cromwell had a select following but it was heterogeneous and lacking in the broad appeal of tradition.[5]

The new element in Cromwell's following which disturbed his enemies was religious conviction. They saw him as the leader of a countrywide conspiracy of heretics, which they described in feudal terms as a retinue. Throughout the country there were protestant-minded gentlemen who supported him. In the Midlands the Markhams and Lascelles, in Yorkshire the eccentric Sir Francis Bigod, in Essex John Pylbarough who described himself as Cromwell's servant and dedicated a pious tract to Cromwell, in Gloucestershire Master Richard Tracy, who was indebted to Cromwell for aid over the posthumous heresy proceedings against his father, were typical of the men who, as Edward Hall put it, knew nothing but truth by Cromwell. Denying that he had a retinue, Cromwell spoke only of the members of his household whom, he claimed, were youths, sent by their parents for an upbringing. Yet parents can have had little doubt about the religion of a household where young men, like Bartholomew Traheron, who had visited Calvin and Zwingli and had brought back books from Bullinger for Cromwell, were accepted into service.[6]

Cromwell had a religious following but it was not an organised retinue. Those who shared Cromwell's evangelical and protestant attitudes were too few and not sufficiently of one mind to provide the sort of support which the puritans gave to Elizabethan lords. Cromwell could not give them a leadership based on outright doctrinal changes. He was inhibited from exploiting such religious support by his obedience to the King and the necessity of preserving the concord and unity of the realm. He was not prepared to precipitate a religious war. The need for moderation prevented him from fostering religious divisions. He could not afford to provoke another Pilgrimage of Grace.

It was as an heretical counsellor of the King rather than as a leader of a 'retinue' of heretics that Cromwell's religious influence was most often decried. At a time when humanist intellectuals saw counsel as the essence of politics, individual counsellors acquired especial importance. Yet the personalised politics of Henry's court derived as much from the dynasticism of the aristocracy as from the individualism of the humanists. The King's insistence upon the responsibility of each of his servants to himself and his failure to promote mutual trust among them encouraged lone wolves. His preference for a dominant minister threw into relief the figure of his chosen servant and prevented the emergence of a stable balance of faction.

In such a setting of personalised politics Cromwell's career looks like a series of duels. He defeated Thomas More in parliament and council by 1532, when More retired, and destroyed him in legal battle in 1535. He undermined the financial authority of Norfolk, the Lord Treasurer, took over his role in managing parliamentary elections and drove him from council by 1534. In 1536 he weakened the Howard connection by destroying the power of the Boleyns, eliminating Norfolk's influence in Ireland and attainting the Duke's half-brother, Thomas Howard. In the next year he thwarted Norfolk's ambitions in the North. His rival, Gardiner, he defeated over ecclesiastical policy in 1532 and robbed of the office of Secretary in 1534. Both Norfolk and Gardiner, however, retreated and lived to fight and to triumph over Cromwell on another day.[7]

Behind the clash of personalities there waxed and waned the forces of faction. Interests of family and status and profession, ambitions of haves and have-nots, mingled with religious convictions and assumptions about the proper ordering of society and government to produce an ever shifting pattern of association among those around the King. The role of the nobility in a strong royal government and of the local establishment in the face of royal intervention became issues in faction strife both at the court and in the provinces. The importance of diversity of opinion in religious matters in the creation of faction became clear in the 1530's, when religious commitment was seen to involve the royal authority and succession, foreign alliances and regional prosperity, as well as personal salvation. When a coalition of groups could be drawn to espouse policies and principles then faction became a political instrument.

Cromwell's dominant position made him at once an outsider and a key figure in faction politics. His hold on royal favour and the administration made him a man whose support or removal all factions desired. Yet he had to avoid the appearance of being a faction leader and represent himself as the servant of the King. His power ensured him a following of time-servers, eager for spoils, and the reluctant acquiescence of enemies, who were biding their time to strike him down, but it did not in itself inspire loyalties to him. His dependence on the King made him strong against opponents but weak in his commitment to his followers, since he was obliged to obey the King regardless of their expectations. Both his social rank and his political position made it difficult for him to organise or lead a strong faction.

While constitutional conventions recognised no accepted role or expression of opposition, Cromwell enjoyed the advantage of being able to define what was loyal and what was disloyal. His position enabled him to adopt an opportunist attitude towards factions, which was determined by his need to preserve his ascendancy. Obedience to the King had its advantages but its penalty was that Cromwell had to play a lone hand. He acted with factions but never surrendered his position above faction as the King's loyal servant.

The motives behind the faction strife were expressed within the framework of matrimonial politics which was imposed by the King. Since royal favour could best be won by support for his dynastic aims, the making of queens became a focus of politics and the queens became the figure-heads of faction. In the personalised politics of royal matrimony it was not surprising that some believed that the King's lust was the motor of his policies. Those with a deeper appreciation of politics knew that the change of a Queen meant a change of men about the King and an opportunity for new policies. A new Queen was the next best thing to a new King. They realised that dynastic manoeuvres affected both foreign and domestic politics and the King's attitude to a wide range of reforms.

Cromwell came to power by working with those who replaced Catherine of Aragon by Anne Boleyn. Catherine and later her daughter, Mary, came to stand for obedience to the Pope, alliance with the Emperor and the preservation of traditional religion. Her supporters became a loose-knit conservative opposition faction. Warham, Fisher and More opposed royal policy and gained some support in parliament, among certain religious houses in London and among those involved in the affair of the Maid of Kent. In defeating such opposition Cromwell secured the triumph of those who had destroyed Wolsey and established them as rivals of his influence.

By weakening the influence of Norfolk who with Suffolk gave strong noble support to the Boleyns, Cromwell sapped the strength of the new Queen's faction. A conspiracy, beginning amongst place-seeking courtiers, gave Cromwell the opportunity to investigate the rumours of the Queen's infidelities and to release Henry from his already irksome marriage. Norfolk and Suffolk saved themselves by abandoning the Queen. The Boleyn faction disintegrated. His opportunist intervention in court politics made Cromwell stronger than ever and placed him well to profit by the accession of the new Queen, Jane Seymour.[8]

The death of Catherine of Aragon and Anne Boleyn removed the old figure-heads of faction and allowed Cromwell to establish himself with the Seymours. His son's marriage to the new Queen's sister gave Cromwell a dynastic link with the dominant court circle. It was significant that Norfolk failed to make the marriage alliance with the Seymours, which he sought. Cromwell further consolidated his position by robbing the opposing factions of a figure-head, by inducing Mary to submit to the King. In this he had the aid of Jane Seymour who played the role of pacifier. Henry was persuaded to keep his wife out of politics and so to neutralise the political influence of the court.[9]

While Cromwell controlled the court through the Seymours, his dominance was challenged by certain northern nobles who had long been excluded from the counsels of the King. They used the Pilgrimage of Grace to bring their grievances to Henry's notice. Having failed to win Norfolk's support, they were doomed to be treated as a provincial rebellious faction. Their defeat made Cromwell strong enough to deny Norfolk the rewards of his loyalty to the King. It was the death of Jane Seymour late in 1537 which by freeing Henry to marry again seemed to open the way to a renewal of faction struggle.

Cromwell's diversion of Henry's interest to foreign marriage alliances removed queen-making from the cockpit of the court to the remoter prerogative field of foreign policy. At home it remained for Cromwell to deal with the legacy of lost causes in the domestic dynastic politics of the past, Yorkist hopes, loyalties to the memory of Catherine of Aragon and the grievances of the Pole family. The adherents of such lost causes were destroyed by the exposure in 1538 of the so-called Exeter conspiracy.[10] The evidence of their support for a treasonable claim to the throne was in the dynastic idiom which masked the varied motives of the politics of the time.

Cromwell made Anne of Cleves Henry's next Queen in 1539. In the dynastic politics at court it seemed as if Cromwell was now supreme. He had, however, underrated the tenacity of Norfolk and Gardiner who had always backed down before his challenges in the past. Between them they managed the coup which brought Cromwell down. The alliance of traditionalist clerics and nobles created a faction which Cromwell was powerless to counter because for the first time his rivals had the support of the King. It was characteristic of court politics that even the triumph of Norfolk and Gardiner was cast in the dynastic mould. Their trump card was Catherine Howard, the King's next Queen.

Up to 1539 Cromwell had been both fortunate and successful in the removal of his opponents. In 1532 Archbishop Warham died, More retired and Gardiner lost the King's trust. Following Wolsey's example in employing rivals away from court, Cromwell had contrived to keep Gardiner on ambassadorial and Norfolk on military duties far from the royal presence. On Anne Boleyn's fall he had prevented her devoted Thomas Cranmer from seeing the King. He managed to deprive the opposition to himself of effective leadership at court and to isolate the King from his rivals in moments of decision. It was his failure to prevent the return of Norfolk and Gardiner to court in 1539 and 1540 that had proved fatal to him.[11]

If Cromwell's absorption in parliamentary business in early 1540 gave his enemies their chance to mount a coup against him, it was an understandable lapse. Parliament was his chosen instrument of policy and in his hour of peril it was in parliament that he was most likely to vindicate himself and prove himself indispensable to the King. Throughout his career in the royal service he had devoted himself to the management of parliament. His own entry to the Commons in 1529 showed that he knew enough about elections to dodge the unwelcome patronage of the Duke of Norfolk and still gain a seat. Lacking Norfolk's power to dispose of a dozen seats, Cromwell set about organising direct royal intervention in elections. He expected candidates to have the royal approval which he had sought for himself in 1529. He kept lists of members and noted vacancies. In 1533 his call to patrons to serve the King by providing seats for approved candidates at by-elections was well received. That the passage of the Act of Appeals was later remembered as being due to the fact that 'few would displease my Lord Privy Seal' was a sign of his grip upon parliamentary patronage by 1533.[12]

To the election of 1536 Cromwell applied his electoral experience. He was outraged that the royal interest had not been consulted at Canterbury, where members had been elected with a haste that rightly suggested to him a local coup. He refused to tolerate the flouting of royal patronage and demanded another election. The city authorities, acknowledging their fault, ensured the unanimous election of Cromwell's nominees. In 1539 he mobilised friendly nobles, such as the Earl of Southampton, and sheriffs and county gentry to produce knights and burgesses who knew their duty. He challenged the sway of hostile patrons, such as Gardiner, who, as Bishop of Winchester, had his own candidates. He placed his spokesman, Richard Morison, in the Commons and mustered the support of those who would take advice as the price of a seat. With his usual enthusiasm he informed the King that he and his fellow councillors had done their duty and that his Majesty 'had never more tractable parliament.'[13]

In informing the electoral authorities at Canterbury in 1536 of the King's 'trust and expectation', Cromwell disregarded local patronage. The complaint of Robert Aske, leader of the Pilgrimage of Grace, that 'the old custom was that none of the King's servants should be of the Commons house; yet most of that House were King's servants' revealed the reaction to Cromwell's successful electoral management. Demands made in the Pilgrimage of Grace showed that there was a belief that local representation had suffered. The resentment was not against patronage but against the predominance of royal patronage.[14]

The complaints were exaggerated for Cromwell's electoral management did not produce parliaments which were quite as tractable as he claimed. It was necessary to silence dissident voices by inducing their owners to absent themselves at certain times. In 1534 Cromwell induced Sir George Throgmorton and Sir Marmaduke Constable, who with other papist gentlemen discussed parliamentary affairs in the Queen's Head tavern, to stay away from the Commons. In the same session Bishops, Fisher, Nix, Lee and Tunstall deemed it wise not to attend in the Lords, as did the Earl of Northumberland, the lords Darcy and Hussey and the majority of the abbots in 1536. Cromwell made it plain that the better part of loyalty was absence.[15]

Cromwell had experience of business in the Commons in 1523 and in the eight sessions from 1529 to 1536. Cavendish's claim that Cromwell swayed the Commons on behalf of Wolsey, Cromwell's care in preparing a speech for the Commons in 1523 and his eagerness to place his propagandist, Richard Morison, in the Commons in 1539 suggest that he did not underrate the power of rhetoric to persuade the Commons. Perhaps, more important as a means of carrying the House with him was his meticulous preparation of legislation. By careful drafting, forceful preambles of justification and clauses, safeguarding vested interests, he sought to expedite the passage of bills. His expertise was recognised as early as 1531, when he was reported as having 'penned certain matters in the parliament house which no man gainsaid'. In preparing the Act of Appeals he held preliminary talks with clerics and laymen. In these ways he reduced amendments and the chances of opposition. To him the advantages of taking the initiative with a well prepared programme were clear.[16]

When Audley followed Thomas More as Speaker, Cromwell was assured of the support of the man who controlled the debates and procedure of the Commons. Humphrey Wingfield, a burgess for Yarmouth, followed Audley in 1533. In the brief parliament of 1536 Cromwell's protégé, Richard Rich, took the chair. Nicholas Hare was Speaker in 1539. Wingfield and Hare had been lawyers for Wolsey and became Cromwell's men. A confused report suggests that contemporaries suspected that Cromwell arranged the election of speakers in accord with the tradition that he should be a man acceptable to the King.[17] Their suspicions were, no doubt, justified.

Of most importance in the handling of parliament were the powers of its most influential member, the King. Cromwell used them to summon, prorogue and dissolve parliament and to prolong or postpone sessions. In the King's speech he could take the initiative in parliamentary business. The King himself could give a lead, as he did over the Answer of the Ordinaries, use blackmail, as he did over the Statute of Uses, and make personal appearances, and press for unusual moves, like a division as over the bill on annates. Henry was not Cromwell's puppet in dealing with parliament. He showed a sure touch both before and after Cromwell's ascendancy. Yet the Commons were right to suspect that, when Henry was well prepared to meet their deputation, it was Cromwell who had informed the King of what was afoot. In the last resort Cromwell managed parliament for the King, who alone could command its loyalty. In 1539 Henry's intervention had secured the Act of Six Articles and in 1540 he gave his assent to the Act of Attainder which condemned Cromwell of treason.[18]

It had been Cromwell's task to maintain the loyalty to the King. In it he had the aid of the King who was an accomplished showman in his own right. The court demonstrated royal power and magnificence. Cromwell, however, was too conscious of the cost to elaborate the spectacle of court life. While he took part in the ceremonial of great occasions, he did not encourage the King to indulge in the extravagant pageantry and lavish court life which Henry had enjoyed in his youth. The military review which he led in London was no Field of the Cloth of Gold. He arranged an impressive welcome for Anne of Cleves, but the wedding was a quiet affair. He did not cultivate the costly splendour which Wolsey made characteristic of his propagandist gestures.

The actions taken to enforce policy were staged to affect public opinion. Trials, executions and burnings which had been traditionally used to impress the public were continued. The trial of Elizabeth Barton discredited the King's opponents. The execution of Fisher and More was an assertion of the King's claims in defiance of foreign opinion. Cromwell took part in the much publicised demonstration in Smithfield against popery and superstition, when Dr Forest and the Welsh image Darvell Gadern were burned in the presence of the Council and a large crowd, assembled to hear Latimer preach. Another telling display in 1538 was the exposure at Maidstone, then before the Court, and finally before the populace of London of the mechanisms which gave the Rood of Boxley its deceptively miraculous responses. At the peak of the campaign against superstition in that year Cromwell presided over the burning of images in Chelsea.[19]

Foxe spoke of Cromwell as 'seeking all means and ways to beat down false religion and advance the true'. His methods ranged from the destruction of shrines and the ruin of great religious houses to the toleration, if not the active encouragement of anticlerical plays and interludes. He gave some small patronage to the author John Bale, of the antipapal play, *King John*. His campaign against the memory and memorials of St Thomas Becket had a symbolic significance which was not lost upon the public. Dramatic iconoclasm made plain for those with eyes to see the changing emphases of reform.[20]

If Cromwell had not encouraged the artistry of pageantry and his iconoclasm had been destructive of medieval art, he nevertheless fostered the contemporary arts of portraiture, engraving and printing. His patronage of Holbein, leading to the appointment of Holbein as King's painter in 1537, provided an impressive regal image for the King, which was a masterpiece of visual propaganda. He arranged for Holbein to depict the King's prospective brides and his secretary, Richard Morison, composed lines, appended to the artist's portrait of the infant, Edward Tudor. Holbein designed the frontispiece for Coverdale's Bible and another artist engraved that of the Great Bible of 1539.[21]

Cromwell's taste for biblical exposition in the protestant manner revealed his preference for the literal interpretation. Direct action and words and realism in art rather than the still popular symbolic and allegorical approach characterised his propaganda. He was a man of the Word who found in the printed and spoken word the most appealing means of information and persuasion. His conduct of public relations in government relied heavily on a protestant emphasis on preaching and the use of the newer medium of communication, the printing press.

Through the licensing of preaching and by injunction and proclamation he was able to determine largely the topic and message of sermons. In London from 1535 to 1539 he was able to ensure through Bishop Hilsey that favourable preachers were chosen for the popular outdoor pulpit at St Paul's Cross. He did not go so far as to accept a proposal to print sermons for every curate, but he did show an interest in printing any sermon by well known traditionalists, like Tunstall, which supported government policy. The Church provided him with a large audience which he persuaded and instructed through the pulpit and the Church door, where proclamations and acts of parliament were posted.[22]

Besides realising the importance of argument and assertion, Cromwell understood the value of making clear the King's intentions and demands. The royal policies, announced to the body of the realm in parliament, were publicised by the distribution of printed statutes, proclamations and pamphlets. Care was taken to ensure that such publications were publicly read in places where there were the largest audiences. Cromwell's peculiar instrument was the circular letter. Under signet seal and sign manual circular letters were sent to bishops, justices of assize and of the peace to make them aware of the King's views and requirements.[23] For Cromwell information as much as argument was an important means of government.

In 1529 the Council began to exercise censorship so that Cromwell was able to continue an activity which had formerly been the province of the ecclesiastical authorities. In 1534 an Act of attainder was used as authority for the destruction of hostile works. Proclamations on censorship were issued in 1535, 1536 and 1538. Recognising that the printing press made the suppression of books difficult, Cromwell preferred to confine censorship to works, like service books, which were subject to official checking, or to prosecute the authors or possessors of offensive works, who were vulnerable to charges of heresy or treason. He encouraged the voluntary surrender of, and condemned in general, 'seditious and over-thwartly framed books' but he did not follow Wolsey's practice of listing prohibited works. Unrestricted by such lists, he was free to tolerate works which his opponents condemned as heretical.[24] It was indicative of his sympathies that he felt that he had more to lose by strict censorship than by allowing a comparatively free circulation to the products of the printing press.

On the orchestration of official pamphleteering,[25] Cromwell probably began to exercise his influence in 1532 with the publication of *The Glass of Truth*, reputed to be the King's composition and devoted to his case for annulling his marriage. Late in 1533 came the *Articles* from the Council, asserting the rectitude of recent actions and emphasising the competence of parliament and the limitation of papal claims. By mid 1534 a *Little Treatise* was issued at Cromwell's instigation to defend the Supremacy against the charge of innovation. In the same and following year he attempted without much popular success to raise the level of debate by having prepared by William Marshall English translations of the old antipapal classics, *De Donatione Constantini Magni* by Lorenzo Valla and an edited version of the *Defensor Pacis* by Marsilio of Padua.

To meet continental criticism Cromwell in 1534 induced Edward Fox and Richard Sampson to produce latin treatises defending the supremacy. To justify the execution of Fisher and More he was constrained to prepare latin letters to the English ambassadors at the French and Papal Courts. In 1537 he published a latin work by Morison replying to an attack by Cochlaeus on the King's divorce. The papal call for a General Council forced responses in a *Protestation*, declaring that no prince is bound to attend the pretended council, and in *An Epistle from Henry VIII to the Emperor,* issued a year later in 1538.

Opposition at home produced the magnificently disdainful royal Answers to the Lincolnshire and Yorkshire rebels, which asserted royal policy and declared the support of parliament and council for them. Morison attacked the same rebels in his *Lamentation* and *Remedy for Sedition.* He was employed again to write against the traitors of the Exeter Conspiracy in his *Invective* and to rally support for foreign policy in *An Exhortation to stir all Englishmen to the defence of their country.* In 1538, presumably for the benefit of lawyers, the King's printer published *A Treatise proving by the King's laws that the Bishop of Rome had never right to any supremacy within this realm.*

Among all these pamphlets there was *An Exhortation to Unity* by Thomas Starkey, issued in 1536, which had particularly attracted Cromwell's attention. It countered the charge by Pole that the Supremacy had ruptured the unity of Christendom. It was not particularly good propaganda and was not an important source of adiaphoristic thinking in England. It was, however, typical of Cromwell's attitudes and elicited the advice from him to the author to emphasise the need for moderation. It was an example of the Erasmian thinking which Cromwell found congenial.

Although Cromwell seems to have cared little about his personal popularity, he was sensitive to public opinion on matters of policy. In his office arguments were prepared and cases were drafted ready for publication, if required. He took the need for propaganda seriously and provided justifications at all levels and for all audiences. He made pamphleteering an official activity and directed it with a sense of occasion. Yet it was ironical that, despite his patronage and commissions, he failed to produce the classic pamphlets of the time. Royal prejudice forced him to turn down the chance of employing Tyndale, one of the most effective writers of the age in 1531. Christopher St German, the most percipient of legal writers, appears to have worked independently. Although Cromwell may have helped in persuading him to write, Stephen Gardiner, his enemy, was to produce in *De Vera Obedientia* the classic defence of the Supremacy.

Cromwell's concern with propaganda went deeper than a purely political purpose. He wished to bring a moral order to the political and social world. His reason and his moral sense required some satisfaction. The conviction that true religion was connected with the political success and the physical well-being of the Commonwealth through the ways of Providence, encouraged Cromwell to go beyond the officially sponsored propaganda. He patronised the moderate Lutheran author, Richard Taverner. He lent his support to the translation into English of

works by Erasmus and Capito. His cultivation of pious works of
Erasmian and Lutheran origin went beyond the call of political duty
and laid him open to the charge of circulating 'great numbers of false
erroneous books'. As well as the tactics of political persuasion he
employed the strategy of religious conversion.[26]

In pursuit of this stategic aim Cromwell produced his most effective
piece of propaganda, the Great English Bible in 1539. With the aid of
his old Lutheran friend, Miles Coverdale, he procured an English Bible
which, he hoped, would banish the 'old ignorance and blindness'. The
design to place an English Bible in every parish church was an attempt
to enlighten the public. He believed that the setting forth of the Word
of God was a duty of the King, vital to the 'virtuous maintenance of his
commonwealth'. In the imperialist image of the King, armed with a
sword and a book, Cromwell saw the sources of temporal and spiritual
power, because he took it for granted that the book was not the Codex
of the Laws, but the Bible.[27]

If virtue was fortified by a knowledge of the Word of God, learning
was the product of education. For Cromwell the purpose of education
was to train both the laity and the clergy to 'profit the commonwealth
with their counsel and wisdom'. His was the humanist view of
preparation for the active life. For his son, Gregory, he approved a
curriculum including the study of the works of Erasmus, English and
Ancient history, music, dancing and exercise with arms. He provided
for his son the sort of education which Sir Thomas Elyot was advocating
for the ruling class. While Starkey proposed a compulsory education for
all, which would be suited to rank and talents, Cromwell accepted the
need for children to be brought up to some occupation so that idleness
would be avoided and the prosperity of the commonwealth
promoted.[28]

In the personal patronage of schools Cromwell did not show the active
concern of his colleague, Thomas Audley. Only on behalf of Wolsey did
he help in the founding of a college and a school. By the dissolution of
the monasteries he reduced the provision of education. He had little
enthusiasm for the conversion of religious houses into schools, but he
did consider with Cranmer plans to expand the facilities for the
education of the clergy in collegiate institutions. He followed Wolsey in
promoting the provision of a standard latin grammar for schools.
Perhaps, his own experience suggested that encouragement of the desire
for education was more important than the provision of the means. It
was notable that his demand for higher standards from the clergy
stressed self-education by Bible reading rather than the provision of
theological training.[29]

On the universities Cromwell's policies had considerable effect. While
the number of students was reduced by the abolition of the religious

orders, he made provision in the injunctions of 1536 for students to benefit by the patronage of the secular clergy. The fear that the dissolution might threaten the possessions of the colleges was not realised. By his support for scholars at both universities and by sending his son to Cambridge, Cromwell showed some encouragement for the education of laymen at the universities. His abolition of degrees in canon law and his fostering of humanist and biblical studies strengthened the move towards the New Learning which was already affecting scholars and adding new subjects to the range of teaching at the universities. The purging of the libraries in the universities led his commissioners to exaggerate their victory over the scholastic tradition and to declare that at Oxford they had 'set Duns in Bocardo'. It is, however, clear that, if, as Chancellor of the University of Cambridge from 1536, Cromwell maintained the old discipline in behaviour and in the relations of town and gown, in the discipline of studies he favoured the humanist reformers. His advocacy of regius appointments extended royal patronage in the universities and stressed the ideal of education for the profit of the commonwealth.[30]

While Cromwell bore the responsibility for the execution of policy, he had to do whatever was possible to carry the King's subjects with him. He learned to bend their ambitions to the tasks of government by his exercise of patronage. He knew how to exploit the rivalries of faction to his own ends. His management of parliament enabled him to win the assent of those who represented the body of the realm to the laws which enshrined policy. His propaganda appropriated the powerful reforming ideas, associated with Erasmus and Luther, to forwarding his aims. His demand of education was that it should provide learned and wise servants of the King to counsel him in performing the duty of rulers 'to advance, set forth, and increase their commonwealths'. That he achieved so much in so short a tenure of power suggests that Cromwell understood how to manage and persuade his countrymen.

11   ZENITH AND NADIR

At the beginning of 1539 Thomas Cromwell could look back on the decade since the fall of Wolsey with some satisfaction. By 1534 he had become secretary to the King and had ousted his opponents from the council. During the next two years he became Vicegerent in Spirituals and Lord Privy Seal. Generally his policies had prospered. The strongest gesture against them, the Pilgrimage of Grace had been suppressed. Yet Cromwell was aware that he could not afford to drop his guard. He had taken great risks and he warned his servants of the ever present threat, posed by his enemies in the church and amongst the nobility.[1]

The struggle to keep his hold upon affairs at home was made all the more difficult by the changes abroad. The isolation of England which had resulted from his break with Rome was made plain in January, 1539, when Francis I and the Emperor, Charles V, agreed in the treaty of Toledo not to negotiate with England separately. During his years of office Cromwell had built up the defensive power of the realm but he had failed to establish any permanent system of alliances on the continent to counter the hostility of the Emperor. His energies had been concentrated upon domestic affairs and he had not been able to gain the King's full confidence in foreign policy. In 1523 Henry had not been responsive to his advice upon the need to concentrate upon the conquest of Scotland. During 1530's the King had not been ready to commit himself to an alliance with the German princes.[2]

Although in moments of crisis Henry had been prepared to entertain negotiations with the Lutheran princes as a temporary expedient, he had never shared Cromwell's leaning to a European protestant alliance. That alliance which Barnes had worked to obtain by negotiations in Germany and Denmark as early as 1532 was, it seemed to Cromwell, continuously thwarted by the King's refusal to make the doctrinal concessions to Lutheranism, which were the price of an alliance with the Schmalkaldic League of German protestant princes. Cromwell's hopes of stabilising English foreign policy foundered upon Henry's suspicion of heresy and the King's preference for the risky game of manipulating the divergent interests of Valois and Hapsburg rulers. Henry liked to treat the King of France and the Emperor as his equals.

The threatening situation created by the treaty of Toledo gave Cromwell his chance to revive at least an indirect alliance with the German princes and to take the lead in foreign policy and to become a Queen-maker. In placing the personal and political charms of Anne of Cleves above those of Christina, the widowed duchess of Milan, he was urging Henry to ally with a German prince rather than with the Emperor. Anne of Cleves was the daughter of Duke John of Cleves, who had, like Henry, thrown off the papal authority without adopting an avowedly heretical doctrine and who was father-in-law to the Elector of Saxony, the leading member of the Lutheran Schmalkaldic League. As Cromwell saw, a treaty with the Duke of Cleves was not a direct alliance with open heresy but would, nevertheless, provide a strong link with the protestant princes. It would also make Cromwell a Queen-maker and foster protestant hopes at home.

It did not prove an easy solution. Duke John died in February 1539 and his successor, Anne's brother, roused the Emperor's wrath by uniting his inheritance, Gelderland, with Cleves. The union of the Duchies was a provocation which drew Francis I and the Emperor closer together. They warned Henry off the Cleves alliance by withdrawing their ambassadors from the English court in late February and by arresting English shipping in the ports of the Netherlands. In March Cromwell responded by mobilising the levies of the southern and south-western counties and by raising the forces on the Border to deter Scottish intervention. The threat of invasion seemed real but it slowly subsided. In late March the French ambassador returned to England, but it was not until an imperial fleet, concentrated in the Downs, withdrew in late April that the immediate danger seemed to be past.[3]

Meanwhile Cromwell prepared for parliament on 28th April. In managing the elections he was obstructed by Gardiner, who, as Bishop of Winchester, wanted to make his own nominations. It did not stop Cromwell from obtaining a tractable parliament but it was a sign of the opposition that he could expect from Gardiner, who led the conservative bishops. Since Cromwell had in mind a device in parliament for unity in religion, Gardiner's hostility was significant. While Cromwell was issuing the Great Bible in April, Gardiner was preaching at court. A struggle for influence over ecclesiastical policy between the two was to be predicted in the coming parliament.[4]

When parliament opened, Cromwell from his place in the Lords had a full programme to support. There were further schemes for the defence of the realm. The aftermath of the Exeter conspiracy had to be cleared up by attainders which put the Countess of Salisbury and Lady Montague in the Tower and convicted Reginald Pole of treason.

Cromwell supervised the passage of the attainders and produced the evidence. There was a bill to legalise past and future surrenders of monastic houses. Another bill to set up new bishoprics and provide for education and poor relief was introduced to demonstrate that monastic wealth was being put to good use. While the problem of vagabondage was tackled in another measure for poor relief. On such matters Cromwell encountered little opposition.[5]

When the council tried to put through a bill to make proclamations more effective, there was a rumpus. Gardiner later recalled the long debate in the Lords. Legal quibbles, it would seem, gave Cromwell's opponents a chance to attack the government. Despite redrafting, the council obtained the measures which they desired to give force to proclamations.[6] More serious opposition to Cromwell came over the plan to obtain uniformity in doctrine and practice in the Church of England. While everyone was united upon the need for unity and concord in religion the terms upon which they should be established were open to profound disagreement.

Cromwell with the two archbishops and six bishops formed a committee to give effect to the King's desire to abolish diversity of opinion. The balance of innovators and traditionalists in the committee suggests that Cromwell was hoping to establish a compromise and that the middle way which had been hinted at in proclamations on 26th February and 1st April would become the law of the land. Cromwell's device for unity in religion depended for its success upon his control of each stage in the process of authorising the middle way.[7]

In the event it was an auspicious moment for those who wished to reassert tradition and halt religious change at home and withdraw from a protestant connection abroad. In the light of Charles V's truce with the Lutherans at the diet of Frankfort and the return of the French ambassador Henry deemed it wise to dissociate himself from heresy. His conservative instincts told him that the dangerous diversity of opinion which destroyed the unity and concord of his realm arose from recent innovations. If those, who regarded Cromwell's middle way as half way to heresy, could manoeuvre the King into taking the initiative there was a strong chance that the unity imposed by parliament upon religion would be an affirmation of traditional doctrine and practice.

Without waiting for a pronouncement by Cromwell's committee, Norfolk launched a debate in the Lords on six points of religion. Cranmer and the reformers were overwhelmed in parliament and in convocation. Worse still for Cromwell's hopes, Norfolk and Gardiner were able to persuade the King to take an interest and to prorogue parliament for a week, while he could be persuaded by them to make up his mind on the issues before parliament. When the King, prompted by Norfolk and Gardiner, took the initiative, Cromwell lost control. Henry even appeared in parliament to air his theological learning and sway it in favour of the traditionalists' formulation of six articles which emerged in debate.[8]

The resulting Act of Six Articles, affirmed the real presence in the sacrament of the Altar, and asserted that communion in both kinds was not necessary for the laity, that priests should not marry, that vows of chastity ought to be observed, and that private masses and auricular confession should continue. Cromwell could do no more than leave it to Audley to try to ease the effect of the Act upon reformers. The orthodox view of the mass had been established and the position of the priesthood restored. Cromwell had failed to obtain parliamentary authority for the middle way.

The Act was a setback to reformers at home. Cranmer sent his wife back to Germany. Latimer and Shaxton resigned their sees. The Lutheran envoys departed and withdrew their support for the Cleves alliance. Abroad Melanchthon and the Elector of Saxony expressed their dismay. Cromwell's domestic policy on a religious settlement and his foreign policy of alliance with Cleves appeared to be ruined. Although ill with fever in late April and early May, Cromwell had not, as More had done, pleaded ill-health and resigned.[9] He was too experienced a politician to abandon hope. His determination to survive revealed his ambition and love of power but it also showed his sense of calling. In his political defeat he may have recognised the random stroke of Machiavelli's Fortuna but he knew from his Bible about the strange workings of Providence.

With the prorogation of parliament the temporary ascendancy of Gardiner and Norfolk over the King in religious matters disappeared. Cromwell reasserted his position as Vicegerent by appointing moderates and reformers to the episcopate. Capon and Bell replaced Latimer and Shaxton and Bonner was appointed to the important see of London, when the die-hard Stokesley died. He twice postponed parliament in order to keep Gardiner and Norfolk from the court and the King. He evaded any widespread persecution of reformers under the terms of the Six Articles Act. By October it was being said on the continent that the Six Articles Act was the work of a minority which had already lost royal favour. Cromwell retained his hold on the levers of power.[10]

Meanwhile Duke William of Cleves declared in July his assent to the marriage of his sister to the King of England. Another rapprochement between the Valois and Hapsburg monarchs made the offer politically attractive. Cromwell argued that the alliance with Cleves would mean the support of the Elector of Saxony, that it would give Henry the opportunity to exercise a moderating influence on religious extremism in Germany and that it would produce heirs to strengthen the Tudor succession. Henry was won over to the need for allies in Germany but he tried in great secrecy to explore the chances of marrying his daughter, Mary, to Philip of Bavaria. His failure led him to accept the marriage alliance with Cleves in October. Cromwell had succeeded in regaining control of foreign policy.[11]

On 27th December Anne of Cleves landed in England. Cromwell's presence in the forefront of the welcome to the royal bride was a sign of his desire to identify himself with the triumphant culmination of negotiations. On 1st January, Henry, unable to restrain his curiosity, unexpectedly rode to Rochester to view the bride. It was a disastrous encounter. Henry had taken a dislike to Anne. But with Charles V being cordially entertained in Paris it was a time for political considerations to triumph. Within a week Henry was wedded to Anne in her room at Greenwich. Henry made it plain that his bride was not as attractive as she had been represented. As the architect of the alliance Cromwell spoke of Anne's regal bearing and did nothing to encourage the King's regret. Since there was no personal basis to the King's marriage it remained to see how long the political basis for it would last.[12]

In the spring of 1540 Francis and Charles were once again at loggerheads and Henry took the initiative in stirring up the hostility between them. In February Henry sent Norfolk to Paris to win Francis to the Anglo-Cleves alliance and foment suspicions between Francis and Charles. Cromwell could do little but follow the King's lead. On his return Norfolk exploited his diplomatic success by advertising the French King's opinion that the dismissal of Cromwell would do much to promote better relations between himself and Henry. Henry did not abandon Cromwell to please Francis I, but, when in April he ignored a friendly letter from the Elector of Saxony, it was clear that he had abandoned Cromwell's policy.[13]

Meanwhile at home Gardiner set a trap for Cromwell. He accused Barnes, Cromwell's friend and the champion of the German protestant alliance, of heresy and managed to draw the King into the theological disputation. After recanting, Barnes proved defiant and Gardiner called upon the King once again. Henry put Barnes and two supporters in the Tower while he considered the matter.[14] Gardiner had delivered a series of indirect blows at Cromwell. He showed up Cromwell's inaction over enforcing the Six Articles and gained from the King a condemnation of Lutheran doctrine. He had put in the Tower a known supporter of Cromwell's friendly policy to protestant powers and had cast doubt upon Cromwell's good lordship and ability to protect his supporters.

Cromwell could only avoid Gardiner's trap by refusing to identify himself in the eyes of the King with the heretical Barnes. He met Gardiner's attack by a gesture of reconciliation. On 30th March they dined together in apparent amity. Their meeting indicated that

Cromwell was no longer sure of his superiority and that he was aware that he was being obliged to share the royal favour with dangerous rivals. At court there was resentment at his reform of the Household which had taken effect late in 1539. His reluctant farewell to the envoys of Saxony and Hesse in January had further depressed the morale of his protestant supporters. The challenge to his influence in ecclesiastical and foreign policy led to rumours that he was to be replaced by Tunstall in the Vicegerency and that he was only holding on to power by doing whatever Henry demanded regardless of his own policies.[15]

Yet those, who believed that Cromwell was finished, underrated his high place in Henry's esteem. When the twice delayed parliament met on 12th April, Cromwell had the opportunity to demonstrate once again his mastery of affairs. He immediately sought to reestablish his lead in religious matters by a long speech on the need for unity and concord in religion. After attacking both superstition and heresy, he asserted that the King rejected both and was determined to establish true doctrine and the rule of the Scriptures in order to achieve unity. Cromwell was announcing in public the King's adherence to the middle way, based on the authority of the Bible and avoiding the new heresy and the old superstition. Although he had succeeded in reopening the question of religious uniformity, the two commissions set up to deal with doctrine and practice were not under his control and that on doctrine was dominated by Gardiner and his supporters.[16]

In handling the rest of the parliamentary business Cromwell seemed determined to secure as many of his measures as he could. In major matters he finished off the last of the religious orders, the Order of Knights Hospitallers of St John, bestowing their wealth upon the King, and proposed massive taxation.[17] His sense of purpose and grasp of legislative policy was as strong as ever. It was clear that he was still the most effective and competent of the King's servants. Henry had no doubts about Cromwell's ability and, however disastrous the alliance with Cleves had proved, was prepared to reward him.

On 18th April, 1540, Cromwell was created Earl of Essex in the palace at Westminster and given the office of Lord Chamberlain. They were the great rewards with which Henry recognised his loyal servant's past services. They followed quickly upon Cromwell's relinquishment of the secretaryship. They confirmed that he did not leave his office under a cloud. The King allowed him to nominate his successors, Sadler and Wriothesley, to the now shared secretaryship.[18] He had 'made the secretaryship his centre of power but in vacating it he was not losing power. He carried his personal influence with him. With high office in the Royal Household and with an earldom Cromwell was changing from the drudgery of administration to the task of counselling which befitted an elder statesman and great noble. His influence enhanced by his new honours was reinforced in council by his two protégés in the secretaryship.

When on 23rd April, on the Feast of St George, Cromwell sat in his stall, one of the five earls present at the chapter of the Order of the Garter, it seemed to all appearances that he had reached the zenith of his career.[19] He knew that Fortune's wheel did not stand still and that the mighty were humbled. He was aware of the forces ranged against him and of the growing initiative of his rivals, Gardiner and Norfolk, but he cannot have anticipated how close he was to the sudden descent to his nadir. In April, 1540, it seemed just and appropriate that he had been granted the social honours to match his political achievement, his wealth and his style of life.

The splendour of Cromwell's status was the fruit of political power. It was, however, a glory that reflected the royal favour. No other loyalties supported him. He was not rooted in social esteem like the older nobility whose role was taken for granted. He had risen too rapidly to become established in his new nobility. Norfolk worked to ensure that no one forgot the origins of the Earl of Essex. Of the nobles who had been friendly towards Cromwell, Wiltshire had died, Southampton had turned against him and Russell was to prove disloyal. He had served only the house of Tudor. In the eyes of the common people and many of the clergy he remained a parvenu. Amongst his colleagues in the government personal ambitions and rivalries outweighed any regard they had for him. Bureaucrats who were loyal to the King did not expect to fall along with their masters. Cromwell was unable to inspire the loyalty which Wolsey had drawn from him. Only Ralph Sadler who owed him so much and the Archbishop, Thomas Cranmer, who sympathised with some of his aims were to make belated gestures of friendship when he fell from favour.[20]

Even as he was making his first ceremonial appearances in his dignity as Earl of Essex, Cromwell was aware of a new and dangerous rival for the King's favour. In April Norfolk had put forward his kinswoman, Catherine Howard, to catch the King's fancy. Gardiner arranged meetings between the King and Catherine at Winchester House in Southwark, where the King's visits made it apparent to all London that he had a new mistress. Norfolk and Gardiner believed that they had found a young woman who could not only gain the King's affections but also the Queen's throne. Henry's emotions had been engaged to the advantage of Cromwell's opponents.[21] The prospects of a new dispensation at court under a Howard Queen drew support towards Cromwell's enemies.

The continental situation favoured the plans of Cromwell's rivals. Having crushed the uprising in Ghent, Charles V was turning his attention to the Duke of Cleves who called upon his ally Henry VIII. To be dragged into conflict with the Emperor on behalf of Cleves was not in Henry's view the purpose of the alliance with the Duke. While Francis I was building fortifications in the neighbourhood of Calais, Henry had no wish to be embroiled with the Emperor. By May Henry decided to approach Charles V, who was now at loggerheads with the French King over Milan, and disclaim support for Cleves.[22] The collapse of the political basis for the royal marriage was now as apparent as the failure of the personal relationship between the King and his wife.

The hopes of those whose prospects centred upon Catherine Howard grew. To retain the political initiative Cromwell was in the position of having to propose some way of ending the marriage of which he had been a strong advocate. Yet to remove Anne was to clear the way for Catherine Howard and through her for Norfolk and Gardiner to the favour of the King. It was a dilemma which inhibited Cromwell from action. This was the dangerous consequence of the Cleves marriage for Cromwell. The marriage had not been successful in any way but it had not alienated the King. Cromwell had just been rewarded with an earldom. The danger arose from the fact that, because the marriage had not been to the King's personal liking, he was all the more susceptible to an infatuation for Catherine Howard, the candidate of Cromwell's rivals. Cromwell had no alternative to Catherine. His only hope was to discredit the would-be Queen-makers.

The charge to which his enemies with their conservative sympathies were most vulnerable was that of supporting papal pretensions. But Norfolk and Gardiner were too close to the King to be openly accused by Cromwell who had to begin by stirring up suspicions and striking as near to them as he dared. Lord Lisle, the King's deputy at Calais, was brought to the Tower on a charge of intrigue with Cardinal Pole. There were rumours that another high personage was involved in treason and Lisle's links with Norfolk pointed in the direction which Cromwell intended. London was roused by the arrest of a well known merchant for employing a papalist chaplain. In the panic two other merchants fled abroad. The next revelation of popish sympathies was the arrest of Richard Sampson, bishop of Chichester, a candidate for the new see of Westminster. Along with him to the Tower went Dr Watson. Both were known supporters of Gardiner and of tradition in church affairs. Rumour had it that Cromwell had declared that he was after five more bishops and it was obvious that Gardiner would be among their number.[23]

The counter-attack, launched by Cromwell, looked promising. Unable to act in the King's matrimonial affairs, he had taken the initiative in the ecclesiastical sphere by rousing suspicions about the papalist sympathies of his opponents. It seemed as if his threats might influence the shaken episcopate at a time when doctrine and practice were again under consideration. It was expected that Latimer would be freed from restraint and Barnes from the Tower. Yet Cromwell's tactics amounted to a diversion rather than a decisive blow. Norfolk and Gardiner had not been dislodged from their position of strength. Nevertheless at the beginning of June the French ambassador still believed that in the crucial struggle with his enemies Cromwell would win.[24]

Yet whatever panic Cromwell had caused among his antagonists, the King's actions were ominously non-committal. When informed of Sampson's imprisonment in the Tower, Henry had admitted that the attested charge of having exalted papal authority above that of the King was sufficient to condemn the bishop, but he did not permit the decisive confiscation of the bishop's goods to follow. He postponed a decision on Latimer's release. Cromwell had failed to precipitate the King into action. His absence from court in the second half of May, while he busied himself with preparations for parliament, had allowed Gardiner and Norfolk to establish themselves further in Henry's favour through the seductive Catherine Howard.[25]

The more Henry became absorbed by his matrimonial predicament the more he turned to Norfolk and Gardiner. Looking back it was easy to blame Cromwell for the unhappy consequences of the Cleves alliance. There was much to be said for making Cromwell the scapegoat for recent foreign policy and for making a fresh start in diplomatic relations by dismissing Cromwell. There were political arguments enough with which to denigrate Cromwell but they did not serve the purpose of his enemies. The dismissal and disgrace of Cromwell on the grounds that his policies had failed reflected on the King and was not what his opponents desired. They had no intention of allowing Cromwell to survive, as Wolsey had done, and to keep them in agonising suspense over the chance of a return to royal favour. They sought to take Cromwell's life.

In early June Norfolk and Gardiner were collecting evidence to convict Cromwell of capital offences and to support charges of treason and heresy. They obtained the necessary sworn testimony to make their charges stick. Throgmorton, Rich and, it seems, Wriothesley too were ready to betray Cromwell and give the damaging evidence on oath. With the testimony of Cromwell's colleagues in the bureaucracy a case for his abuse of office was made. Evidence of his support for Lutheran views was obtained and it was informally insinuated that he was even a sacramentary.[26] Momentarily obsessed by marital problems Henry was prepared to give rein to the men who seemed most ready to solve them. Swayed by his greatest noble and his ablest cleric, the King found that he wanted to believe the suspicions which had been aroused concerning Cromwell.

With confidence in the King's support, Norfolk struck at Cromwell on 10th June, 1540. When Cromwell entered the council chamber a little late after dinner, Norfolk shouted, 'Cromwell, do not sit there, traitors do not sit with gentlemen.' Immediately the guard entered and arrested Cromwell in the King's name on a charge of treason. Taken unawares, Cromwell demanded if this was the reward for his services and appealed to the councillors to answer whether he was a traitor or not. Their accusations made Cromwell realise that he was the victim of a prepared plot. Disclaiming intention of offence, he renounced all pardon and made a plea for a quick end. Unable to resist humiliating Cromwell, Norfolk tore the insignia of St George from his enemy's neck, while Southampton, eager to renounce his former favour towards Cromwell, ripped the Garter from him. Cromwell was then conveyed to the Tower by barge along the Thames.[27]

The same day the King's men seized Cromwell's house at Austin Friars. It was taken as a sign that Cromwell's fall was final and planned. It was now safe to denigrate the fallen minister and to spread rumours about how he was to be stripped of his titles and called plain 'shearman', of how he was to be drawn, hanged and quartered like a commoner and of how the King refused to see him or have mention made of his name. Those who had suffered under his rule were glad to see him go. Only those 'who knew nothing but truth by him both lamented him and heartily prayed for him'.[28]

Cromwell knew the King too well to have any illusions about the fate that awaited him. He could do no more than plead for mercy. On 17th June a bill of attainder against him was introduced in the Lords. Two days later it went to the Commons, where a new bill, probably adding other charges, was concocted with a proviso to safeguard the property of the deanery of Wells, held by Cromwell. The bill was passed on 29th June. Although hostile rumour insisted that Cromwell had created a precedent fatal to himself by attainting the Countess of Salisbury without previous trial, prior sentence by a court was not required by law in attainder by parliament. His enemies had shown due regard for the legalities.[29]

The charges against Cromwell represented him as 'a most false and corrupt traitor, deceiver and circumventor against' the King. They alleged corrupt and unauthorised practices in administration and leniency and slackness in justice which amounted to an abuse of royal trust and authority. Cromwell was further accused of acting for personal gain, of promoting heresy and of showing disdain towards the nobility. But the proof of the serious charges of treason and heresy rested not upon Cromwell's actions but upon reports of his words. It was declared that he had affirmed that the teaching of Barnes and other heretics was good and that 'if the King would turn from it, yet I would not turn; and if the King did turn, and all his people, I would fight in the field in mine own person, with my sword in my hand against him and all other'.[30]

Cromwell's reported words were a treasonable utterance in defence of heresy. They contained all the elements of treason for prosecution under the treason act of 1534. They were too pat a self-incrimination to be anything other than a fabrication. The skilled economy with which the phrases, attributed to Cromwell, had been contrived, required only a minimum of perjury to provide legal ground for Cromwell's conviction by attainder in parliament. Sworn evidence of treason by words was necessary to turn the complaints against him into a lethal condemnation.

The bill of attainder reveals Gardiner's interest in its insistence upon heresy and the connection with Barnes. It was as if, having failed to catch Cromwell at the first attempt to involve him with Barnes, Gardiner was determined to trap him a second time. Norfolk's animosity towards the upstart earl is detectable in the accusation of disdain towards the nobility. That Cromwell had said that 'if the lords would handle him so, that he would give them such a breakfast as never was made in England', may well have been true. But it was a gratuitous charge, designed to discredit him for it would not have stood up in court as evidence of treason.

Their case evidently seemed to Cromwell's accusers to rest on slender evidence, for, while Cromwell lay in the Tower, they laboured to collect further proof. His papers were searched to ascertain whether there was any incriminating matter in his correspondence with Lutherans. Enquiries were made in France about reports of treasonable words by Cromwell, concerning his designs to make himself king and to marry the lady Mary. He was accused of betraying the King's confidences concerning his marriage to Anne of Cleves.[31] The efforts to denigrate Cromwell showed how desperate Norfolk and Gardiner were to ensure that Cromwell should not be reprieved.

In the Tower Cromwell behaved with caution and dignity. He did not attempt to incriminate others. Two days after his arrest he was allowed to write to the King, following an interrogation at which some of the charges against him were revealed. He denied that he had ever willingly committed treason and assured Henry that he had striven with all his might to serve, strengthen and enrich the King. He denied that he had spoken of 'such matters' with his betrayers Rich and Throgmorton whose veracity and characters he impugned with restraint but with effect. While regretfully admitting slackness in enforcing legislation against heretics, he denied that he had ever been a sacramentary. In mitigation he claimed that he had 'meddled in so many matters' that he could not answer for all. He declared that he had not divulged the

King's confidences. He dismissed the idea that he had maintained a great retinue. Finally he made a plea for mercy.[32]

Cranmer wrote to the King trying to sow doubt about Cromwell's guilt and wondering whom the King might trust if Cromwell had indeed betrayed him. Ralph Sadler undertook to carry a letter from his master to the King who had it read out three times and appeared moved, but not enough to exercise his mercy. Intent upon the nullification of his marriage, Henry thought of Cromwell only as a witness who could substantiate the royal claim never to have consummated his marriage. Subjected to interrogatories drawn up by the King, Cromwell out of loyalty and in hope of mercy confirmed the intimate details of Henry's revulsion from his bride in a letter on 30th June. It was the day after the attainder was passed and Cromwell confessed that 'the frail flesh' incited him to continually call upon the King for mercy and pardon. Neither mercy nor a quick end were granted. Not until the King's matrimonial case was completed and it was certain that Cromwell's testimony was no longer required was the date for execution fixed.[33]

On 29th July after seven weeks of imprisonment Cromwell was led out to be beheaded on Tower Green. On the scaffold he made the speech and prayer, expected of the condemned. Acknowledging the judgement of the law, he confessed that he had offended his prince. But he was far more concerned with his sins against God. He denied aiding heretics and claimed to die in the Catholic faith of the Holy Church. 'And then made he his prayer which was long, but not so long, as both Godly and learned and after committed his soul into the hands of God and so patiently suffered the stroke of the axe . . . . '[34]

Cromwell's head on London Bridge was a sign to Londoners that another squalid intrigue for power at court had come to its bloody end. It was recognised as such by Henry some six months later, when he complained, 'On light pretexts, by false accusations they made me put to death the most faithful servant I have ever had.' It was a tribute typical of the egotistical King. The greatest English historian in the Tudor period suggested the wider significance of Cromwell's career, when he wrote, 'We may well say this, that England had a Cromwell.'[35]

12 PROBLEMS OF ASSESSMENT

While it appeared to historians that the Reformation dominated modern European history, it was to be expected that their interest in Cromwell would be focused upon his contribution to the religious and ecclesiastical changes in the reign of Henry VIII. Although John Foxe established Cromwell's position in the English Reformation for his protestant countrymen, later ecclesiastical historians, such as Thomas Fuller, tended to pay more attention to Henry VIII, the Supreme Head, and to Thomas Cranmer, the Archbishop of Canterbury, than to Cromwell, the Vicegerent. Nevertheless Foxe's picture of Cromwell as an active reformer endured. Of Cromwell Foxe wrote, 'His whole life was nothing else but a continual care and travail how to advance and further the right knowledge of the Gospel and reform of the House of God.'[1]

When in the second half of the nineteenth century historians came to accept that the Renaissance was the beginning of modern times, Cromwell was seen in a new context. He was now judged by his contribution to the making of the state. The interest of historians in state-making led them to interpret the politics of the sixteenth century in the light of the works of Machiavelli who was regarded as the originator of modern political thought. Cromwell was cast as a Machiavellian and it was Pole's attack upon him as such a politician which seemed to provide the contemporary endorsement. By the beginning of the twentieth century it was accepted that Cromwell was a wholly secular minded politician. In 1902 his biographer, R.B. Merriman concluded that Cromwell remained outside the religious movements of his time and used them only to serve his own political ends.[2]

The interpretation of Cromwell's motives in the light of the idea of the Renaissance, established by Jacob Burckhardt, not only changed the champion of the Reformation into a Machiavellian but also altered the estimate of his character. The warm zeal and idealistic enthusiasm of a reformer was replaced by the cold calculation and emotionless cunning, appropriate to a practitioner of Renaissance statecraft. Cromwell's biography was not unrelated to the wider problems of historical interpretation. The difficulty of reconciling the Reformation Cromwell with the Renaissance Cromwell persists. It can be seen in the continuing practice of qualifying his idealism as secular and his approach to religion as strictly rational. Such different Cromwells tend to confuse the picture of his character and the determination of his role.

Starting with the Reformation as his interest, A.G. Dickens has done much to restore the acceptance of Cromwell as a religious reformer. He has brought out Cromwell's evangelical enthusiasm and seen in his policies not only the establishment of the Church of England but also the beginnings of an Anglican ethos of the via media and of adiaphorism. G.R. Elton began by considering Cromwell's role as a state-maker and was inclined to look upon him as a secular minded man, but his later researches have persuaded him that Foxe was right in presenting Cromwell as a man of the Bible. Even if Cromwell is accepted as more of an Erasmian than a protestant sympathiser, it is clear that modern scholarship concludes that Cromwell had a serious religious attitude. There is now a wider agreement on how to interpret the spirit in which Cromwell wrote, 'He that either feareth not God nor esteemeth the King's Majesty's injunctions, precepts, ordinances and commandments is no meet herb to grow in his Majesty's most Catholic and virtuous garden.'[3]

Another great theme of historical interpretation which has affected Cromwell's reputation was that of the development of parliament, the central concern of Whig constitutional history. In the framework of constitutional development, set forth by William Stubbs, the reign of Henry VIII belonged to the 'Tudor dictatorship'. A concept of the European historians of Renaissance state-making, the New Monarchy, suited and reinforced the notion that the Tudor monarchy was despotic. In such a setting Cromwell's parliamentary activities were summed up by J.R. Green who wrote, 'Parliament assembled only to sanction acts of unscrupulous tyranny, or to build up by its own statutes the great fabric of absolute rule'. It was a conclusion in which R.B. Merriman concurred.[4] Cromwell, it seemed, had used parliament as an instrument of absolutism.

Since the middle of this century G.R. Elton has been building up the case against regarding Cromwell as a devotee of despotism and has shown him as an advocate of lawful government and the champion of a sovereignty which resided in the King in parliament. Cromwell's adherence to the due process of law and to the authority of statute have been revealed as the constitutional limitations within which he sought to work. Far from appearing as a means of consolidating a Tudor despotism Cromwell's achievement has been presented as the guarantee of the future of a parliamentary monarchy.[5]

Cromwell's practice of the ways of lawful government and exercise of the sovereignty of the King in Parliament has a bearing on the question of whether English constitutional development was different from that of the continental monarchies. If in Europe absolutism was developing in the early sixteenth century, it might seem unlikely that England was immune from such a trend. On this question the promoters of the uniform and general interpretations of history have argued with the defenders of the peculiar and various. Leaving aside the wider issues, it might be pointed out that Cromwell with his training in the common law and his parliamentary experience would appear to be suited to perpetuate a tradition of government which since the fifteenth century was consciously contrasted with the absolutism of the French monarchy and which rejected despotism. The recent reappraisal of parliament's role in the reign of Henry VIII would seem to confirm Cromwell in his whig respectability.

The tendency to regard parliament as the vehicle of political and social pressures has distracted attention from the constitutional importance of the institution itself. If political crises, generated abroad, rather than parliamentary habits and institutional sophistication determined the perpetuation of parliament, then it might be argued that Cromwell's parliamentary performance was thrust upon him by the political deadlock, created by the Pope and the Emperor. If the importance of parliament was merely a reflection of social change in the political nation, then it might seem that Cromwell's task was to hold the parliamentary mirror up to society. Political crises and social change had an effect upon the perpetuation of parliament but the existence of a representative assembly with established functions and traditions imposed ways of thinking and a *modus operandi* upon King, Lords and Commons which were of constitutional importance. It was that constitutional importance which Cromwell chose to exploit and so to establish for himself an important role in preserving a parliamentary tradition.

In the interpretation of the conduct of the monarch in government the consideration of the relationship of the King and his servant, of Henry VIII and Cromwell has been influential. Stubbs, who saw Henry as a royal dictator, declared, 'I am inclined to regard Henry himself as the main originator of the greatest and most critical changes of his reign; and I am sure that, after the fall of Wolsey, there is no minister, great or small, who can claim anything like an original share in determining the royal policy'. He added, 'I am obliged altogether to reject the notion that he was the interpreter of the wishes of his people'.[6] In this picture of the complete despot, ruling in his own personal interest, there was no room for Cromwell, except as the subservient agent of the King.

James Anthony Froude had, however, regarded Henry as the

interpreter of his people's wishes and he allowed Cromwell a large role. Of Cromwell he wrote, 'For eight years his influence had been supreme with the King — supreme in parliament — supreme in convocation; the nation, in the ferment of revolution, was absolutely controlled by him; and he left the print of his individual genius stamped indelibly, while the metal was at white heat, into the constitution of the country'. He summed up in the words, 'Cromwell's intellect presided — Cromwell's hand executed'.[7]

The evidence of Cromwell's control of the means of government and of his intellectual ability to formulate and initiate policy would seem to support Froude's estimate. But the effect of the emphasis upon Cromwell's political and administrative mastery has affected the estimate of the King's capacities and role. Consequently Henry has been presented as less capable and astute. The question as to whether the King or his minister was the ruler and originator of policy led to the replacement of the picture of an omnipotent King by that of an all powerful minister. It was clearly too simple a picture. If Cromwell could persuade the King, so could others, as was demonstrated by Cromwell's fall. The growing appreciation of the importance of faction and of court politics is leading to a revision of views on the nature and practice of Henry's rule. The King and minister both worked amidst the tensions created by all the interests at court.[8] The full measure of the political complexity behind monarchical and ministerial rule has yet to be fully explored.

When the Victorian historian J.R. Green wrote, 'The history of this great revolution, for it is nothing less, is the history of a single man', he was writing of Cromwell and his achievement. 'The ten years which follow the fall of Wolsey are among the most momentous in our history', he added.[9] The notion of the momentous and revolutionary importance of the 1530's remains with historians, but the significance of those years is debated in different terms. The character of the revolution, attributed to Cromwell, has been altered and elaborated.

The discussion of the significance for the state of the revolution of the 1530's is no longer conducted in terms of its relevance to the creation of the New Monarchy but in its relevance to the more ambiguous notion of the modern state, The idea of the establishment of the modern state in the sixteenth century has provoked both the medievalists and the modernists to stress on the one hand the continuity of the practice and theory of the state and on the other hand the differences and changes. Bureaucratic and parliamentary government were medieval, it is claimed, while sovereignty is modern. While the characteristics of the New Monarchy were anchored in the early modern period those of the modern state belong to a vaguer time scale, hence the difficulty in establishing the decisiveness of Cromwell's actions in establishing a modern state.

A decisive step towards the creation of the modern state with which Cromwell has been credited was the establishment of bureaucratic government. His revolution in government arose from his changes in the administration which altered the nature of government by allowing for a bureaucratic initiative in the conduct of government. The course of the revolution in government was plotted in the decline in the role of the departments of the royal household and in the increase in the part played by the departments of state. The process was envisaged as a shift from a royal to a national and bureaucratic government.[10]

The debate over the revolution in government has tended to diminish the revolutionary nature of Cromwell's activities and present them as a step in a longer evolution of administrative change.[11] It may be argued that they were the result of political and financial circumstances and of the King's style of rule rather than of any idea of what the nature of government should be. Whether administrative change led to the emergence of bureaucratic initiative in policy as distinct from routine administrative functions may also be debated. It would seem that Cromwell ruled by virtue of royal favour rather than by bureaucratic authority and that the council however bureaucratic its composition was dependent on the will of the King in matters of policy.

Yet, while the King did not allow the initiative in government to pass to the administration and government remained monarchical and not bureaucratic in principle, the lack of royal interest in the administration did allow the organisation of the administration to pass into the hands of the bureaucrats. The exercise of the royal power to utilise whatever agencies he pleased ceased. The King's creative force in the administration was no longer personal. The Privy Chamber did not emerge as a new agency of the prerogative. Henry's readiness to leave administration to Cromwell meant that bureaucrats shaped the administrative machinery. It was a step which strengthened the bureaucracy but which did not make the state bureaucratic.

Cromwell's treatment of the administration did not amount to a preparation for bureaucratic government. He did not reorganise the bureaucracy. He was an improver and exploiter of what existed. His new institutions, the Court of Augmentations and the Council of the West, were based on existing models and neither survived as institutions for long. It may be claimed that in the Secretaryship and the Privy Council he produced what were virtually new institutions and that he altered the centre of gravity in the administration. Yet these changes appear to be more nearly related to the practical needs of his personal ascendancy and the position, allowed to him by the King, than to any plan for a national bureaucratic government. They were to the advantage of royal rather than bureaucratic rule. Cromwell was capable of broad political vision but in the administration he focused his mind upon the business methods of separate institutions, not upon the bureaucratic structure as a whole. He saw bureaucrats as servants of the King and not as the masters of national policy.

A preoccupation with a revolution which inaugurated the modern state may well tend to exaggerate the novelty as well as the secular nature of Cromwell's activities. Cromwell's own preoccupation was with the enforcement of a reformation which affected the religious life and practice of clergy and laity and in the zeal with which he pursued that task his own religious views played no small part. The Royal Supremacy was first acknowledged by the clergy who were not blind to the implications which went beyond a claim to secular sovereignty. The intensification of an awareness of religious issues rather than the secularisation of outlook in affairs of state might well seem to be the immediate result of the revolution of the 1530's. The stress upon the divine right of royal authority showed scant recognition of the emergence of the predominance of secular sovereignty in a secular state.

Historians of the 1530's have generally agreed that it was a period of momentous change. Those who have studied the changes in government, in the state and in political thought have tended to describe them by the politically appropriate term, revolution. Those who have been interested in the changes in ecclesiastical government, the Church and religious thinking have usually seen them as constituting a reformation. All acknowledge the overlapping of the history of the church and the state, but have allotted the prime significance to their chosen view of events. Most recognise the importance of Cromwell either as secular politician or reformer in either the revolution in the state or the reformation in the church. Yet the old struggle of the temporalty and the spiritualty persists in the different interpretations and reflects the secular or religious views of the authors.

Whether the church was reformed to suit a changing view of the state or the state was reformed to meet an altered concept of the church remains a difficult question to decide. Both church and state were undergoing changes and were continuously interacting. Since both claimed divine authority and both the clergy and the laity were concerned with their salvation, there was a mutual interest in reform. The medieval usage of the term *Ecclesia Anglicana*, the vestiges of Wycliffite heresy, the Erasmian criticism of institutional religion and the debate between Thomas More and William Tyndale, all helped to publicise attitudes towards the church as radical as those which the revival of imperialism and the emergence of machiavellianism induced towards the state. The idea that a political reformation preceded a religious reformation in England is based on the narrow interpretation that the official adoption of protestantism constituted the religious reformation. In 1529 the King declared his intention to reform the church. The preamble of the Act of Appeals in 1533 made clear the concept of a Church of England and both the King and Cromwell assumed the significance of the break with Rome for doctrinal authority from 1531, when the Royal Supremacy was mooted.[12]

Cromwell recognised the inextricable union of church and state by fostering a unitary view of a body politic which embraced both church and state. He saw the division between the temporalty and spiritualty as nominal, when he came to theorise about the result of his actions. It was a diagnosis which had much to commend it in the paradoxical situation which emerged. By giving, as it seems, more influence to the state in ecclesiastical affairs, it ensured that religious matters became the preoccupation of the state. By making the King Supreme Head the divine right of monarchy came to be stressed. The rejection of papal sanctions made way for those of the Bible. While the clergy became the subjects of the King, the laity became members of the Church of England and were committed to doctrines, declared and enforced by statutory authority. Cromwell's view of the body politic extended the mixed polity to include not only the politic and regal dominion but also the temporal and spiritual.

The study of some of the intellectual origins of the activities of Cromwell or of the revolution of the 1530's has drawn attention to what might be called the Enlightenment and away from the Terror. The consideration of ideas rather than events has tended to stress the elements of conscious planning by Cromwell and to minimise the effect of the pressure of circumstance upon the shaping of policy. Humanist intellectuals were apt to cast their patron, Cromwell, in the role of idealised philosophic counsellor. While Thomas Starkey reflects the good intentions and intellectual sincerity, Richard Morison demonstrates the propagandist expediency of thought, which produced the mental climate of Cromwell's entourage. The shift of interest from the block to the books has emphasised the rational, idealistic, moderate and programmatic aspects of the revolution of the 1530's.

Seen in the context of the intellectual origins of his actions, Cromwell appears to have been motivated by the rational calculation which was practised by his more academic advisers. The result has been to suggest that Cromwell was intellectually superior to the King. The picture of a brilliant King with Cromwell as his insensitive executioner is thus altered to show an intellectual Cromwell with a wayward royal axeman. Cromwell's well considered programme appears to suffer from the interference of a King who acted in response to his emotions. By crediting Cromwell with a dominance in the realm of ideas, he appears to hold the initiative in policy and so assume the responsibility for it. Presented as thinker, Cromwell acquires the power which the humanists hoped would be exercised by a philosophic counsellor over a shallow minded King.

In the relationship of the King and Cromwell there were more determinants than that of quality of mind. Both Henry and Cromwell showed intellectual curiosity and were aware of the ideas which had a bearing on policy. It was Cromwell's business to be the advocate of policy. It was Henry's task to choose between policies. Royal policy was at its most forceful when the King and an able minister agreed. They worked at different levels. Henry enjoyed the advantage of his superior position; Cromwell that of his legal expertise and knowledge of how to exploit the machinery of government. It may be that Cromwell was better at performing his ministerial tasks than Henry was at fulfilling the duties of Kingship.

In his ministerial capacity Cromwell was responsible for recommending the passage of economic and social measures. That such measures which used to be called mercantilist or paternalist are now discussed in the context of the concept of commonwealth is indicative of a change of historical perspective. Legislation which was once judged by its contribution to the power and security of the state is now assessed by its contribution to the welfare of the community. This change of interpretation does greater justice to the moral and idealistic element in the commonwealth thinking of the time but it is in danger of introducing the anachronistic preoccupations of the modern welfare state into an estimation of Cromwell's policy.

Cromwell's efforts to edify the commonwealth expressed the desire to enrich all men, to educate all, to relieve poverty, banish idleness or unemployment, to bring about moral regeneration and to foster unity and concord. These aims were pursued, however, in a commonwealth which, like Thomas More's *Utopia*, had to be defended against its enemies and in a realm which was united by its obedience to the King. The disposal of the proceeds of the dissolution showed which policies Cromwell put first. Despite the modern attraction of commonwealth thinking its sixteenth century context and sources are utterly remote from those of the welfare state.

Cromwell tackled the problems of poor relief and of the much publicised evil effects of pasture farming and of rising prices with ingenuity, but he did not inaugurate any exceptional programme of economic or social reform. The greater part of parliamentary legislation had long been devoted to social and economic regulation. Wolsey had set up a commission against enclosures and had tried to control them through the courts.[13] Despite his personal experience of the mercantile world, Cromwell remained ready to sacrifice economic to fiscal considerations, as in the Irish debasement. His control of prices was in response to the demands of traders rather than in the interest of consumers. Although he shared and on occasion used the ideas, current among a variety of reforming publicists, he was not the founder of any school of commonwealth men. The varied group of intellectuals who offered him their advice did not constitute a revolutionary party or even a specially recruited corps of propagandists. In his policies the well worn assumptions of governmental tradition predominated over the ideas of the commonwealth men and the humanists.

Cromwell who became a baron and then an earl was not on the strength of his humble birth the herald of a new class rising to power. The prejudice against ecclesiastics and the shortage of trained gentlemen gave him his opportunity. His disdain for nobles and their dislike of him was not a sign of class conflict but an indication of the adherence of both parties to the notion of degree society and to the concepts of nobility by which they judged each others' shortcomings. His readiness to give employment to the gentry was an acknowledgement of their existing potential. Similarly his connection with the merchants of London was not a sign of any sudden emergence of the mercantile class and its interests. The common accusation, aimed at all ranks of society and at the professions, of undermining degree society was levelled at him but his actions belie the charge.

The revolution of the 1530's does not qualify as a social or economic revolution. The most disruptive act of intervention in the inflation of Henry's reign was the debasement of the 1540's, which Cromwell did not predetermine. The measures, supported by Cromwell, attempted to preserve existing society and the economy. Such novelty as there was in his moves was that of method rather than of aim. Even the Dissolution of the Monasteries led to no fundamental transformation of social or economic life. Change of landownership did not bring any change of use which would not have occurred in response to underlying economic trends of the period. Land prices remained remarkably steady. While the dissolution weakened the ecclesiastical component of society, it introduced no new interest in lay society. The distribution of ex-monastic lands consolidated the old social order by strengthening the existing gentry and allowing for the endowment of new nobility. If it caused any alteration in the relationship of the different ranks of landholders, it did so without a revolutionary change in the structure of society as a whole.

If it may be argued that the revolution of the 1530's did not consist in a decisive move to establish a despotic or a secular or a bureaucratic state, that it did not entail any radical change in the social or economic structure and that its political inspiration was in favour of a traditional mixed polity and its religious aim was the moderation of a middle way, it may be wondered how profound a revolution it was. It is clear that the greater the expectations of transformation, embodied in the ideas of revolution, the less the changes, expedited by Cromwell, may be made to appear. There exists, however, another temptation which is to make Cromwell live up to the greatest expectations of change by representing everything that Cromwell did as revolutionary.

Such a temptation exists not only as a result of certain views of what constitutes a revolution but also as a consequence of a widely held idea of what makes an historical period. The idea of the age or period usually demands a consistency of interpretation so that what is regarded as characteristic of the age is seen to be manifest in all its aspects. If the distinguishing characteristic of the 1530's is that it was a revolutionary age then the tendency is to view all its aspects in terms of its essentially revolutionary character. The compulsion to such consistency is necessary to the definition of the age.

The question of periodisation raises the relationship of Cromwell's revolution of the 1530's to the change from medieval to modern times. The 1530's now appear to stand close to the advancing frontier of the Middle Ages and to separate medieval history not from modern history but from the history of the early modern period. While the lengthening perspective of history has inevitably changed the criteria of modernity, it has also tended to minimise the degree of change in the transition from medieval to modern conditions by the introduction of the intermediate stage of the early modern period. It has also facilitated the argument that the early modern period saw the working out of medieval trends rather than the introduction of modern trends.

In the light of changes in periodisation Cromwell might be represented as the last of the medieval imperialists and the reviver of the medieval bureaucratic administration, parliament and monarchy. It is always a problem in the interpretation of the significance of historical personages to decide whether they are the last of a traditional kind or the first of a new breed. Since Cromwell has generally been seen as belonging to the modern period, he has usually been presented as the first of a new breed. As the medieval historians move into the Tudor period, however, he may come to look more like his predecessors. He was the pupil of Wolsey from whose entourage most of the servants of Henry VIII emerged.

If the interpretation of Cromwell's achievement, his revolution of the 1530's, is a complex business, so too is the reading of his character. The historian with his idea of the man of his age will stress the effects of historical environment. But, if he accepts that the individual is capable of shaping history and of exercising a choice, however limited, in the determination of his historical fate, he will attempt to understand the character of the individual because it is a factor in historical explanation.

The difficulty of the psychological approach to historical characters lies in the paucity of the evidence upon which to base a clinical diagnosis. The evidence of Cromwell's behaviour is not sufficient for a scientific psychological analysis. It is, of course, possible to apply descriptive psychological terms to Cromwell. It is perhaps inescapable as part of the idiom of our day. But the use of such terminology must not be regarded as precise, authoritative and scientific, when it is perforce used in an intuitive and speculative manner.

Another approach to the character of the historical individual may be based on his role or status. The merchant, the money-lender, the lawyer, the politician may be held to have certain qualities which enable them to fulfil their tasks. Those in each grade of society may be credited with certain attitudes which enable them to adapt to and accept their status. To apply this kind of approach to Cromwell is difficult because he played so many parts with a protean ability that his role is difficult to determine. Similarly he passed through the different degrees of society from humble to high status with such ease that his social outlook cannot be treated as a constant.

Then there is the intuitive response to appearances and the readiness to interpret physical features as a guide to character which have led to the reading of Cromwell's character from the portrait of him by Holbein. The portrait is, of course, the artist's impression of Cromwell but the realism of Holbein's interpretation is such that the temptation to assess Cromwell's character from it is strong. Such visual evidence may be as good as any written descriptions of his character. Yet the assessment of character from physical traits is notoriously unreliable.

Cromwell's political existence prompts the distinction between his public and private character. It is tempting to picture the private man in his moments of relaxation and to try to catch him off his guard. Cromwell as a fancier of hawks, as a gardener obtaining seeds from Italy, or as an exasperated parent seems to lose the inscrutability of a councillor 'whose office is an eye to the prince'. To parade his common humanity and assemble instances of his kindness and consideration makes him more sympathetic. Glimpses of him sharing the experiences of ordinary life and displaying the emotions of personal relationships appear to suggest that the real character of Cromwell is to be found in his private life. Yet to humanize him in such a way is to accept that public life transformed his personality and to acknowledge how difficult it is to understand the qualities which made him exceptional.

What intensity of feeling drove Cromwell to his absorption in public affairs, to meddle in so many things and to be ever ready to make or mar can, perhaps, be appreciated by considering the motives which he avowed. No doubt, there was much self deception in them and they might be translated into terms of ambition, love of power, the need to prove oneself or into more sophisticated psychological explanations. Yet however sceptically their face value ought to be received, they possessed a compelling force and reality for Cromwell. They were the motives which he recognised.

Cromwell's letters are pervaded with a sense of duty and service. Even when he was demanding the duty and service of others, he conveys his awareness of their compulsion. His sense of duty and service was expressed in personal loyalty to Wolsey and then to the King. That it did not render him subservient was evident in his plain speaking to his masters, who recognised the integrity which it conferred upon their servant by their trust. Such virtues were not only those of personal loyalty but were also those of the social hierarchical world, of the monarchical government and of the religious and ecclesiastical sphere. Cromwell felt a duty to serve causes in the commonwealth, in the realm and in the Church.

Cromwell's acceptance of the conventional ideals of his time was not mere lip-service. He explored their intellectual and religious foundations in search of convictions more satisfying than those of glib propaganda. He found his political convictions in the works of Marsilio of Padua and in his sense of English law and history. He discovered his religious convictions in the Bible, in the works of the followers of Erasmus and Luther and in a sense of calling. Aware that his life was at stake, he needed a strength of mind and spirit as much as all his political skills to sustain him in his 'labours, pains and travails'.

Concerning the nature of the body politic, of the commonwealth and of the church and religion, Cromwell held strong convictions which he enunciated in forceful language. His advocacy of moderation was passionate. His abomination of superstition and treason was the reflex of positive beliefs and not the expression of a destructive instinct. He was saved from fanaticism by his acceptance of the realities of politics. Impatient for decisive action, he nevertheless accommodated himself to the opposition of men and events. Whatever the obstacles he did not lose his sense of direction. His timing and methods made his government unusually effective. He could claim to possess an idealism which gave his policies a force which did not rely wholly upon the sanctions with which he armed them. Knowing that politics were concerned with power, he also understood that they were concerned with ideals. His qualities prompted Cranmer to write to the King that Cromwell was 'such a servant, in my judgement, in wisdom, diligence, faithfulness, and experience, as no prince in this realm ever had'.[14] If Cranmer's judgement was correct, Cromwell had fulfilled his aim in life.

NOTES

Abbreviations in the Notes

BIHR Bulletin of the Institute of Historical Research
CHJ Cambridge Historical Journal
CSP Calendar of State Papers
EETS Early English Text Society
EHR English Historical Review
HJ Historical Journal
JEH Journal of Ecclesiastical History
L.P. Letters and Papers, Foreign and Domestic, of the Reign of Henry VIII, 1509-47, ed. J.S. Brewer, J. Gairdner and R.H. Brodie. (References by page number)
TRHS Transactions of the Royal Historical Society
Place of publication London unless otherwise stated

CROMWELL'S PORTRAIT

1. Roy Strong, *Tudor and Jacobean Portraits* (HMSO 1969), I, 114.
2. John Foxe, *Acts and Monuments* (1870), ed. J. Pratt, V, 395.
3. R.B. Merriman, *Life and Letters of Thomas Cromwell* (Oxford 1902), I, 373.
4. Ibid., II, 162.
5. Ibid., II, 129.
6. L.P., IV (ii), 1535-36; IX, 289; Foxe, *Acts and Monuments,* V, 45-6; *Narratives of the Days of the Reformation,* ed. J.G. Nichols, Camden Soc., LXXVII (1859), 258-9.
7. Merriman, *Life and Letters,* I, 323.
8. *Chronicle of King Henry VIII of England* (1889), trans. M.A.S. Hume, 90-1.
9. L.P., V, 329, 696; IV (i), 65.
10. P. Hughes, *The Reformatiion in England* (1951), I, 328, n.2.
11. C.S.L. Davies, *Peace, Print and Protestantism* (1976), 159; L.P., VII, 55-6; IX, 156-7; P. Van Dyke, *Renascence Portraits* (1906), 234.
12. L.P., IX, 19, 30.
13. John Stow, *A Survey of London* (Oxford 1908), ed. C.L. Kingsford, 88-9.
14. L.P., XV, 164.
15. William Roper, 'The Life of Sir Thomas More', ed. E.V. Hitchcock, *EETS,* Original Series, CXCVII (1935), 71, 81.
16. L.P., XII, 12.

17. Merriman, *Life and Letters,* II, 267.
18. L.P., XV, 512.
19. Foxe, *Acts and Monuments,* V, 364.
20. L.P., V, 554, 484; XIV (ii), 343, 344, 328.
21. L. Gottesman, *Four Political Treatises of Sir Thomas Elyot* (Florida 1967), 206.
22. *Shakespeare in his own Age* (Cambridge 1964), ed. A. Nicoll, 233-5.
23. L.P., XIV (i), 110.
24. G.R. Elton, *Reform & Renewal* (Cambridge 1973), 17.
25. Merriman, *Life and Letters,* I, 415; L.P., XV, 511.
26. Elton, *Reform & Renewal,* 26 n.61, 27.
27. Ibid., 11-12.
28. Thomas Elyot, *The Boke called the Governour* (Everyman 1907), 16-17.
29. L.P., XII (ii), 113, 171.
30. L.P., XV, 373, 376, 416; XI, 25.
31. Merriman, *Life and Letters,* 30-44.
32. Charles Wriothesley, 'Chronicle', ed. W.D. Hamilton, Camden Soc., New Series, XI (1875), 117.
33. Ibid., 96-7; Stow, *A Survey of London,* I, 91.

Chapter 1   WAYS TO ADVANCEMENT

1. See Merriman, *Life and Letters,* I, ch. 1.
2. Foxe, *Acts and Monuments,* V, 398; G.R. Elton, *Policy and Police* (Cambridge 1972), 192.
3. Merriman, *Life and Letters,* II, 265.
4. Foxe, *Acts and Monuments,* V, 365.
5. Ibid., V, 367.
6. S.E. Lehmberg, *Sir Thomas Elyot: Tudor Humanist* (Austin 1960), 30.
7. L.P., III (i), 377; III (ii), 1523, 832, 843, 1035.
8. Merriman, *Life and Letters,* I, 30-44.
9. Ibid., 313.
10. Van Dyke, *Renascence Portraits,* 142-3.
11. Merriman, *Life and Letters,* I, 319.
12. L.P., IV (ii), 1456.
13. Ibid., 1344.
14. Merriman, *Life and Letters,* I, 53-4.
15. Ibid., I, 56-63.

Chapter 2   IN THE KING'S SERVICE

1. A.J. Slavin, *Politics and Profit* (Cambridge 1966), 22.
2. George Cavendish, 'Life and Death of Cardinal Wolsey', ed. R.S. Sylvester, *EETS,* CCXLIII (1959) 104-7.
3. G.R. Elton, *The Tudor Revolution in Government* (Cambridge 1953), 77-80; Merriman, *Life and Letters,* I, 67-8; L.P., IV (iii), 3180.
4. S.E. Lehmberg, *The Reformation Parliament 1529-1536* (Cambridge 1970), 102-4.

5. L.P., IV (iii), 2780, 2702.
6. Merriman, *Life and Letters*, I, 327.
7. L.P., IV (iii), 2730.
8. Merriman, *Life and Letters*, I, 332-3.
9. Ibid., I, 328.
10. Cavendish, 'Life and Death of Cardinal Wolsey', 104.
11. Foxe, *Acts and Monuments*, V, 366.
12. *CSP*, Spanish, V (i), 569.
13. T. Phillips, *The History of the Life of Cardinal Pole*, 2nd ed. (1768), I, 82-87; Van Dyke, *Renascence Portraits*, 152-4.
14. Foxe, *Acts and Monuments*, V, 366.
15. L.P., IV (iii), 2676.
16. J.J. Scarisbrick, *Henry VIII* (1968), 267.
17. Elton, *The Tudor Revolution in Government*, 88.
18. Edward Hall, *Chronicle* (1809), 764.

CHAPTER 3. THE MAKING OF THE SUPREMACY

1. Scarisbrick, *Henry VIII*, 261; L.P., IV (iii), 3004.
2. G.R. Elton, *Studies in Tudor and Stuart Politics and Government* (Cambridge 1974), I, 179-82.
3. Merriman, *Life and Letters*, I, 334.
4. J.J. Scarisbrick, 'Pardon of the Clergy 1531', *CHJ*, XII (1956), 33.
5. Lehmberg, *The Reformation Parliament*, 114.
6. L.P., V, 387; *Cabala sive Scrinia: Mysteries of State and Government* (1691), 227-30.
7. Hall, *Chronicle*, 774.
8. L.P., VI, 146; V, 381; *CSP*, Spanish, IV (ii), 405.
9. Merriman, *Life and Letters*, I, 343.
10. Elton, *Studies*, II, 107-36; J.P. Cooper, 'The Supplication against the Ordinaries reconsidered', *EHR*, LXXII (1957), 616-41; Lehmberg, *The Reformation Parliament*, 139.
11. Ibid., 153; L.P., V, 343.
12. Foxe, *Acts and Monuments*, V, 366; Hall, *Chronicle*, 788.
13. M. Kelly, 'The Submission of the Clergy', *TRHS.*, 5th Series, XV (1965), 115-17.
14. G.R. Elton, *Policy and Police* (Cambridge 1972), 178; N. Pocock, *Records of the Reformation* (Oxford 1870), II, 418-19.
15. Elton, *Studies*, II, 85.
16. Ibid., 82-106.
17. Thomas Cranmer, *Works*, ed. J.E. Cox (Cambridge 1846), II, 242.
18. Elton, *Policy and Police*, 180; Pocock, *Records of the Reformation*, II, 523-31.
19. *Statutes of the Realm* (1817), III, 471-4.
20. Elton, *Policy and Police*, 182; J. Strype, *Ecclesiastical Memorials* (Oxford 1822), I (i), 162-75; P. Janelle, *Obedience in Church and State* (Cambridge 1930), 67-171.
21. *Statutes of the Realm*, III, 812.

Chapter 4   THE AUGMENTATION OF THE KING'S REVENUES

1. Merriman, *Life and Letters*, I, 30-44; II, 265; Elton, *Reform & Renewal*, 12; L.P., VII, 344, 580.
2. Thomas More, 'The Apologye of Syr Thomas More', ed. A.I. Taft, *EETS*, Original Series, CLXXX (1930), 83-8; Cavendish, 'Life and Death of Cardinal Wolsey', 118.
3. L. Stone, 'The Political Programme of Thomas Cromwell', *BIHR*, XXIV (1951), 1-18.
4. *Valor Ecclesiasticus* (1810), I-X.
5. J. Youings, *The Dissolution of the Monasteries* (1971), 20.
6. *Statutes of the Realm*, III, 575-8.
7. Merriman, *Life and Letters*, II, 265.
8. Elyot, *The Boke called the Governour*, 195-6.
9. F.C. Dietz, *English Government Finance 1485-1558* (1964), 106; L.P., VIII, 315.
10. Elton, *The Tudor Revolution in Government*, 160, 433-8; Hall, *Chronicle*, 821.
11. Lehmberg, *The Reformation Parliament*, 208; *Statutes of the Realm*, III, 516, 812; L.P., XIV (i), 405.
12. *Statutes of the Realm*, III, 517.
13. Merriman, *Life and Letters*, I, 313.
14. Dietz, *English Government Finance 1485-1558*, 162.
15. J.J. Goring, 'The General Proscription of 1522', *EHR*, LXXXVI (1971), 681-705; L.P., XIV (i), 330.
16. J.J. Scarisbrick, 'Clerical Taxation in England 1485-1547', *JEH*, XI (1960), 41-54.
17. L.P., VII, 64; W.C. Richardson, *Tudor Chamber Administration 1485-1547* (Baton Rouge 1952), 388; *Statutes of the Realm*, III, 611-19; J. Hurstfield, 'The Revival of Feudalism in Early Tudor Period', *History*, New Series, XXXVII (1952), 137; E.W. Ives, 'The Genesis of the Statute of Uses', *EHR*, LXXXII (1967), 673-97.
18. Elton, *Policy and Police*, 67-71; M.H. and R. Dodds, *The Pilgrimage of Grace 1536-1537 and the Exeter Conspiracy 1538* (Cambridge 1915), I, 76-7.
19. Elton, *Reform & Renewal*, 114-15; T.S. Willan, *A Tudor Book of Rates* (Manchester 1962), xx-xxii; P. L. Hughes and J.F. Larkin, *Tudor Royal Proclamations* (Yale 1964), I, 381-3.
20. W.G. Hoskins, *The Age of Plunder* (1976), 181-2.
21. L.P., VII, 342; IX, 57; XI, 463, 492; XII (i), 539; XII (ii), 31, 409-10; Merriman, *Life and Letters*, I, 38; Elton, *Reform & Renewal*, 117-19; *A New History of Ireland* (Oxford 1976), ed. T.W. Moody *et al.*, III, 409.
22. Elton, *The Tudor Revolution in Government*, 98-119, 160-223.
23. B.P. Wolffe, *The Crown Lands 1461-1536* (1970), 133-7.
24. *Statutes of the Realm*, III, 45-7, 182-92.
25. W.C. Richardson, *History of the Court of Augmentations 1536-54*, (Baton Rouge 1961), passim; 'The Papers of George Wyatt Esquire, ed. D.M. Loades, Camden Soc., 4th Series, V (1968), 159-60.

26. G.R. Elton, *England under the Tudors,* 2nd ed. (1974), 180-4, 479-81.
27. Elton, *The Tudor Revolution in Government,* 433-4.
28. *Statutes of the Realm,* III, 729.
29. *The Report of the Royal Commission of 1552* (Morgan Town 1974), ed. W.C. Richardson, xxii-xxiii.
30. L.P., VII, 53.
31. *Statutes of the Realm,* III, 812; Merriman, *Life and Letters,* I, 373.

Chapter 5   LIMITATIONS AND OPPOSITION

1. Cavendish, 'Life and Death of Cardinal Wolsey', 179.
2. R. Koebener, 'The Imperial Crown of the Realm: Henry VIII, Constantine and Polydore Vergil', *BIHR,* XXVI (1953), 29-52; L.P., XIV (i), 475.
3. Merriman, *Life and Letters,* II, 268.
4. Cranmer, *Works,* II, 359; Foxe, *Acts and Monuments,* V, 691; Merriman, *Life and Letters,* I, 232; L.P., X, 291-2; Elyot, *The Boke called the Governour,* 261, 293.
5. Elton, *Studies,* II, 215-35.
6. D. Hay. 'The Church of England in the later Middle Ages', *History,* LIII (1968), 35-50; Elton, *Studies,* II, 85-6, 230.
7. E.W. Ives, 'Faction at the Court of Henry VIII: the Fall of Anne Boleyn', *History,* LVII (1972), 183.
8. *Statutes of the Realm,* III, 542-4; Elton, *The Tudor Revolution in Government,* 270-6.
9. *The Report of the Royal Commission of 1552,* ed. W.C. Richardson, xxx-xxxi.
10. G. Burnet, *The History of the Reformation of the English Church* (Oxford 1865), ed. N. Pocock, I, 443-4.
11. M.E. James, 'Obedience and Dissent in Henrician England: the Lincolnshire Rebellion, 1536', *Past and Present,* XLVIII (1970), 7.
12. L.P., XI, 272; XII (i), 441; Dodds, *The Pilgrimage of Grace,* II, 186-7.
13. *Statutes of the Realm,* III, 729-30; L. Stone, *The Crisis of the Aristocracy* (Oxford 1965), 29.
14. W.G. Zeeveld, *The Foundations of Tudor Policy* (1969), Ch. 8; Merriman, *Life and Letters,* II, 129; Hall, *Chronicle,* 839.
15. Van Dyke, *Renascence Portraits,* 152; L.P., XI, 305; VI, 577; VII, 20.
16. Merriman, *Life and Letters,* II, 265; M.L. Bush, 'The Problem of the Far North: a Study of the Crisis of 1537 and its consequences', *Northern History,* VI (1971), 40; L.P., XII (i), 519.
17. L.P., XI, 504-5, 505-7; Dodds, *The Pilgrimage of Grace,* I, 358-9.
18. G.R. Elton, 'Tudor Government: the Points of Contact. III. The Court, *TRHS,* 5th Series, XXVI (1976), passim.
19. C. Pythian-Adams, 'Ceremony and the citizen: the communal Year at Coventry 1450-1559', *Crisis and Order in English Towns* (1972), ed. P. Clark and P. Slack, 57-80.
20. M. Kelly, 'The Submission of the Clergy', *TRHS,* 5th Series, XV (1965),

98; C.Haigh, *Reformation and Resistance in Tudor Lancashire* (Cambridge 1976), 63-75; *Statutes of the Realm*, III, 739-43.

21.   Ives, 'The Genesis of the Statute of Uses', 694-5; R.W. Heinze, *The Proclamations of the Tudor Kings* (Cambridge 1976), 113-15.

22.   Hoskins, *The Age of Plunder*, 87, 161; J.F.D. Shrewsbury, *A History of the Bubonic Plague in the British Isles* (Cambridge 1970), 167-73; Dietz, *English Government Finance 1485-1558*, 143; *Statutes of the Realm*, III, 813.

23.   Cavendish, 'Life and Death of Cardinal Wolsey', 101.

Chapter 6   THE CHURCH OF ENGLAND

1.   L.P., VI, 153.

2.   S.E. Lehmberg, 'Supremacy and Vicegerency: a reexamination', *EHR*, *LXXXI* (1966), 225-35; Elton, *Policy and Police*, 247-8; C.S. Kitching, 'Probate Jurisdiction of Thomas Cromwell as Vicegerent', *BIHR*, XLVI (1973), 102-6.

3.   H. Gee and W.J. Hardy, *Documents Illustrative of English Church History* (1910), 269; *Statutes of the Realm*, III, 427-8; Merriman, *Life and Letters*, II, 197.

4.   *Statutes of the Realm*, II, 427-8.

5.   Ibid., 559, 493-9; Gee and Hardy, *Documents Illustrative of English Church History*, 173.

6.   Elton, *Policy and Police*, 230-46; Hughes and Larkin, *Tudor Royal Proclamations*, I, 215-16, 224-5, 227-8, 229-32, 235-7, 260-1, 270-6, 278-80, 284-7.

7.   Elton, *Reform & Renewal*, 133-35; F.D. Logan, 'The Henrician Canons', *BIHR*, XLVII (1974), 99-103.

8.   J. Phillips, *The Reformation of Images: Destruction of Art in England 1535-1660* (1973), 1-81; C. Pythian-Adams, 'Ceremony and the Citizen'.

9.   *Statutes of the Realm*, III, 575-8, 559-60; Burnet, *History of the Reformation*, I, 296-300.

10.   'England in the Reign of Henry VIII: Starkey's Life and Letters', ed. S.J. Herrtage, *EETS*, XXXII (1878), liii-lix.

11.   *Statutes of the Realm*, III, 728; Youings, *Dissolution of the Monasteries*, 85.

12.   Merriman, *Life and Letters*, II, 131-2; Youings, *Dissolution of the Monasteries*, 66-75, 88-9.

13.   N. Orme, *English Schools in the Middle Ages* (1973), 254; Gee and Hardy, *Documents Illustrative of English Church History*, 271, 278, 272, 277, 276.

14.   L.P., X, 17; Elton, *Policy and Police*, 244.

15.   J. F. Mozley, *Coverdale and his Bibles* (1953), 115, 125; S.L. Greenslade, ed., *Cambridge History of the Bible* (Cambridge 1963), II, 141-51.

16.   Mozley, *Coverdale and his Bibles*, 201-20.

17.   M. Deansley, *The Lollard Bible* (Cambridge 1966), 351-73; Gee and Hardy, *Documents Illustrative of English Church History*, 279.

18.   *English Historical Documents 1485-1558* (1967), ed. C.H. Williams, V, 795-805.

19. Foxe, *Acts and Monuments*, V, 378-82; Cranmer, *Works*, II, 366-7.
20. Hughes and Larkin. *Tudor Royal Proclamations*, I, 273-5; Elton, *Studies*, I, 205 n.2; L.P., XIV (i). 329.
21. Merriman, *Life and Letters*, II, 162
22. Cavendish, 'Life and Death of Cardinal Wolsey', 106.
23. Merriman, *Life and Letters*, I, 56-63; L.P., IV (ii), 1457.
24. Elton, *Reform & Renewal*, 38-41.
25. Merriman, *Life and Letters*, I, 374; II, 128-9.
26. Ibid., I, 279.
27. L.P., XIII (i), 476.
28. *Statutes of the Realm*, III, 427; Merriman, *Life and Letters*, II, 66.
29. Hall, *Chronicle*, 839; Foxe, *Acts and Monuments*, V 378.

Chapter 7   THE GOVERNANCE OF THE REALM

1. L.P., XIV (ii), 139; Merriman, *Life and Letters*, I, 87.
2. L.P., XIII (i), 42.
3. M.E. James, 'Change and Continuity in the Tudor North', *Borthwick Papers*, XXVII (York 1965), passim.
4. J. Youings, 'The Council of the West', *TRHS*, X (1960), 41-59.
5. Ibid., 56; Haigh, *Reformation and Resistance in Tudor Lancashire*, 104-5; N. Williams, *Thomas Howard, Fourth Duke of Norfolk* (1964), 64-79.
6. M.L. Bush, 'The Problem of the Far North', 40-63; James, 'Continuity and Change in the Tudor North', 15-16.
7. Ibid., 9-10, 16-19; D.M. Loades, *Politics and the Nation* (1974), 175-6; L.P., XII (ii), 235.
8. L.P., XII (i), 284.
9. R. Reid, *The King's Council in the North* (1921), 116-17; G.T. Lapsley, *The County Palatine of Durham* (1899), 196-8.
10. Reid, *The King's Council in the North*, 147-65.
11. L.P., VI, 644-5; M. MacCurtain, *Tudor and Stuart Ireland* (Dublin 1972), 6-10.
12. L.P., VII, 447-9; S.G. Ellis, 'The Kildare Rebellion and the Early Henrician Reformation', *HJ*, XIX (1976), 807-29.
13. B. Bradshaw, *The Dissolution of the Religious Orders in Ireland under Henry VIII* (Cambridge 1974), 56-9.
14. R.D. Edwards, 'The Irish Reformation Parliament of Henry VIII', *Historical Studies* (1968), ed. W.T. Moody, VI, 61-2.
15. B. Bradshaw, 'The opposition to the ecclesiastical legislation in the Irish Reformation Parliament', *Irish Historical Studies*, XVI (1969), 285-303.
16. B. Bradshaw, 'George Brown, first Reformation Archbishop of Dublin 1536-1554', *JEH*, XXI (1970), 309-15; MacCurtain, *Tudor and Stuart Ireland*, 22-38; *New History of Ireland*, III, 29-31, 39-63.
17. L.P., XV, 419; *State Papers, King Henry the Eighth* (1830-1852), II, 554.
18. L.P., VI, 177, 322; T.B. Pugh, *The Marcher Lordships of South Wales* (Cardiff 1963), 46-7.

19.   L.P., VI, 95; C.A.J. Skeel, *The Council in the Marches of Wales* (1904), 49-80; P. Williams, *The Council in the Marches of Wales under Elizabeth I* (Cardiff 1958), 14-35.
20.   D. Williams, *A History of Modern Wales* (1950), 35; *Statutes of the Realm*, III, 563-9.
21.   Ibid., III, 555-8, 563-9.
22.   G. Williams, *The Welsh Church from Conquest to Reformation* (Cardiff 1962), 555-7.
23.   *Statutes of the Realm*, III, 632-50; Merriman, *Life and Letters*, I, 391; II, 148-9, 226-7; A.J. Eagleston, *The Channel Islands under Tudor Government* (Cambridge 1949), passim.

Chapter 8   THE CHARACTER OF GOVERNMENT

1.   Van Dyke, *Renascence Portraits*, 151-3; Foxe, *Acts and Monuments*, VI, 46; Scarisbrick, *Henry VIII*, 247; J.A. Muller, *Stephen Gardiner and the Tudor Reaction* (1926), 298; L.P., VII, 580.
2.   L.P., VI, 14.
3.   *Statutes of the Realm*, III, 649, 568.
4.   Ibid., 464-71.
5.   S.E. Lehmberg, 'Early Tudor Parliamentary Procedure: Provisos in the legislation of the Reformation Parliament', *EHR*, LXXV (1970), 10; Hall, *Chronicle*, 774-5, 784-6.
6.   J. Hurstfield, 'Was there a Tudor Despotism after all?', TRHS, 5th Series, LII, (1967), 83-108.
7.   Heinze, *The Proclamations of the Tudor Kings*, 41-2, 56, 118-52.
8.   Ibid., 165-7.
9.   *Statutes of the Realm*, III, 726-8.
10.   M.L. Bush, *The Government Policy of Protector Somerset* (1975), 138-39, 140 n.65.
11.   Hurstfield, 'Was there a Tudor Despotism after all?', 94-7; Elton, *Studies*, I, 341-5, 270-4.
12.   Merriman, *Life and Letters*, I, 410.
13.   S.B. Chrimes, *Sir John Fortescue: De Laudibus Angliae* (Cambridge 1942), 5-7; Elyot, *The Boke called the Governour*, 150; Merriman, *Life and Letters*, I, 437.
14.   R. Steele, *King's letters from the early Tudors with letters from Henry VIII and Anne Boleyn* (1904), 236; Merriman, *Life and Letters*, I, 361; *Chronicle of King Henry VIII*, 61.
15.   L.P., VII, 603; Elton, *Studies*, II, 69-71.
16.   Merriman, *Life and Letters*, I, 360; Van Dyke, *Renascence Portraits*, 242-4; Elton, *Policy and Police*, 328-9, 396-7; Haigh, *Reformation and Resistance in Tudor Lancashire*, 113, 138.
17.   Elton, *Policy and Police*, 264, 288-9; J.R. Bellamy, *The Law of Treason in England in the Later Middle Ages* (Cambridge 1970), 119-23.
18.   I.D. Thornley, 'The Destruction of Sanctuary', *Tudor Studies* (1924), ed. R.W. Seton-Watson, 203.
19.   Elton, *Policy and Police*, 263-326, 392-3.

20.   S.E. Lehmberg, 'Parliamentary Attainder in the reign of Henry VIII', *HJ*, XVIII (1975), 675, 702.
21.   Ibid., 684.
22.   W.K. Ferguson, *The Articulate Citizen and the English Renaissance* (Durham N.C. 1965), 133-61; W.R.D. Jones, *The Tudor Commonwealth 1529-1559* (1970), passim.
23.   Elton, *Studies*, II, 236-58.
24.   *Statutes of the Realm*, III, 430-2, 545-6, 760-3, 663, 421-2, 655, 725.
25.   Elton, *Reform & Renewal*, 120-1.
26.   *The Agrarian History of England and Wales 1500-1640* (Cambridge 1967), ed. J. Thirsk, IV, 217.
27.   *Statutes of the Realm*, III, 558-62; F.R. Salter, *Some Early Tracts on Poor Relief* (1926); Elton, *Studies*, II, 137-54.
28.   *Statutes of the Realm*, III, 819.
29.   Mozley, *Coverdale and his Bibles*, 254.
30.   *Statues of the Realm*, III, 464.

Chapter 9   THE APPARATUS OF POWER

1.   Merriman, *Life and Letters*, I, 344.
2.   *State Papers, King Henry the Eighth*, I, 79-80; Elton, *The Tudor Revolution in Government*, 299.
3.   Ibid., 298-300.
4.   *State Papers, King Henry the Eighth*, II, 553; Conyers Read, *Mr. Secretary Walsingham and the policy of Queen Elizabeth* (Oxford 1925), I, 439.
5.   *Statutes of the Realm*, III, 729.
6.   Elton, *The Tudor Revolution in Government*, 127-33; W.J. Jones, *The Elizabethan Court of Chancery* (Oxford 1967), 164.
7.   *The Complete Peerage* (1913), ed. V. Gibbs and H.A. Doubleday, III, 556.
8.   Elton, *The Tudor Revolution in Government*, 132-3, 138.
9.   Ibid., 298.
10.   Ibid., 385-97, 413-15.
11.   Ibid., 433-8, 439-41; *Statutes of the Realm*, III, 542-4.
12.   Burnet, *History of the Reformation of the English Church*, IV, 416-17; Merriman, *Life and Letters*, II, 266.
13.   L.P., XII (i), 299; Pocock, *Records of the Reformation*, II, 523-31.
14.   *State Papers, King Henry the Eighth*, II, 508; L.P., XV, 377.
15.   *Proceeding and Ordinances of the Privy Council of England* (1837), ed. H. Nicolas, VII, 4; D.E. Hoak, *The King's Council in the reign of Edward VI* (Cambridge 1976), 265.
16.   Elton, *The Tudor Revolution in Government*, 201, 118, 202, 314, 279-80.
17.   Lehmberg, *The Reformation Parliament*, 249-53, 132, 190, 208.
18.   S.B. Chrimes, *Henry VII* (1972), 135; M. McKisack, *The Parliamentary Representation of the English Boroughs during the Middle Ages* (Oxford 1932), 118; G.W.O. Woodward. 'The Role of Parliament in the Henrician Reformation', *Government in Reformation Europe 1520-1560*

(1971), ed. H.J. Cohn, 113-25.
19. J.E. Neale, *The Elizabethan House of Commons* (1949), 301-20; Elton *Studies*, II, 43-5.
20. R. Holinshed, *Chronicles* (1808), III, 826.
21. J.W. Allen. *Political Thought in the Sixteenth Century*, 2nd ed. (1941), 167.
22. Muller, *Stephen Gardiner and the Tudor Reaction*, 93-4; Roper, *Life of Sir Thomas More*, 85.
23. H. Brinklow, 'Complaynt of Roderyck Mors', ed. J.M. Cowper, *EETS*, Extra Series, XXII (1874), 35.

Chapter 10   THE MANIPULATION OF POWER

1. Elton, *The Tudor Revolution in Government*, 122-3; L.P., XI, 203; Elton, *Reform & Renewal*, 24.
2. Slavin, *Politics and Profit*, 133, Merriman, *Life and Letters*, I, 390-98.
3. *The Complete Peerage*, III, 555-7.
4. *CSP*, Spanish, V, 569; Ives, 'Faction at the Court of Henry VIII: the Fall of Anne Boleyn', 176; Elton, *The Tudor Revolution in Government*, 381-2; L.P, XIII (ii), 497.
5. Elton, *Reform & Renewal*, 24-6, 61-2, 65; Merriman, *Life and Letters*, I, 397-8; Wriothesley, *Chronicle*, 96.
6. Burnet, *History of the Reformation of the English Church*, III, 419; D. Wilson, *A Tudor Tapestry* (1972), 107; A.G. Dickens, *Lollards and Protestants in the Diocese of York 1509-1558* (Oxford 1959) 69; C.H. Smyth, *Cranmer and the Reformation under Edward VI* (Cambridge 1932), 83-4; J.K. McConica, *English Humanists and Reformation Politics under Henry VIII and Edward VI* (Oxford 1965), 192; Hall, *Chronicle*, 838, Merriman, *Life and Letters*, II, 267.
7. Elton, *Studies*, I, 166-72; L.P., VIII, 104; *Statutes of the Realm*, III, 680-1; Bradshaw, *The Dissolution of the Religious Orders in Ireland under Henry VIII*, 57-8; Muller, *Stephen Gardiner and the Tudor Reaction*, 46-8, 54-5.
8. Ives, 'Faction at the Court of Henry VIII: the Fall of Anne Boleyn', 169-88; G.R. Elton, 'Tudor Government: the points of Contact, III, The Court', *TRHS*, 5th series, XXVI (1976), 221-3, 226-7.
9. L.P., XIII (i), 510.
10. Dodds, *The Pilgrimage of Grace*, II, 277-327.
11. Ives, 'Faction at the Court of Henry VIII: the Fall of Anne Boleyn', 179; Elton, *Studies*, I, 213-14.
12. Merriman, *Life and Letters*, I, 67; A.F. Pollard, 'Thomas Cromwell's Parliamentary Lists', *BIHR*, IX (1931), 31-43.
13. K. Pickthorn, *Early Tudor Government: Henry VIII* (Cambridge 1934), 404-05; Elton, *Studies*, I, 200-5; L.P., XIV (i), 210.
14. Merriman, *Life and Letters*, II, 13-14; Dodds, *The Pilgrimage of Grace*, I, 359; L.P., XI, 504-5.
15. Lehmberg, *The Reformation Parliament*, 17-18, 254.
16. Cavendish, 'Life and Death of Cardinal Wolsey', 113; L.P., XIV (i), 405; V, 288; Elton, *Studies*, II, 99-100.

17. Wriothesley, *Chronicle*, 32.
18. Lehmberg, *The Reformation Parliament*, 137, 254-5.
19. Wriothesley, *Chronicle*, 80-1, 75-6; Burnet, *History of the Reformation of the English Church*, VI, 194-5; S. Anglo, *Spectacle, Pageantry and Early Tudor Policy* (Oxford 1969), 263-77.
20. Foxe, *Acts and Monuments*, V, 403; Hughes and Larkin, *Tudor Royal Proclamations*, I, 275-6.
21. R. Strong, *Holbein and Henry VIII* (1967), 14.
22. Wriothesley, *Chronicle*, 104; M. Maclure, *The Paul's Cross Sermons 1534-1642* (1958), 14, 26-8; Heinze, *The Proclamations of the Tudor Kings*, 28-9.
23. Elton, *Policy and Police*, 217.
24. *Statutes of the Realm*, III, 451; Hughes and Larkin, *Tudor Royal Proclamations*, I, 229-32, 235-7, 270-6; Gee and Hardy, *Documents Illustrative of English Church History*, 145; Elton, *Policy and Police*, 220-1.
25. For the following three paragraphs see Elton, *Policy and Police*, 173-207.
26. McConica, *English Humanists and Reformation Politics*, 117-20, 170; Elton, *Reform & Renewal*, 35.
27. A.G. Dickens, *Thomas Cromwell and the English Reformation* (1959), 109-23; A.G. Dickens, *The English Reformation* (1964), 133-8; Hughes and Larkin, *Tudor Royal Proclamations*, I, 286.
28. Gee and Hardy, *Documents Illustrative of English Church History*, 272, 274; L. Stone, *The Crisis of the Aristocracy*, 679-80.
29. J. Simon, *Education and Society in Tudor England* (Cambridge 1966), 182-4; Orme, *English Schools in the Middle Ages*, 262-4.
30. Merriman, *Life and Letters*, I, 431-2, 437-8; 'Letters relating to the Suppression of Monasteries, ed. T. Wright, Camden Soc., XXVI (1843), 70-1; H. Kearney, *Scholars and Gentlemen* (1970), 18-21.

Chapter 11   ZENITH AND NADIR

1. Foxe, *Acts and Monuments*, V, 401.
2. Merriman, *Life and Letters*, 212-80; R.B. Wernham, *Before the Armada* (1966), 111-48.
3. L.P., XIV (i), 151-3, 206, 219, 241, 264-330, 339, 349, 424-5.
4. Mozley, *Coverdale and his Bibles*, 261-2; Wriothesley, *Chronicle*, 113; L.P., XIV (i), 224, 246-7, 331-7.
5. *Journal of the House of Lords*, I, 110.
6. Heinze, *Proclamations of the Tudor Kings*, 153-77.
7. *Journal of the House of Lords*, I, 105; Hughes and Larkin, *Tudor Royal Proclamations*, I, 278-80, 284-6; L.P., XIV (i), 329.
8. *Journal of the House of Lords*, I, 109, 111; L.P., XIV (i), 475.
9. J. Ridley, *Thomas Cranmer* (Oxford 1962), 148; L.P., XIV (i), 545; Merriman, *Life and Letters*, I, 258; II, 214.
10. *Handbook of British Chronology*, 2nd ed. (1961), ed. F.M. Powicke and E.B. Fryde, 262, 252, 240; L.P., XIV (i), 149.
11. Merriman, *Life and Letters*, I, 267-8.

12. *Chronicle of King Henry VIII*, 90-1; L.P., XV, 4-6; Merriman, *Life and Letters*, II, 269.
13. L.P., XV, 369-70; Strype, *Ecclesiastical Memorials*, I (ii), 437-42.
14. Foxe, *Acts and Monuments*, V, 430-3; Muller, *Stephen Gardiner and the Tudor Reaction*, 85-9.
15. L.P., XV, 164, 206; Merriman, *Life and Letters*, I, 266.
16. *Journal of the House of Lords*, I, 129; Elton, *Studies*, I, 216; R.W. Dixon, *History of the Church of England* (1895), II, 233-4.
17. Elton, *Reform & Renewal*, 96; *Statutes of the Realm*, III, 778-81, 812-24.
18. L.P., XV, 242-3; Wriothesley, *Chronicle*, 115; Slavin, *Politics and Profit*, 46-9.
19. L.P., XV, 251-2.
20. Foxe, *Acts and Monuments*, V, 404; Cranmer, *Works*, II, 401.
21. L.B. Smith, *A Tudor Tragedy* (1962), 108.
22. L.P. XV., 349-50; Merriman, *Life and Letters*, II, 261-3.
23. L.P., XV, 350-1, 326.
24. Ibid., 351.
25. L.P., XV, 336; *State Papers, King Henry the Eighth*, I, 627-8.
26. Scarisbrick, *Henry VIII*, 379.
27. L.P. XV, 377; *Chronicle of King Henry VIII*, 96-100.
28. L.P., XV, 377; Hall, *Chronicle*, 838.
29. Elton, *Studies*, I, 221.
30. Burnet, *History of the Reformation of the English Church*, IV, 415-23.
31. L.P., XV, 376, 386.
32. Merriman, *Life and Letters*, II, 268-70.
33. L.P., XV, 338-89; Cranmer, *Works*, II, 401; Foxe, *Acts and Monuments*, V, 404.
34. Hall, *Chronicle*, 839.
35. L.P., XVI, 285; Wriothesley, *Chronicle*, 120; Foxe, *Acts and Monuments*, V, 396.

Chapter 12 PROBLEMS OF ASSESSMENT

1. Foxe, *Acts and Monuments*, V, 384; T. Fuller, *The Church History of Britain* (1842), ed. J. Nichols, III, 98-100.
2. Merriman, *Life and Letters*, I, 305.
3. Dickens, *The English Reformation*, 133-5, 179-82; Dickens, *Thomas Cromwell and the English Reformation*, 109-23, 179-82; Elton, *Reform & Renewal*, 36; McConica, *English Humanists and Reformation Politics*, 199, Merriman, *Life and Letters*, II, 227.
4. W. Stubbs, *Lectures on Medieval and Modern History* (Oxford 1887), 386; J.R. Green, *A Short History of the English People*, 2nd ed. (1905), 332; Merriman, *Life and Letters*, I, 308.
5. Elton, *Studies*, II, 215-35; Elton, *England Under the Tudors*, 167-70.
6. Stubbs, *Lectures on Medieval and Modern History*, 281.
7. J. A. Froude, *History of England*, 3rd ed., (1864), II, 531-2.

8. Elton, 'Tudor Government: the Points of Contact. III. The Court', 221-2.
9. Green, *A Short History of the English People*, 331, 332.
10. Elton,. *England under the Tudors*, 180-4.
11. P. Williams and G.L. Harriss, 'A Revolution in Tudor History?', *Past and Present*, XXV (1963), 3-58; Elton, *England under the Tudors*, 479-82.
12. Scarisbrick, 'The Pardon of the Clergy, 1531'.
13. M. Beresford, *The lost Villages of England* (1954), 102-33.
14. Cranmer, *Works*, II, 401.

FURTHER READING

J.W. Allen, *Political Thought in the Sixteenth Century*, 2nd. ed., (1941).

S. Anglo, *Spectacle and Pageantry and Early Tudor Policy* (Oxford 1967).

F. Le van Baumer, *The Early Tudor Theory of Kingship* (New York 1966).

H.E. Bell. *An Introduction to the history and records of the Court of Wards and Liveries* (Cambridge 1953).

B. Bradshaw, *The Dissolution of the Religious Orders in Ireland under Henry VIII* (Cambridge 1974).

C.S.L. Davies, 'A New Life of Henry VIII', *History*, LVII (1969).

A.G. Dickens, *Thomas Cromwell and the English Reformation* (1959).

A.G. Dickens, *The English Reformation* (1964).

F.C. Dietz, *English Government Finance 1485-1558* (1964).

M.H. and R. Dodds, *The Pilgrimage of Grace 1536 and the Exeter Conspiracy 1538* (Cambridge 1915).

P. Van Dyke, *Renascence Portraits* (1906).

G.R. Elton, *The Tudor Revolution in Government* (Cambridge 1953).

G.R. Elton, *England under the Tudors* (1955), 2nd ed. (1974).

G.R. Elton, *Star Chamber Stories* (1958).

G.R. Elton, *The Tudor Constitution* (Cambridge 1960).

G.R. Elton, *Policy and Police* (Cambridge 1972)

G.R. Elton, *Reform & Renewal* (Cambridge 1973).

G.R. Elton, *Studies in Tudor and Stuart Politics and Government* (Cambridge 1974).

G.R. Elton, 'Tudor Government: The points of Contact: I. Parliament', *Transactions of the Royal Historical Society*, 5th series, XXIV (1974).

G.R. Elton, 'Tudor Government: The Points of Contact: II. The Council', *Transactions of the Royal Historical Society*, 5th Series, XXV (1975).

G.R. Elton, 'Tudor Government: The Points of Contact: III. The Court', *Transactions of the Royal Historical Society*, 5th Series, XXVI (1976).

J. Foxe, *Acts and Monuments*, ed. J. Pratt (1870).

C. Haigh, *Reformation and Resistance in Tudor Lancashire* (Cambridge 1976).

D. Hay, 'The Church of England in the later Middle Ages', *History*, LIII(1968).

R.W. Heinze, *Proclamations of the Tudor Kings* (Cambridge 1976).

W.G. Hoskins, *The Age of Plunder* (1976).

J. Hurstfield, 'Was there a Tudor Despotism after all?', *Transactions of the Royal Historical Society*, 5th Series, LII (1967).

W.E. Ives, 'The Genesis of the Statute of Uses', *English Historical Review*, LXXXII (1967).

W.E. Ives, 'Faction at the Court of Henry VIII; the Fall of Anne Boleyn', *History*, LVII (1972).

W.R.D. Jones, *The Tudor Commonwealth* (1970).

M. Kelly, 'The Submission of the Clergy', *Transactions of the Royal Historical Society*, 5th Series, XV (1965).

R. Koebener, 'The Imperial Crown of the Realm; Henry VIII, Constantine and Polydore Vergil', *Bulletin of the Institute of Historical Research*, XXVI (1953).

S.E. Lehmberg, 'Supremacy and Vicegerency: a re-examination', *English Historical Review*, LXXI (1966).

S.E. Lehmberg, *The Reformation Parliament 1529-1536* (Cambridge 1970).

S.E. Lehmberg, 'Sir Thomas Audley: a Soul as Black as Marble?', *Tudor Men and Institutions* (Baton Rouge 1972), ed. A.J. Slavin.

S.E. Lehmberg, 'Parliamentary Attainder in the reign of Henry VIII', *Historical Journal*, XVIII (1975).

J.K. McConica, *English Humanists and Reformation Politics under Henry VIII and Edward VI* (Oxford 1965).

R.B. Merriman, *Life and Letters of Thomas Cromwell* (Oxford 1902).

J.F. Mozley, *Coverdale and his Bibles* (1953).

J.A. Muller, *Stephen Gardiner and the Tudor Reaction* (1926).

W.C. Richardson, *History of the Court of Augmentations 1536-54* (Baton Rouge 1961).

J. Ridley, *Thomas Cranmer* (1948).

J.J. Scarisbrick, 'Pardon of the Clergy 1531', *Cambridge Historical Journal*, XII (1956).

J.J. Scarisbrick, *Henry VIII* (1968).

A.J. Slavin, *Politics and Profit* (Cambridge 1966).

A.J. Slavin, *Thomas Cromwell on Church and Commonwealth* (New York 1969).

N. Williams, *The Cardinal and the Secretary* (1975).

P. Williams and G.L. Harriss, 'A revolution in Tudor History?', *Past and Present*, XXV (1963).

J. Youings, *The Dissolution of the Monasteries* (1971).

W.G. Zeeveld, *Foundations of Tudor Policy* (1948).

INDEX